W9-AZA-274

One Small Starfish

A Mother's Everyday Advice, Survival Tactics
& Wisdom for Raising a Special Needs Child

ANNE ADDISON

All marketing and publishing right guaranteed to and reserved by

FUTURE HORIZONS INC.

721 W. Abram Street
Arlington, Texas 76013
817-277-0727
800-489-0727
817-277-2270 (Fax)
E-mail: info@futurehorizons-autism.com
www.FutureHorizons-autism.com

Cataloging in Publication Data is available from the Library of Congress.

ISBN 1-885477-87-2

This book is dedicated to parents and children
who face extraordinary challenges

Table Of Contents

ACKNOWLEDGEMENTS

In hindsight, every step along my own journey has in some shape or manner, prepared me for what I face each day with Jack. I have been greatly blessed with friends, teachers, colleagues and earthly angels. Each has provided strength, direction, wisdom and love. Thank you, one and all.

Specifically, I thank Liz Murphy, who suggested early on that I keep a diary of my experiences; Sally Eberhardt who showed me how to get through this labyrinth with grace and determination; Linda Wilkenson, Michelle Gresia, Erika Cebulski, Eileen McMullen and Anne Karfopoulos, the amazing teachers who helped Jack grow; Deborah Alberti, the speech and language pathologist who was the guiding light of our professional team and an outstanding clinician, Drs. Jeanne Dietrich and Nanci Spector, psychologists, and Dr. Jean-Paul Marachi, the psychiatrist who has been at the helm since nearly day one.

I could not have kept my spirit and countenance without a wide-flung circle of friends and supporters, including the Hagerbrant family, the Zadik family, the Harrington family, Gosia Mroz, Julien Jary, Charlotte Graves, Virginia Marzonie, Cindy Key, Lori Jary, Patricia Marion, Aubin Wilson, Deborah Ward, Lynn Mayer, Hugh Underhill, Seagun Maku, Candice Timpson, Cooperative Education Services, North Street School and the Board of Education, Camp Northwood, First Presbyterian Church, St. Michael's Church, and the order of the Society of Jesus.

To my family, who have stayed in the boat with us even during those gatherings when the boat became a little too rocky. Thank you for your support and unconditional love; especially to my mother and father, who gave me the lay of the parenting land.

To Anne Yeager and Barry Fiewel, who shared with me their literary wisdom, and to those parents and professionals who read manuscripts and reviewed cover designs; you gave me invaluable direction. To Wayne Gilpin, publisher; Amanda Sobel, editor; Lauren Graessle, cover and layout designer; and Stacy McLaughlin, communications liason. This team brought the book to a whole new level.

A special thanks to my husband, John, who has helped me keep perspective and made me laugh along the way. To Sarah, who has been a shining light in our lives, and to Jack, who has given me the opportunity to grow in ways I could never have imagined.

But above all, my thanks to the Lord, who inspired me to write this book, as it is.

Introduction

An old man stands at the edge of a beach, gazing down at thousands of starfish, left behind by the changing tide. He methodically picks up starfish after starfish, tossing each back into the ocean. A young man comes up to the older one and asks, "Why are you bothering to throw a few starfish back into the water? You can't possibly make a difference." The old man looks at the younger one, picking up the littlest starfish and holding it up for his questioning visitor to see. As he tosses the starfish back into the water he replies, "Well, it sure makes a big difference to this one."

You can make a difference against difficult odds. It takes someone like the wise old man, who is patient, committed and focused, regardless of what others think or how impossible the situation may look. If you are parenting a special needs child, many days you can feel like you are operating in a state of controlled crisis. Every drop of energy is spent trying to keep a small sense of calm in the home, knowing full well that success is unlikely. By the time the last power struggle and bedtime battle is over, it is work enough to get the house in order before collapsing in bed. The thought of sitting down to try to find the kernel of meaning in this unexpected turn of life is just too mentally and physically exhausting to attempt. Yet, through this struggle there are lessons much greater than what they seem, if only we can step back and see the countless gifts hidden amidst the pain.

I often become sad when I read a book that traces a family's struggle. The tale always seems to move evenly forward and end with a neatly packaged story of success. For us, where the past nine years have only been consistent in their inconsistency, such stories of steady progress are not encouraging. Where are the slips backward just when you're getting comfortable that you've got the thing under control? Where are the unexpected twists that no one prepared you for? And most important, how do you get through the basic day-to-day living?

This book is designed to give you some practical strategies for working and living with children who present challenging behaviors. Beyond this, I hope that it gives you the fire inside to be the coach for your child that you need to be. More than advocate. Coach. Your child needs someone who is never satisfied with the way things are, who is always searching for more answers to get to what could be. Someone who can maintain a calm and a sense of order since the child may——to a greater or lesser degree—have little ability to create that organization within. And your child needs someone who always, and forever, will believe in him and cheer him on. At times, you may be the only one in his world who is on his side.

It might seem unfair that in addition to having a child with such profound needs you now have to take on this greater emotional role. But this is not a question of fairness.

I threw the fairness question out the second summer that our son, Jack, was known to us as a special needs child, having ADHD. Sarah, our daughter, was three years old and Jack was two.

We were vacationing on a tiny island off the coast of Georgia, a marvelous place to spend time. The setting is restful, there are all sorts of water-based activities for the children, and the entire island is just three square miles—a critical requirement for the wandering Jack. One day on the beach we met a family of four. The little girl, Helen, was in a baby jogger. Because of her small size, I didn't realize that she was actually seven—she looked four. Then we saw her father carefully lift her so that she could put her toes in the ocean. The child had cerebral palsy.

The more closely we observed the family, the more we saw the tremendous physical and emotional energy they invested in their little girl. Not only did they have to work with the behavioral component, they were responsible for the little girl's daily maintenance. This mother was my first hero in the world of special needs. She was realistic yet unrelenting in her hope for her child. She didn't try to hide or sugar coat their daily struggles. Nor did she look upon herself as a martyr. She was a practical, here's what needs to be done, type.

At the end of the week, two things struck me. First was the energy and enthusiasm that the family invested in Helen. Second was the courage, centeredness and upbeat attitude of Helen's mother. I hoped these images would stay with me as I prepared to guide our own uncertain boat with Jack through the coming years.

No matter how courageous you are, you will grieve. You have to cry, and you will, again and again. You will grieve each time you see a friend's child reach a new benchmark that you know your child never will. You will sob when you have a setback. Your heart will ache when you give into a few minutes of daydreaming about what life could be like, if only. You have to cry. You live with a grave loss that you feel day after day.

I have a big banner going across the wall of our kitchen. It says, Attitude Is A Little Thing That Makes A Big Difference. It's been up for about six months. One day, when we were going through our worst dip with Jack and I was giving in to tears, the child turned to me and said, "Looks like your attitude needs a little adjusting." No kidding. He actually got it! So, maybe this book will provide an attitude adjustment when you need it.

I have tried to incorporate the survival tools that I use, as well as those shared with me by other parents, professionals and teachers in my world. However, I don't want you to think that this book is merely about survival.

Just surviving isn't good enough for anyone and it certainly isn't good enough for special children. These children are like those starfish. Each day that we bring them a step forward, they are further away from being lost on the beach. And although a little step isn't a big thing today, or tomorrow or the next day, if you keep taking little steps, you will see one day that you have walked a great distance with your child.

I. The Diagnosis Process

WHAT'S GOING ON HERE?

THE EVALUATION TANGO

READ THE LABEL, MABEL

ARE WE THERE YET?

What's Going On Here?
When You First Sense Something
Is Not Right

I wasn't even supposed to be able to have children. Or so the doctors said.

I was thirty when my husband John and I first began trying to begin our family. I noticed that I was having hot flashes. When you get them, there is no question as to what they are, you just know. After some basic testing, my doctor informed me that I was one of the 1 in 15,000 women in premature menopause.

Hopeful that we could capture some of the final ovulatory cycles, we began exploring fertility processes. One of my friends shared the name of a homeopath in Ontario, Canada, who had had luck helping women like me conceive. Coincidentally, I had to go no more than thirty minutes away from this doctor to visit one of my company's manufacturing plants. This was an easy way to take a long shot at trying to bring my body back in sync.

After examining me and conducting a number of tests, Dr. George[1] determined that my system was overactive in some areas and underactive in others. Loaded with brown bottles filled with natural remedies, I returned to the States and became pregnant. I know it sounds too easy and a bit of hocus-pocus but honestly, after my visit to Dr. George and a regular recitation of the rosary, I was pregnant within a month.

That was the beginning of life with Sarah. We called her Miss Happy-Go-Lucky right from the start. It seemed like she aimed to please from the first day. Sarah was healthy, bubbly and right on schedule from feedings to first words. "Parenting? A snap!" I remember thinking to myself.

1. The names of some of the professionals have been changed for privacy purposes.

Mindful of my possible physical limitations, John and I did not want to waste any time trying to expand our family. And although my mother tried to tell me that having children close together was not as easy as it looked, we moved forward with our plan to expand. Luck held and by the time Sarah was nine months old, Jack was on the way.

In those early years, conception was about the only similarity between our two children.

Jack's first days of life would typify his attitude through his toddler years. He was the sweetest day-old newborn, winning over the nurses with his precious face. He was so sweet that I begged the nurses to let him stay in my room most of the day.

As sweet as he was, however, there were moments, coming out of nowhere, when Jack became distant and out-of-sorts, lying in the hospital bassinet. He had a marvelous hospital nurse who was masterful at calming him down. Although it was a little unnerving to see this child's countenance change so quickly, the nurse advised me to swaddle him tighter to give him a little added security. As the new mothers on the ward were blissfully establishing the first bond with their newborn, there was a little nagging at the back of my mind. Three days after Jack's birth, I returned home, and my quiet nags proved to be uncannily on target.

I've managed to block out many of the experiences and pain of those years but I do remember in Jack's first months that nothing could keep this little child happy. Jack seemed to be constantly out of rhythm with the world, from his sleep cycle to his general mood. We would swing him endlessly in the old-fashioned Swing-O-Matic from my mother, which had lulled four children and four grandchildren to sleep. No magic for little Jack. Strollers, playpens and other everyday baby things upset him.

We moved to bottle feedings after the first exhausting week, but it took us five formulas before we found something that Jack could tolerate. Car rides were the only thing that calmed him and produced sleep. We circled a lot of neighborhoods in those days. On some level, I knew that this wasn't the way it should be with even the most difficult of babies.

What fooled me, and can still catch me today, is that there was no constancy or predictability to Jack. A child with Down's syndrome has a pretty clear trajectory. A parent knows what to expect developmentally and emotionally. Jack wasn't an obvious anything. He was just constantly off and constantly in motion. Maybe he was just a cranky or colicky child, I hoped.

Developmental delays and other disorders off the typical scale were completely unknown to John and me. Nothing in our backgrounds gave us any clue as to what was abnormal childhood development. Jack's disinterest in toys and unresponsiveness to most people struck us as unusual, but did not raise any flags. If he had not bonded to me I might have picked up that something was awry. But he was clearly bonded. My mother called it the hip attachment. It seemed that I was always schlepping Jack, and that as long as he was on my hip he was relatively soothed. Not scheduled, mind you, but soothed.

Unfortunately, by the three-month mark we had not achieved any sort of schedule that was regular or comfortable for the family. It seemed that Jack, with his finicky personality and no need for sleep was slowly determining the tenor and schedule for the entire family. We were being run by a child.

Jack had constant ear infections so I blamed a lot of his behavior and crankiness on the fact that he often wasn't feeling well. We visited the pediatrician nearly every week. Each time, I naively hoped that he would have an ear infection. At least that would explain why the child was constantly up at night, not taking naps, and generally fussy. My hope came true. In the first eighteen months of life, Jack had fifteen ear infections and more than fifteen rounds of antibiotics.

It wasn't just the irregularity of his physical system that struck us as odd. Even in his earliest years, Jack seemed to have no regard for authority. I had tracked Penelope Leach, Dr. Brazelton, Dr. Dobson and a number of other professionals to build my parenting philosophy. This philosophy was similar to the approach that my parents had successfully used. No major surprises—keep a clear structure with stated rules and expectations, be consistent in your message, give warnings for misbehavior, follow through on consequences that you state, maintain a shared parenting approach and above all, lather on love and support. That was day-in, day-out parenting to me.

Our parenting method was working effectively for Sarah. Sarah was very much her own person with distinct opinions, but she respected authority and knew the meaning of the phrase "Hop to it!"

With Jack, the same parenting approach wasn't effective at all. To begin with, it was impossible to gain Jack's attention. He made absolutely no eye contact with us and it was difficult to tell if he had even heard us. Though I don't believe that this accounted for the entire problem, we did learn that Jack, in fact, could not hear that well. When Jack was two, we finally had tubes inserted in his ears in an effort to reduce the number of ear infections. This is a common procedure for young children who suffer frequent ear infections. It turned out that he had a thirty percent hearing loss before the tubes were inserted. The pediatrician pointed to the hearing loss as the reason why Jack wasn't following even the simplest of directions. Jack probably couldn't hear anyone. Not knowing any better, we accepted the pediatrician's explanation and looked no further.

Taking Charge

 *Strategies*

- KEEP A JOURNAL RECOUNTING MAJOR THEMES, BEHAVIORS AND POSSIBLE THEORIES THAT YOU HAVE, PARTICULARLY DURING TIMES THAT ARE VERY ON OR VERY OFF FOR THE CHILD.

I bought a notebook and kept a daily log of what Jack ate (thinking perhaps an allergic reaction was causing behavior problems), and what major behavioral problems we encountered throughout the day, including what set him off and how the incident was resolved. I also noted the amount of sleep he had had that night. A sample daily log is provided in Appendix II, Logs and Tracking Tools.

- TALK TO YOUR PEDIATRICIAN ABOUT BEHAVIORS AND WORRIES THAT YOU HAVE. DON'T BE SATISFIED WITH A LACKLUSTER RESPONSE OR AN ANSWER THAT DOESN'T SUIT YOUR GUT.

Do not wait until your next well-child check up or a sick visit to bring the doctor's attention to what you are noticing. If you have kept a diary, bring the doctor the information that you have gathered and think through what the major developmental, behavioral and emotional issues are. I usually bring a list of issues that I would like to discuss in to the doctor's office with me, as it is easy to forget my questions when I get caught up in a discussion.

- READ. ACQUAINT YOURSELF WITH LITERATURE RELATED TO THE ISSUES YOUR CHILD IS HAVING.

There are many good books, general as well as specific to a diagnosis, which you can read to gather information. If you have a good bookstore with knowledgeable salespeople you might tell them what sort of information you are looking for. Your doctor might also have book suggestions for you, based on the problems that you tell him you are having.

• NETWORK WITH PARENTS WHO HAVE INFANTS EXHIBITING SIMILAR SYMPTOMS.
You will need to be a bit of a detective on this one. If the pediatrician indicates a preliminary diagnosis, seek out a local chapter of the organization for that disorder. The internet is also a great place to find other parents. The daily chat rooms of a parent group serving a suspected disability can give you immediate, real life feedback. These are the parents who are in the trenches every day. I have found them to be knowledgeable, well-resourced, compassionate and practical.

• TRY TO ESTABLISH A STRUCTURE TO THE DAY AND A ROUTINE THAT THE CHILD CAN GET USED TO.
Fragile children may have difficulty with transitions and changes in their routine. These are not children who enjoy spontaneity and last minute changes. Try to keep your day structured and without surprises, so that the child knows what to expect.

• KEEP THINGS SIMPLE.
Although your other children might be able to go from one activity to the next, probably just one daily outing is enough for an exceptional child. If you can, leave the exceptional child at home with a sitter or spouse when you need to run errands or pick siblings up. It will save wear and tear on everyone. Perhaps you can group errands together and do them all at one time when you have babysitting support or a spouse available to help.

• TAILOR YOUR ACTIVITIES TO THE ENVIRONMENT THAT BEST SUITS THE CHILD.
You will begin to see what sorts of things trigger behaviors or reactions, or are uncomfortable for your child. For example, some children have trouble with sensory overload and cannot handle noise and commotion. If you have a child with hypersensitivity, forget the circus or other activities that could trigger problem behaviors.

• KEEP AN EYE ON SIBLINGS.
Most likely, you are spending a tremendous amount of time and energy on the out-of-sync child. Siblings may sense that something is awry, and notice that they are getting less time and attention from their parents than they are used to.

John and I divide-and-conquer on Sundays, after church services. We each take a child and do something special. This approach gives siblings a chance for special one-on-one time and also gives them a break from their tiring brother or sister.

• MAKE SURE THERE ARE SUFFICIENT BREAKS FOR THE PARENT WHO BEARS THE BRUNT OF THE RESPONSIBILITY AND SPENDS THE MOST TIME WITH THE EXCEPTIONAL CHILD.

If you are worn out, frustrated and tired, your child is likely to feel the effect of your stress. Be sure that the primary caretaker gets time away each week by him or herself to regroup and recharge his or her batteries.

• BE CREATIVE IN LOOKING FOR SUPPORT SO THAT YOU CAN GET A BREAK.

Think beyond regular babysitters to what your town might provide for support. Our town began an agency last year to serve parents who have children on the autistic spectrum. They provide respite care and run a mentor program. Often, these agencies have funding available to qualifying families, to help reduce some costs, such as childcare.

• SPEND TIME WITH YOUR SPOUSE AND WITH FRIENDS.

Parents of special needs children often tell me that their relationships with their spouse and friends have suffered the most. Because your child may be difficult in public, you may end up declining social invitations for the family. Babysitters who can work with more demanding children can be hard to find, making it difficult for you to go out with your spouse and friends. Again, find the social services agency in your town that can provide you with the appropriate care at an affordable price for you. It is critical for your own mental health that you are able to relax, and that you maintain your sense of who you are apart from your children.

The Evaluation Tango
The Evaluation Process

Before we began the evaluation process to see what was going on with Jack, we muddled through. Each day seemed too long and each night seemed too short. Nothing we did made a difference in Jack.

In fact, I argued with Jack's pediatrician for two years that the child's inward focus, lack of communication, and complete disregard for directions were more than a precocious little boy with constant ear infections. By that time, our family was in a crisis. Something had to change.

Even the simplest of household routines, bathing a child, was a two-hour ordeal. I would coax, plead, bribe and frequently cry as I tried to get Jack into the bathtub. And it wasn't just baths. Getting Jack dressed was a similar game of catch-as-catch can. Dinnertime, the part of the day that we used to look forward to, was spent cajoling Jack to the table and then entertaining him to stay longer than two minutes. Trying to orchestrate getting Sarah to school or the family to church would completely exhaust me.

Looking back, I am surprised that we tolerated this craziness for so long. You shouldn't have to. There is a multitude of help just an office visit away. Today, the theory is: the earlier the intervention, the better. We will never know how much more could have been accomplished if we had not lost those early months.

There have been tremendous gains in understanding the neurologically based disorders that affect the behavior, emotions, and learning capabilities of a child. A competent pediatrician can look at your child's presenting symptoms and refer you to a psychologist, psychiatrist or neurologist for an initial evaluation. From there, specialists might be called in for more in-depth evaluations. A description of the medical professionals in this field is provided in Appendix III, Medical Information.

Our Journey with Doctors

It is frightening to be in charge of a ship that you do not know how to sail. We had no diagnosis for Jack, no plan, and no team of professionals to run the boat. We needed a plan, and since a plan is only as good as the people who work on it, the first step was to get the right professionals.

The first professional to assess Jack was a neurologist. The pediatrician recommended that we start with a neurologist to rule out any significant neurological illnesses. The neurologist determined that Jack had Attention Deficit Hyperactivity Disorder (ADHD) and suggested a thorough psychological assessment. We interviewed several psychologists and settling on one for the evaluation.

The psychologist conducted a complete psychological and emotional assessment. The evaluation took eight office visits. Jack was given a number of tests which enabled the psychologist to understand his cognitive thinking abilities, intellectual capacity, emotional and behavioral states and developmental levels. The evaluation confirmed that intellectually, Jack was in the superior range. The vast discrepancy between his verbal and written performance highlighted significant language and communication deficiencies. He had motor planning and sensory issues that affected his organizational planning abilities and he had severe ADHD, resulting in all sorts of behavioral and emotional concerns.

A whole new world was presented to us. Its existence shattered dreams we had not yet had the joy of defining. Predictions about what life would be like down the road devastated us. The unknown of the situation was frightening.

We decided to tackle the ADHD first. We needed to get Jack to a place where he could attend to what people were asking of him, and to where he could slow down his engine and focus. The neurologist and psychologist decided to use Ritalin to treat these symptoms of ADHD. It seemed to make sense to use the neurologist (rather than bring in a psychiatrist) to monitor and prescribe the medication since it was such a straightforward treatment plan.

The psychological evaluation pointed to a number of significant deficits that needed to be addressed. Any one of these deficits—or any combination of them-- could have contributed to Jack's anger and non-compliance. Jack couldn't tolerate many sensations against his skin. Maybe this was enough of an irritation-- he could not get beyond the discomfort from the feel of clothes and the touch of another person. Maybe his inability to communicate beyond putting a few words together was so frustrating that he was acting out his thoughts and emotions instead of verbalizing them.

Based on the psychologist's observations, we prioritized the concerns and came up with an attack plan. In addition to the medication to treat the symptoms of ADHD we would begin working with an occupational therapist to go after the tactile defensiveness issues and motor planning deficits. A speech and language pathologist would work with Jack to develop his language skills, which were nine months delayed when he was 2 ½ years old.

The plan worked until Jack was in kindergarten, when his behaviors became even more difficult. The behaviors, in fact, began to get in the way of his progress in occupational and speech therapy. Jack would fixate on what he wanted to do and would refuse to cooperate with the therapist. At that point, we turned to a noted pediatric psychopharmacologist (a psychiatrist who is a guru in children's psychiatric medications), who had a large patient population of children with autistic disorders and ADHD. The doctor insisted that we bring Jack to the first visit. I think that was our big mistake. We never had a chance to speak freely and without interruption.

Jack demonstrated many of our causes for concern in that first fifty-minute session: unsafe behaviors, failure to follow directions, propelling self-agendas, obsession with an idea or activity, and tantruming. The doctor described what he saw in front of him, read the evaluations conducted thus far, and, from what he read and saw, agreed with the ADHD diagnosis but prescribed a change in medication from Ritalin to Adderall.

Although some reactions to psychiatric medications require several weeks to reach an accurate blood level Adderall usually takes effect within a few days. Initially we seemed to get a positive response: the symptoms of the disorder were reduced.

Sometimes, if Jack is in the middle of a down period or is heading towards a dip, it is very, very tough to tell if a negative response to a new drug is due to the drug, or if it is just part of the downturn. The drug might be effective in a stable period but you can't tell that during a downturn.

Jack had been having difficulty in school, which had initially prompted us to see the new doctor. After the medication change, he continued to have difficulties. The doctor was hesitant to make any changes. John and I asked ourselves, "Is this doctor doing the best that he can for Jack? Is there something more that we can be doing? Should we get a second opinion?"

Since it was time for an updated psychological evaluation, we began there, with a fresh psychologist. I called a well-regarded school for special needs children, asked our speech and language and occupational therapists for names, and drew upon my support group to find a psychologist that was exceptional in evaluations. Through my search, we found Dr. Sawyer.

Dr. Sawyer did a comprehensive psychological evaluation, similar to the one that had been done three years prior. The higher verbal scores on the IQ test revealed that Jack had made solid speech and language gains. He had also made improvements in the sensory integration area. Dr. Sawyer concluded that, as determined three years earlier, Jack had severe ADHD. Additionally, she felt he might have another neurologically based disorder called Asperger's Syndrome (AS), a form of high-functioning autism.

With the discovery of a possible second neurological impairment John and I decided to once again change psychopharmacologists, since we were not completely happy with the one we were seeing. Dr. Sawyer worked closely with Dr. Hornsby, a psychopharmacologist who had a private practice and taught at a well respected medical college. He had a sterling reputation in our county. Besides good credentials, we needed a doctor who could click with Jack—and with us.

John and I learned from experience that it would be best if we met Dr. Hornsby alone to review the history. At the first meeting, we brought copies of past evaluations, a short write-up from the school outlining Jack's current issues, and updates from outside therapists. The chemistry was good and Dr. Hornsby was familiar with children like Jack.

Jack's first meeting with Dr. Hornsby was eventful. The child seemed to have a knack for calling forth his worst behaviors at doctors' offices. Dr. Hornsby had an inviting play area separated from his main office by a divider. In no time, Jack discovered a small basketball game and refused to be parted with it. Dr. Hornsby saw firsthand the range of worsening behaviors: Jack's refusal to comply with a request deteriorated to a full-scale tantrum and climaxed with the announcement that he was leaving the office and (as he said) "that's that."

Jack saw Dr. Hornsby every week for a year. In the early days, the sessions did not have much conversation. The only thing Dr. Hornsby could get Jack to do was to play a game of his choice. We were tempted to terminate the weekly meetings but Dr. Hornsby felt that he needed to get a feel for Jack's rhythm and to try to establish a rapport. Later, when Jack had a significant collapse, Dr. Hornsby's firsthand knowledge of Jack served as a good benchmark as he looked at Jack's response to new medications.

Now, anytime I see Jack changing behaviorally, I am in touch with Dr. Hornsby immediately. We are prepared for action.

Similarly, Jack's sessions with Dr. Sawyer, the psychologist, did not involve meaty conversations or delve into deep issues. They were more like play therapy and social skills lessons. Jack truly had a hard time understanding and discussing situations that had to do with how people might feel. One day, a friend's father became very angry with the boy for leaving his hockey equipment outside. The father threw the boy's equipment in the trash. The boy later fished it out. Jack was upset for hours about this incident and worked at the computer, typing something that none of us could see. Later that day I found the file, which he had named "Dork 2." Here is what it said:

Tom's dad is very mean. He made Tom cry.
He threw out Tom's hockey equipment because Tom left it outside.
I don't like Tom's dad.

Although it was progress that Jack could sit down and write about something that affected him, the letter was mainly descriptive, not really about Tom's—or Jack's—feelings. So, back at age two, three, four and five, trying to talk to Dr. Sawyer about his feelings was too many layers below what Jack was able to connect to. We actually found that the social skills class which the school social worker ran once a week was more useful, since it involved live situations with peers.

As you can tell, we created a program that involved a lot of private therapies. We were extremely fortunate that insurance covered much of Jack's treatment program. Speech and occupational therapy were both covered one hundred percent, and the psychologist was covered fifty percent for weekly sessions. This great coverage did not happen automatically. I wrote letters to the insurance company when Jack was first evaluated, outlining what Jack's disorder was about and explaining the role of each therapy. Every six months or so, I sent an update to the insurance company, to let them know how Jack was progressing. Keeping the insurance company well informed seemed to help our reimbursement.

Even if you do not have such generous insurance coverage, don't despair. First, your child will most likely be eligible for school-based therapies. Second, local agencies have therapies that may be available to you at a greatly reduced cost. Every state and town differs. Local agencies, such as your department of social services, the department of special education at your board of education, Easter Seals, and the department of health, may be able to help you find federally or state funded programs offering therapy services (meaning a low cost to you).

EVALUATION
★ Strategies

Whether you use a private therapist or an agency supplied therapist, there are certain traits to look for in the professionals that you bring on board:

• THE PROFESSIONAL HAS SOLID PRACTICAL EXPERIENCE IN THE FIELD.
Neurological disorders on the attention-autism spectrum are very complex. If you had a heart disease, you would probably select a physician who is a cardiologist, and as you learned more and more about your illness, you might seek out a cardiologist who has a subspecialty in your area of concern. Similarly, professionals who have a large patient population and who are treating children like yours will be most helpful.

• THE PROFESSIONAL IS CURRENT IN THE FIELD.
Advancements happen so quickly in the field. If your professional is working with old methods and mindsets your child could be missing important interventions. If the doctor or therapist is attending conferences, involved with a teaching university or center, active in his field, or linked to other professionals in the community, you can probably bet he is on top of what's new.

• THE PROFESSIONAL'S PHILOSOPHY AND METHOD OF TREATMENT MAKE SENSE TO YOU.
While John and I don't pretend to be mental health professionals, we can listen and decide what makes sense. If you don't agree with an approach from the get-go you may end up butting heads throughout your relationship with the doctor or professional. There are many good professionals; find one who has an approach that you agree with.

- BE SURE THAT YOU FEEL COMFORTABLE WITH, AND CAN RELATE TO, EACH PROFESSIONAL ON THE TEAM.

You will probably end up talking to doctors and therapists more than some of your closest friends. You will go through strong emotional periods; having therapists and doctors who can support you will be invaluable. Again, there are many good professionals so don't just settle for someone who hits part of your criteria list. Hold out until you are excited about your choice. A word of caution: don't just go for the big reputation doctor. The one with the longest publishing list or most impressive resume may not be the best doctor or fit your family needs. The department of special education at your board of education might be a resource as well as the word-of-mouth network of parents of special needs children.

- WHEN YOU RECEIVE THE FINAL EVALUATION IT SHOULD BE WRITTEN IN AN EASY-TO-UNDERSTAND WAY; A MEETING TO HAVE THE EVALUATION EXPLAINED IN DEPTH SHOULD ACCOMPANY A DETAILED REPORT.

The psychologist will have a detailed report that reflects the child's history as you have reported it, the test results and their interpretation, and recommendations. It is very important that you understand the test results and what they mean since YOU, ultimately, will be your child's case manager. The recommendations should be clear. You should be able to develop a plan of next steps with the psychologist at the end of the evaluation. For example, will the child need more specialized testing? (speech and language, occupational therapy, etc.) What areas are most important and should be addressed first?

- DEVELOP A PRIORITY PLAN WITH THE PSYCHIATRIST AND/OR PSYCHOLOGIST AND STICK TO IT.

Your child's diagnosis will dictate what things should be attended to first. Be careful that you don't try to take on too many new doctors and therapies at once. Give your child time to get comfortable with one modality before moving on to the next.

- **MAKE THE INSURANCE COMPANY'S JOB AS EASY AS POSSIBLE.**

I found that once the insurance company understood Jack's condition and needs, we were reimbursed for the bills that we submitted much more quickly and with fewer questions. Probably the bills made more sense to the claims adjuster. You will find examples of letters to the insurance company in Appendix I, Sample Presentations and Letters. In addition, when submitting bills I make sure that they are very well organized. After all, isn't it easier to deal with something that is neat and logically organized than to sort through a mess? I put all of the bills for each kind of therapy together and submit the stack with a short letter that updates the insurance company on Jack's condition and progress.

- **ACKNOWLEDGE THE EMOTIONAL STRAIN OF THE SITUATION AND GET THE HELP THAT YOU NEED.**

No doubt about it, this stuff is not easy. Don't hesitate to bring in a psychotherapist or someone who can help you and your spouse cope with the stress.

- **SIMPLIFY OTHER PARTS OF YOUR LIFE.**

Look for ways you can cut down on your regular responsibilities. For example, in a normal routine you may love cooking meals for the family. During this time period, picking up already cooked dinners may be easier all around. I usually use the time when Jack is in a doctor's or therapist's office to run to a nearby grocery store or take-out food store. (Remember, pizza is considered to have all the food groups). Don't try to be Supermom or Superdad by doing it all yourself.

- **GATHER RESOURCES.**

You don't need to wait until the evaluation is over to begin learning. Ask the professionals you meet for relevant books and articles. Reading as much as possible will equip you to ask better questions.

• BE MINDFUL OF WHEN ENOUGH IS ENOUGH.

Jack needed speech therapy, occupational therapy and psychotherapy. But, the demands of being picked up at school early, adjusting to a car ride, transitioning to a therapist's office, working intensely with a therapist, and then transitioning back to school, were all too much for a child who could not accomplish even the simplest transitions smoothly. Pace the day. Less is often more with these children.

• PACE YOURSELF.

You don't have to get to all the therapists and doctors in round one. Each visit entails transitions and changes for the whole family. Try to keep your home as stress free and normal as possible. Don't make therapies the center of your home life.

READ THE LABEL, MABEL
Understanding the Diagnosis

The best thing and the most important thing about having an evaluation and a diagnosis is that it tells you what you are dealing with. And that's your starting point. From there you can figure out what you are going to change in your own approach—and in the larger environment—to try to overcome the obstacles that your child faces. There will be many ideas among your therapists and perhaps between you and your spouse on how to go about all of this.

When you have a name to put to all the things that have baffled you, you realize two things. One, the behaviors are not your child's fault. And two, his behaviors are not a reflection of your parenting style. Sure it may be something in the genetic code of your family or your spouse's family, but that's hardly your fault. Hearing the diagnosis should take the blame off you, your spouse, and your child. You can then move on.

I never played the blame game but it wasn't until we received an official diagnosis and we developed an action plan that I felt good about how I was handling the situation. I think one of the first things that you might want to do is to take yourself out of the equation. Your child's disorder is not your fault.

When Jack was one year old we had a babysitter, Mabel, who told me after one week on the job, "This child is already ruined." Two years later, we had a reason for the behaviors. How unfair to Jack!—He hadn't been ruined. He was just reacting to an environment that didn't understand his special requirements and limitations. If you can free yourself from the guilt and the fault-finding and move to a place where you are focused on finding ways to help your child, you will be much more useful to yourself, to your family, and to your special child.

The first thing that I did when we received the Asperger's Syndrome (AS) diagnosis was to learn as much as I could about it. In our case, although the psychologist put the Asperger's name to Jack's condition, she added a caveat that he was a very complex person and didn't really fit neatly into the AS diagnosis. She said that it would be useful to think of him having one toe in this group, as some of his symptoms were common to AS people. This could help guide us in treatment and school decisions.

Asperger's Syndrome is a social disability. A person with AS does not pick up social cues, does not know how to read social cues, and has little idea how to establish relationships. In short, the world, with all of its social nuances and unspoken rules, must make an AS person feel like he is living on a foreign planet.

I remember taking Jack to the playground and, like all moms, suggesting that he take turns with the other children on the always popular monkey bars. He would look at me like I was the one from the other planet. Why should he give up a turn doing something that he loved? It just made no sense to him. I'd cajole, countdown, rationalize and finally give the ultimatum that we would have to leave the park if turn taking was not employed. The threat of leaving usually did the trick, but the motivation for giving up the bars wasn't to be a good sport—it was to stay and play.

Typical behaviors of a person with AS include an absorption in a single subject to the point of obsession (usually a very narrow and unusual topic such as train schedules, transportation vehicles, electrical conductors, etc.), little empathy and understanding of others' feelings, difficulty making and keeping friends, a tendency to lecture versus holding a back and forth conversation, poor eye contact, great rigidity to sameness in schedule and activities, and being easily frustrated.

Asperger people are often brilliant. However, that high intellect may only be realized in the subject area that they are consumed by. Their lack of an internal motivation for societal approval often results in little effort to excel in things that don't really interest them. It is not unusual for AS people to be unable to channel their intelligence in a way that would result in a strong school performance or a meaningful career.

Jack's AS-like symptons seemed to be at a mild level. Yes, there was certainly the lack of empathy for others. In fact, Jack generally seemed totally unaware of others, period—feelings, interests and even presence. He had poor eye contact, no interest or ability in making friends (not even with his sister unless she happened to want to do what he was doing), and a fragility that translated into easy frustration. As long as Jack was allowed to follow his own agenda, he was fine. In fact, he was more than fine. He was happy in his own world, doing his own thing.

Jack has a zeal for learning and discovering things around him that is infectious. He becomes fully absorbed, but it's not an all-out, one hundred percent of the time obsession. Even during his worst periods, Jack is fun to hang out with. He looks at the world in such a different way, pulling out ideas that are often fresh and funny.

At three years old, Jack could put together 1,000 piece puzzles with amazing speed. I would sit near him reading a book or trying to help, and we'd chitchat—on his topic of choice of course—lazing the day away. His temperament was even and easy. It stayed that way until I asked him to do something that he didn't want to do or he became wound too tight from wild play. Either scenario resulted in Jack's not responding to my requests to calm down or to leave what he was doing when requested, or to do anything else that involved his ability to modulate his behavior and/or put aside his own wants. When any of these situations arose, frustration spilled into anger that led to hours and hours of pleading, begging, and often physically picking him up to get him where I needed him to be.

During this time period, we felt less like parents and more like the police force. While our friends were teaching their children the first steps of being part of a community through play dates and children's activities, we were on disaster control. We went through sign-up after sign-up for swimming, story time, skating and other classes, only to have to pull Jack out of the program as we realized that he could not follow directions as required. The constant cajoling and patrolling, with many eyes watching us, was too much pressure.

There was never a single moment or defining point when we realized Jack was not typical. But we knew that life with Jack's inwardness, complete lack of cooperation, and his never slowing motor was not the same experience as our friends were having. He was a geode—one of those beautiful crystals hidden inside an ordinary rock. Our friends could already see the precious gifts blooming in their children; we would have to work to bring Jack's out.

My intuition told me that if we were going to get Jack to break through that rock we would need to push, forcing a crack here and a crack there, to break through the barriers holding him back from fully experiencing the world.

And that is how I approached Jack's deficits. The goal of speech and language therapy was to gain simple and then pragmatic language. The goal of occupational therapy was to help Jack overcome his tactile defensiveness and motor planning disorganization. We knew that if he could conquer these obstacles, Jack would be able to begin to connect with the world and we could begin to work on the second layer of goals: following directions, turn-taking, and listening. As the therapies progressed and I began to see a crack here or there, I would push on Jack a little. I would make a request that forced him to interact with me and meet me somewhere that wasn't exactly where he wanted to be.

$\mathcal{S}$trategies FOR DEALING WITH THE DIAGNOSIS

• DON'T BLAME YOURSELF OR START TO IMAGINE WHAT COULD HAVE BEEN.
It is not your fault and it has nothing to do with your parenting, it is just the luck of the draw. Once you begin to accept your situation, you will be free from the emotional strongholds that can get in the way of the parent that you need to be.

• LEARN AS MUCH AS YOU CAN ABOUT YOUR CHILD'S DIAGNOSIS.
Don't stop at the description of the diagnosis. Find out what the strengths as well as the limitations are for people with your child's disorder. Read about people who have successfully lived with the disorder and learn what things helped them grow.

• DON'T LET THE OPINIONS OF OTHER PEOPLE LIMIT THE POSSIBILITIES FOR YOUR CHILD.
People unwittingly say things that can snuff out hope. In most cases, their understanding of your child's disorder is based on some one or two people that they know. Turning a judgment into an opportunity for educating that person a little more about the disorder is doing a service to every child that shares your child's diagnosis.

Are We There Yet?
Setting Up a Therapy Program

If your week is filled running from therapist to therapist you may feel that you are making progress. Don't relax just yet. It is up to you to see to it that goals are articulated, a plan is made, and that the most important things are done, and done correctly. A small investment of time and resources up front will ultimately make your life easier, and will probably help your child make better progress.

Start by making sure that each health care professional has specific goals for the work that they are doing with your child. These goals are generated from the psychological and other evaluations completed. There should be a work plan, supporting the goals laid out by the health care professional. Don't just assume that all of this is in place. As in any job, if no one lays out goals and a plan, the work that gets done may not be the most important work.

When the goals and plan have been established, a timeframe should be set for when the goals will (ideally) be achieved. It's best to put only general time-frames on these, since you have no idea what your child's rate of progress will be. Unfortunately, progress is usually not made without some setbacks and side trips. Don't be surprised by this.

Vague deadlines do not mean vague goals. Goals should be specific and should be measurable. In other words, you want to be able to identify when your child has achieved something and when that something has become a set behavior.

Jack could not greet people. His reciprocal gaze was poor and he would only return a "hello" if you specifically prompted him, several times. One of his speech goals in third grade was to say "hello" to five people, without prompts, four days in a row. To accomplish this, the speech teacher worked with Jack for over six months. Some days, they would spend thirty minutes walking around the school building seeing how many people they could say "hello" to. It took a long period of focusing only on this goal but Jack now greets people very appropriately, and often spontaneously.

Your child will achieve goals established at school and by outside therapists more quickly if you focus on the goals at home as well. The more familiar you are with what the therapist and the school are doing, the more you can reinforce what needs to be accomplished at home.

The school, the outside therapist and our family all worked on Jack's ability to hold a reciprocal gaze. At sessions with our outside therapist, the therapist held up animal cards that she was using as prompts right at her eye level, so that Jack was forced to look at her full in the face. At home, my standard line for awhile was, "Look at my eyes… they are now purple (blue, green, rainbow, polka dot) and flashing!" At school "looking at the speaker" was a standard goal on Jack's individual education goals.

The only way that all this coordination can happen is if YOU make it happen. In today's world, it is very rare that a team of health care professionals located in different settings will be able to meet regularly to review your child's case. Without a communication vehicle, it is hard for each member of the professional team to know how each of their work is fitting in with the others'. While there is no question that I am (and should be) the overall coordinator, I have been lucky enough to have Jack's speech and language pathologist act as the team's point person.

In the early years, it was the speech and language pathologist who raised questions about the overall therapy plan, brought me up to speed with new tools and treatments for Jack's disorder, and unhesitatingly called a doctor or therapist to discuss one thing or another. These days, our psychiatrist plays this role. You will have a feel for who among your team is the right person to lead the effort. When you find the leader, ask him or her if he or she would be willing to act as the coordinator, along with you, for the professionals. Sharing the responsibility gives you emotional support, and professional-to-professional communication can accomplish things that you, as a layperson, cannot. You will find examples of some communication tools for maintaining good team coordination in Appendix I, Sample Letters.

Many times, shared goals lead to therapies that dovetail and build upon one another. For a few years, the list of Jack's therapies included a school-based speech therapist, school-based occupational therapist, a school social worker, a private psychologist, a private psychopharmacologist, a private occupational therapist, a private speech and language pathologist, and a nutritionist. That's a lot of people that could be running in different directions. But with good communication processes, the different therapists worked well together and worked as a cohesive team.

The Logistics

When we first began therapies, the schedule overwhelmed our family. Since children like Jack crave structure and are notorious for being poor transitioners, I thought a visual reminder of the day would be helpful. I made a large poster and taped it to one wall in the kitchen. At breakfast, we reviewed each child's activities for the day. The poster showed the day, time and activity for each child, starting with: 1) Get Dressed, 2) Brush Teeth, 3) Eat Breakfast, and, 4) Go to School.

Although Jack still needed a count down before we left for somewhere ("ten minutes until we leave for speech therapy," "five minutes until we leave for speech therapy," "three minutes until we leave for speech therapy," and, "one minute until we leave for speech therapy") the Breakfast Calendar was a good way to get the children oriented, and it pointed out any quick transition times during the day. Each year I had the children decorate the poster. It is surprising how much more ownership they took once they were part of its creation.

During our hey-day of therapies, I logged twenty thousand miles in ten months. This was not from fun day trips or vacation traveling mind you, just back and forth across town and to and from nearby towns for therapies. During that period, Jack received two speech therapy sessions, two occupational therapy sessions and a psychotherapy session each week, and a once monthly psychiatry visit. Sarah logged many of these miles with us since I didn't have an everyday babysitter. The hour of waiting while Jack was in therapy could have seemed much longer if Sarah and I hadn't had a plan for what to do during that time.

Sarah and I established a separate routine for each of the therapy trips. The speech therapist's office was in a medical building near a shopping center. We spent the first twenty minutes in a bookstore and then got an ice cream cone for the remainder of the time. The occupational therapist's office was not so conveniently located. At occupational therapy, we stayed in the waiting room and did homework.

The bottom line here is: an occupied sibling is a happier sibling. As time went on and Sarah had more after-school activities, I didn't have to bring her with me as often as in those early days. With just Jack, the car ride was quieter, and I could use the time while he was in the therapy session to get errands done, catch up on paperwork, or read. I realized free time was a luxury, so when I had the fifty minutes to myself I tried to use it as prudently as possible.

I never thought about bringing therapies into the home. Once, after we had a particularly difficult time getting Jack to leave the speech therapist's office, the therapist suggested that I look for someone to come to the home for some of our therapies. At the time, there weren't any therapists offering this option in our area. Today, I hear of a lot more people who take this approach. In retrospect, this was a great idea. It would have saved so much of the transitional difficulties that we suffered through several times a week.

When Jack began school, he received some therapies there, but we decided to keep up with the outside therapies so that gains could be made as quickly as possible. It wasn't until Jack entered a therapeutic school in the middle of second grade, where therapists were quite competent and the sessions part of the regular curriculum, that we were able to discontinue the outside therapies.

Strategies FOR ESTABLISHING YOUR CHILD'S THERAPUTIC PROGRAM

• Develop a large wall calendar that shows the activities each day for each child.

It will organize everyone, including you, for the day.

• Make sure that the therapy program reflects the goals and priorities that you have established with the coordinating doctor.

You will only be moving ahead when you are working on the things that need to be worked on.

• Make sure the team is kept informed of goals, progress, and concerns in all the disciplines.

Ideally, the school, outside therapists, and home life should have goals that relate to one another. Working on the same thing over and over again in different environments is what will ultimately bring your child from learning in a specific place to generalizing a behavior.

• Review goals and strategies with your therapists on a regular basis.

This will ensure that everyone stays on track. It will also keep you more conscious of approaching benchmarks (which will mean that it is time to revise goals) and enable you to recognize stalls in the program.

• Set up therapy appointments on a schedule that is least disruptive to your weekly routine.

Between the travel and the transitions, the therapy program will be tiring enough. Try to at least make it minimally intrusive to all of the other things that you juggle in your life.

• Learn ways to incorporate therapies into your natural environment.
All of our therapists would sit down periodically and suggest things we could
do at home to advance their therapy goals.   For example, Jack was tactically
defensive (he couldn't stand being touched or the feel of certain things) when
he was very young.   In occupational therapy, we were trained in a brushing[2]
program used to break down tactile defensiveness.   By learning how to brush
Jack at home, I cut down on the number of times a week I had to bring him
in just for brushing sessions.   Not only was home brushing easier on us, it also
allowed us to overcome the defensiveness more quickly.

• Try to get your therapy needs covered through the school program
and through programs offered through local agencies serving special
needs children.
The more that can be accomplished in one place, the easier it will be on your
child, and ultimately, on you.

• If private therapy is required, consider bringing the therapists into
your home.
If your home is set up in such a way that your child will be able to work with
the therapist without being distracted, this approach could save wear and tear
on everyone.

2. Occupational therapists use a special brush to treat tactile defensiveness; it stimulates the nervous system
and can overcome tactile defenses.

II. SCHOOL DAYS, SCHOOL DAYS

ONE, TWO, THREE STRIKES AND YOU'RE OUT!

A DIFFERENT KIND OF SCHOOL

One, Two, Three Strikes and You're Out!

Getting the Best from Your School

Early School Years

Some parents recognize that their child is not on the typical developmental path before school begins, but for some of us, the school experience is where we must finally face the reality that our child needs special help. It does not matter who identifies your child's needs, you or the school. What does matter is how the two of you work together.

In our case, Jack's school experience was remarkably different each year. Some years, he soared with a program or teacher that fit his needs perfectly; other times, the environment caused a terrible setback. You should pay careful attention to what is going on at school at all times and have a strong communication link with the teacher and team working with your child.

Pre-Kindergarten

When Jack was two years old we moved from the northern suburbs of Chicago to Connecticut. The children had attended a Montessori school in Illinois, and we had been very pleased with the educational philosophy of the program. We found a similar program in our new town and enrolled both children.

It didn't take very long before the teachers at the Montessori school indicated to me that our son's energy level, impulsivity, self-agenda and lack of focus were not even remotely near the edges of what was typical or workable for the school. It was clear that he could easily manage the materials and the academic work, but he could not stay with any task long enough to complete an assignment. Although I reviewed what was happening on a daily basis with the teacher, the situation's severity really became crystal clear at the Thanksgiving assembly of 120 children, where the only pilgrim who couldn't sit at the banquet table was Jack.

I knew then that something significant was going on with Jack. By the time that the teacher, principal and I met after that fateful Thanksgiving assembly, I was prepared for the school's determination that Jack wasn't going to make it there. That is, I thought I was prepared, but I wasn't.

A common comment that I hear from teachers and counselors is that many, many parents simply do not, or cannot, accept the fact that something is wrong with their child. Even if I think I have accepted this fact, I am not always prepared to deal with the implications. It only hits me when Jack does something or I watch him along with typical boys his age. Then I am hit in the belly—again—by what we are dealing with. I think I have accepted our situation, and I probably have at that particular stage and point in time. But each time a new stage or behavior comes upon us, I have to accept Jack all over again. And sometimes, hope gets the better of me and I just forget that what we are living with is not going away—it just changes its face.

You might panic. We did. Don't worry, this is a normal reaction. No one ever wants to hear that their child has issues. If your relationship with the school begins defensively, helping your child—which should be everyone's goal—will be more painful. Try to step back from the situation and look at what is happening objectively. Try to focus on finding answers rather than arguing about the problem.

I know a few parents that have so much anger towards the school system that they are paralyzed. One mother used to bring file boxes to our monthly parent support groups and pull out back up information in case she ever needed to take the department of special education to court. Functioning in an adversarial relationship is exhausting. Your energy will be better spent finding solutions for your child, rather than fighting with the school board.

Our town has a program that is federally mandated for all towns, called the Birth to Three program. This program has various services for children who have identified special needs. We learned that there was an integrated pre-kindergarten program that would be appropriate for Jack. It consisted of six special needs children and seven typical children. The class had a head teacher and two aides. The goal of the program was to work on social skills and behaviors.

Jack was able to spend 1½ years in this pre-school program before kindergarten rolled around and we had to consider other options. In pre-kindergarten, we knew each day how well the program was serving Jack, not only by his home behaviors, but through the use of a daily communication journal that came home with him. Since Jack's issues were almost exclusively social and behavioral, the teacher used the journal to discuss things that had happened in those areas—always sharing strategies that had worked and not worked. I would write back issues that we were struggling with at home so that she could address them in class as well.

Mrs. Wilkinson, the pre-kindergarten teacher, was amazing. She gave me behavior strategies and insights into why Jack might have reacted a particular way. She understood Jack and knew how to get the best out of him. She was able to feed his quest for knowledge and encourage his interest in learning. I think it was her consistency, her even-temper (calm at all times), and clear expectations that were of greatest value to Jack. She was unflappable. The week before school started, Mrs. Wilkinson came to our home to meet Jack and perhaps take a little of the anxiety out of the first day of school. Jack was in the swimming pool when Mrs. Wilkinson arrived. He did a surprisingly nice job of saying "Hello" when she introduced herself. He promptly ran to a bush near the pool to go to the bathroom "au naturale." Mrs. Wilkinson didn't miss a beat and just rolled along with her Getting To Know You agenda.

Kindergarten

Unfortunately, there was no kindergarten class with the integrated format of pre-kindergarten. Both the department of special education and our own team of health care professionals felt that Jack wasn't quite ready for the mainstream class. The only option was a self-contained class with mainstreaming opportunities. The theory was that we'd start off mainstreaming Jack for specials (gym, music and art) and then move into more mainstreaming as Jack proved himself. The format of the special education kindergarten class would be a new one, with two classes combined and team-taught. The class would take place in a different elementary school than where Jack went to pre-school; this particular elementary school was not as familiar with special education services as the first.

It wasn't until we had a year when the daily journal was not used that I realized its real power. Despite my repeated requests that the kindergarten teacher use the daily journal, notes to me were infrequent and sketchy, leaving me with a sense that something was amiss in the class. The clear rules and structure that were the hallmark of Jack's pre-kindergarten class were not so clear in kindergarten. Rather than show-and-tell day, children brought in toys every day. This was 1996 and Star Wars had made a comeback, big time. Jack soon got to know all of the characters and became a devotee, even without having seen the movies. By January, all he could think of during playtime was Star Wars.

While spaceships were swirling in Jack's mind, the self-contained classroom seemed to have taken on its own whirling. One of the two teachers had to take a leave for the remainder of the year for health reasons and the remaining teacher became quite ill for a period of weeks, resulting in frequent substitutes of both head teachers and aides. Lesson plans seemed nonexistent and the general tenor of the class seemed more and more out of control. Amazingly, Jack continued to exceed academic requirements. What he wasn't learning in class he was picking up on his own through academic software programs that I bought, through library visits, and by working once a week with a wonderful teacher from the Montessori school, who taught Jack to read and went on to do special science projects with him. Academics aren't everything, however. It wasn't long before Jack lost his emotional center. Action was needed, and fast.

I was in a meeting at a consumer products company, where I was filling in on a marketing assignment for a woman who was on maternity leave, when I got the first of what would be too many calls to come to school—and right away.

I scribbled a quick note to a quizzical co-worker sitting next to me, explained that Jack was having a difficult time at school, and dashed off for the elementary school.

I was met in the lobby by the principal, the teacher, and the teacher's aide, with the information that Jack had refused to comply with a request in the self-contained classroom. The situation had spiraled down until he was led to the time-out room—a converted custodial closet. I didn't even know such a thing was in existence. It was everything you remember about your elementary school janitor's room. Dark, smelly, and cold. A teacher's aide stood outside the door, holding it slightly ajar.

It seems that when Jack was pushed to comply with a request, some line had been crossed and Jack had been led to the time-out room. With anxiety and sensory issues brimming to overflow, he bit the aide when he was released. Now they were asking me: Could I take him home? My question was not, "Could I?" It was, "Where do we go from here?" Obviously, this method of behavior control was not appropriate for anyone and particularly not for someone with the anxieties of Jack.

The next month was tedious and rocky. Although there were only a couple of other situations that landed Jack in the time-out room, they were dramatic enough that I began to ask myself each morning, "Where will Jack be better off today? Home or school?" Once I had these feelings, it seemed that I lost hold of the trust relationship with the school.

During this time I rather casually, completely unpremeditatedly, turned to Jack's teacher and said, "John and I really wonder if this new drug is doing anything for Jack?" (Jack's doctor had changed his medication for controlling ADHD symptoms just a few months earlier). She said, quite matter-of-factly, "Oh no, he's been a lot worse since starting this new drug." HELLO? Is there some lost satellite hookup between teacher and parents here? Why would the teacher have this sense and not share it immediately? So there we were: three months of regressing behaviors and our child was now so anxious and angry that we were losing more ground.

Following are a few excerpts from a diary that I kept during this time period.

October 7th, Kindergarten

When I picked Jack up today for a psychologist appointment I saw an interaction that continues to reinforce the non-understanding of the nature of Jack's disorder—or the non-understanding of how the teachers should handle his disorder.

Jack had seen a Thanksgiving project at the nurse's office and had asked her for a copy of it. The nurse made ten copies and said, "Here are your copies." It seems that she meant each student in Jack's class could have one; he thought she meant that they were all for him. This pragmatic language-processing problem is typical for Jack.

When Jack came back to the classroom he was asked to hand out the turkeys and he refused, insisting that they were all his. The teacher finally took nine turkeys away and Jack hit her. Other teachers were brought in and his kindergarten teacher took him to the janitorial closet (the time-out room) and held him so tightly that he perceived she was choking him. He became so agitated that he wet himself and the teacher too. The school nurse called me to relay the incident and suggested that I pick him up. He was calm when I arrived and immediately told me that he had asked to go to the bathroom when he was in the time-out room, but no one answered him.

June 5th, Kindergarten

I had Margaret, our masterful babysitter, accompany Jack to school today because it was field day. Knowing that it would be his worst environment, large space, many children, and an unstructured event, I thought that having Margaret there would be useful. She remained with Jack until nearly 11:00 a.m.

The morning was as we expected—lots of waiting, which was difficult for Jack and many others as well. Margaret was struck by the inexperience and negativity of one of the teacher's aides who interacted with Jack. He wanted to help spread some flags out and the aide kept on saying, "No, Jack," although Margaret said there would have been no problem with his helping. She left with him at 11:00 a.m. and they spent a great day together with no transition problems or tantrums. Jack mentioned to her during the day that he had been choked earlier in the year by one of the teachers that Margaret had met. Could incidents such as this have been worrying Jack for more than six months?

Kindergarten ended with all of us—probably not least Jack—breathing a sigh of relief. The school year just didn't gel for Jack. Like many children with special needs, there is a great fragility to Jack; one variable that is slightly off can have a profound impact on his ability to function. The combination of constantly changing teachers, a classroom of high maintenance children, an infrastructure not adept at accommodating special needs children, and a behavior management approach that had scary components like the janitor's room were, taken together, too much for Jack. As a result, he could not hold together his internal environment. We waited through the summer for first grade to begin.

First Grade

The department of special education worked hard with John and me and our team of doctors and therapists to come up with a first-rate, first grade program for Jack. The school staff and administration recognized the disaster of kindergarten, so they did a lot more thinking and planning with us. The result was a first grade program that excited all of us.

We held a series of organizational meetings before the school year began. At the first meeting, Jack's private psychologist and I educated the school team about the needs and requirements of Jack. At the second meeting, I presented the key findings from both our private therapists and a review from the kindergarten teacher. Our psychologist and psychiatrist recommended parameters for a first grade program and classroom structure. At the third meeting, the department of special education coordinator presented options for first grade, including a self-contained classroom with mainstream experiences and mainstreaming with access to a resource room. At the final meeting, we agreed on a program. After each meeting, I prepared a recap of what was discussed and what the next steps were.

For Jack's first grade program, we were in agreement that the class would be no larger than five students. It would have an individualized academic program (challenging his intellectual strength), draw upon a behavioral management system, and have appropriate adjunct therapies.

After the kindergarten disaster, we were all committed to finding a stellar head teacher and classroom aides. However, we didn't hear who the new teacher would be, the location of the classroom, the profiles of the other children, or other details until a few weeks before school started. Our hard work more than paid off. Perhaps most important was the head teacher for Jack's class. Mrs. Gresia was in her mid-thirties and had just completed her graduate work in special education. Although I was dubious about someone who had never taught before, I was pleasantly surprised. Not to say that we didn't start off with a few hiccups.

The first day of school Jack came home with a teacher communication journal filled with problems as opposed to solutions. I panicked—was this going to be a teacher who would only be able to see the difficulties and not be able to address them? Thinking that it might be too offensive to begin with a criticism of the teacher, I called our school district contact. She, in turn, worked with the teacher and encouraged me to give her space and time.

Mrs. Gresia and I had a standing meeting on Fridays to review what had gone on the previous week, identify hot spots and set goals for the coming week. As the Fridays rolled on, Mrs. Gresia bloomed before my eyes and Jack bloomed with her. The class consisted of four students, and, in a natural, unconscious way, each child ended up particularly bonding with a teacher or an aide. Jack lined up with Mrs. Gresia.

Drawing on Jack's strengths to address his needs, Mrs. Gresia created special science projects, pairing a typical student with Jack. The payoff for the typical child was that he could complete projects at a much more advanced level than what was available in the regular classroom. For Jack, it was that he had a model for behavior at very close range.

The largest project, an in-depth study of the solar system, lasted two months. At the conclusion of this wonderful project, Jack and Michael, the typical student, had created a papier-mâché replica of the planetary system. Mrs. Gresia was so pleased with the project that she prepared the children to present the project to the entire first grade class.

Tears streamed down my cheeks as I watched Jack and Michael deliver a formal presentation and then field questions from twenty-three first graders. A moment of lightness ended the presentation, when the vice principal presented each child a certificate of achievement. Jack's response, delivered in the matter-of-fact voice of a child who has seen one too many reward systems, was, "What can I trade this in for?" One of our favorite family evenings for a long time was watching the planet video—including the award ceremony.

As the saying goes, nothing is forever. This is certainly true in elementary education, where the idea of a teacher staying with the same class for more than a year is a rare dream come true. My heart has rarely been as heavy as it was at my last Friday morning meeting with Mrs. Gresia. I knew that it would be beyond luck to find a teacher who was so intuitive and on target with meeting Jack's needs. As for Mrs. Gresia, she shared with me that something had been touched inside of her forever.

Second Grade

There is always a great flurry at the department of special education in May and June. Every parent of a child who has an Individualized Education Plan (IEP) has a mega-meeting with the teachers, school therapists, and coordinators at the department of special education to discuss the child's entire school year from academic, social and behavioral viewpoints. A program for the following school year is developed. It seems strange to me that there is not at least one meeting required during the school year to assess how the program is going and to adjust it as necessary. Unless you, as a parent, push for such a mid-year evaluation, the school will not usually suggest one unless there is a crisis.

In our case, the first planning meeting for second grade was quite comprehensive. Mrs. Gresia reviewed Jack's many goals and gains in first grade, as did the school-based therapists. Jack had completed first grade with participation in the mainstream art, music and gym classes, as well as in a twenty-minute reading and writing group of twelve mainstream students. Mrs. Gresia reviewed the three special science projects that Jack had accomplished with a student from the mainstream, and she also went over the softer gains: playing with children appropriately on the playground, attending after school programs, and more.

The psychologist who ran a social skills group for the three children in the classroom, the occupational therapist and the speech therapist had not had as much success as Mrs. Gresia. Jack needed to have a relationship with someone before he was willing to put his own agenda aside. His inconsistent level of cooperation signaled that his self-agenda could still override requests.

Overall, everyone was feeling very, very good about Jack's first grade performance, so we felt no heat to ramp up planning for second grade. Why would we? He had surpassed grade level expectations from an academic standpoint and was on a very even behavioral keel.

School adjourned for the summer. Despite our suggestion to review a draft of the second grade program before losing Mrs. Gresia, our liaison at the department of special education and the school administrative staff were confident that we could wait until August. All of us looked forward to increasing the mainstream experience, hoping this would be the final bridge before Jack could participate fully in a mainstream class with an aide. What an exciting goal for second grade!

Three days before second grade began, I prepared a presentation for the new teachers and aides who would be working with Jack. I outlined needs and reviewed successful strategies from last year's classroom.

But no final IEP was in place when the doors opened on September 5th. Administrators assured me that a very experienced teacher who had been on staff at this particular elementary school years earlier would be leading Jack's class. The school administration felt that this teacher could determine a program within a few weeks and finalize an IEP Still, I was nervous. The summer had been a little rocky. I thought we had learned our lesson in kindergarten—that being overly prepared was worth the extra trouble—but I went along with the plan anyways.

Two major changes were in place for second grade. These changes my have been the beginning of Jack's complete undoing.

First, Jack would begin each day in the mainstream class and remain there for two hours. The first grade's mainstream class of twelve students was an anomaly, of course. Now he would be part of a regular class with twenty-three pupils. Even with an aide, that was a big jump.

Secondly, Jack's homeroom class would no longer be a self-contained class. In an effort to serve more students, the class was to become a resource room with various students coming in and out throughout the day. This change would require Jack to operate in a much more active environment than he had had to manage in first grade.

With the gains Jack had made in first grade, none of us were prepared for the fragility that showed almost from the first day of school. Little did we know how quickly Jack could lose what he had gained. In Falling Apart at a Stop Sign (see table of contents), you will read what happened to Jack in the autumn of second grade.

It All Starts With Good Communication

Developing a team that is focused and works well together is one of the keys to success for crafting a successful school program. There are more and more children entering the special needs arena, placing greater demands on the administration and teachers to serve all of these children. Jack could easily have fallen into the fray if we had not taken charge and mobilized a team effort.

Communication is critical. With a team of people who are in a variety of settings (school based and private), there needs to be some vehicle for keeping everyone informed about what is going on with your child. Here are a few key communication tools that I use:

Start of the School Year Introductory Letter.
At the start of each school year I prepare a letter to Jack's special education and mainstream teachers and a separate letter to other staff or teachers who come in contact with him. The goal of the letter is to give a snapshot of what Jack is currently like, the key areas that we are working on, and what his summer experience consisted of (including the highs and the lows). I include practical suggestions on how to handle certain situations that have been cropping up and I share some of the successful strategies that the previous teacher used with Jack. Teachers have told me that my letters are very helpful and give them a little insight right off the bat. (I also do the same for Sarah's new teachers and they, as well, have told me how helpful this is.

Quarterly Updates.
Probably the most powerful tool that I use is a quarterly recap memo. In the memo, I review the key goals that we are all working on with Jack for the quarter, discuss how he is performing with regard to these goals, relay achievements and accomplishments that I think are important to the team, and discuss concerns. I also outline any follow-up actions that various team members are working on. Of course, I ask the teachers and our outside health care professionals for their input for these memos. I am just the coordinating and distributing arm for the team. I always provide telephone numbers for all those on the distribution list so that team members can contact each other easily. I am careful to run ideas by folks before they land in print. I make sure that everyone is copied on key communication. I also try to provide articles and information, even recaps of conferences, for the team.

Crisis Memo.[3]

The minute that we sense things are not going well, I write a note to the teacher and/or principal. The note outlines our concerns and suggests that we meet to compare what is happening at home and at school. I date my letter and keep a copy. (Be sure to keep a file of all school correspondence. There are specific laws that require schools to respond to parent concerns like this within a given time frame.) From there, our team meets and adjustments are made as needed.

Meetings.

Another way that I bring providers together is at meetings. It is not unusual for me to bring one of my outside therapists to a school meeting so that she can meet face to face with the school provider of the same discipline. Who I bring depends upon what our top goals are at the moment or where the biggest opportunity might be for some outside input. For example, in first grade one of our key goals was to improve Jack's pragmatic language skills. Our private speech therapist came to a meeting and was able to review and refine goals with the school-based speech therapist, and then discuss what their overarching speech and language program should be. Not unlike the saying that the whole is greater than the sum of the parts, we find that when two therapists bring together their individual programs, a much more comprehensive program can be created.

A sample of each of the written communication tools described above is provided in Appendix I, Letters.

If you feel comfortable being the coordinator of communication, by all means take it on. Someone needs to. If you are not able to be the coordinator, find someone to help you. If your school has a special education committee of the PTA you might start there to look for resources. There may be another parent who is able to attend a meeting with you and guide you through a follow-up memo. There may be someone on your private team of therapists who can perform this role. Finally, there are people who are liaisons or mediators who

3. Email may be the quickest way to get your S.O.S. distributed

might be helpful. Often these are parents of special education children who have been through the process and understand how it works. We have several mediators in our area that charge by the hour to perform this function.

How Does the School Process Work?

There is a U.S. federal law, the Individuals With Disabilities Education Act (IDEA), that was created to insure that children with special needs are provided with an education that meets their particular needs. The spirit of IDEA is to provide our children with equal access to education, in a context that recognizes their special needs. In 1997 this law was amended to clarify the role of parents as partners in the educational process. The more you know and understand about your rights, the more effectively you will be able to effectively advocate for your child.

One of the first things I did when Jack was officially diagnosed and became eligible for special education was to become familiar with the federal and state laws governing our rights. I learned how the process worked and what we could expect. There may be courses reviewing the laws and how they function, offered through the department of special education or a local social services agency. Ask other parents who seem to have good working relationships with the school district how you might get up to speed on the process.

Your child's academic program will be developed by a team of school-based personnel and *you*. You are an important part of the team. Your child will have an Individual Education Program (IEP) as required by state and Federal law. The IEP is a document and a process. It is a written description of the plan that you and the school educators develop. The IEP states, in writing, the resources that the school agrees to provide. The IEP (which may have different names in different states) is developed through meetings where you work as an equal partner with educators to identify your child's needs, decide what resources are required to meet those needs, and list what the anticipated outcomes may be.

The Fundamentals of Working
With The School

To recap, the right medicine, the right classroom setting and the right teacher are each a critical element in a successful school formula. For Jack, pre-kindergarten and first grade saw the right everything, but in kindergarten and second grade we seemed, in retrospect, to be off in every category—medicine, setting and teacher. In these first years of trying to sort out the diagnosis, which influences medication and school setting decisions, a wrong first step can easily have a snowball effect.

At the heart of my role with the school are four fundamentals: 1) keep a positive attitude, 2) maintain a team orientation with the school district, 3) be a good communicator with the teacher, and, 4) stay involved.

I used both art and science to work effectively with the department of special education to get the right services and the right program in place for Jack. I questioned other parents and my coordinator at the department of special education so that I could understand the special education process and to learn how to navigate within the system. Ask your public schools related special education divisions and the special education services committee of your PTA council (if there is one) to meet, so that you can become knowledgeable on the Federal and state law and regulations, learn how your school system works, and determine how you can best advocate for your child.

When your child begins attending public school you will be assigned an administrative person from the department of special education at the board of education (this department has different names in different towns and cities). Being a positive person, I like to think that my counterpart will keep Jack's needs at heart, doing whatever needs to be done to meet Jack's educational goals. We have had good coordinators working on programs for Jack, but they have been constrained by budget, space, staff, etc. They have not been free to carve out a program to suit Jack's unique needs. We found the approach to be more like this: the department of special education has a budget, a certain number of classrooms, teachers, aides, etc. They look at the pool of children who require special services and then try to create classes that fit the general needs of a group of children with similar profiles. In many cases, this approach seems to work. It is not always such a success with a child whose profile is as complex as Jack's.

If you can find parents of children with similar profiles to your child's, you will see what the town has provided for academic services and you will understand its precedence. This doesn't mean that you will be forced to stay within what's been done before. But it does give you a good idea as to what might be a major fight and what will be easy for you to ask for and get. In short, it gives you a point of reference. Additionally, you might get new thoughts on how to fulfill the needs of your child, and a better sense of what might be necessary in the not-to-distant future. I found such contacts to be invaluable throughout my trek with Jack and have discovered them in both focused and accidental manners.

Finally, try to stay consistent with behavior goals, plans, and methods at home and at school. It is difficult for anyone to operate under two different codes of conduct. A child who has natural difficulties in this area will be significantly more confused if school's expectations do not line up with those at home. The more that you and the school are in sync in the behavior management area, the clearer the social world will appear to your child. We turned a significant corner when we were able to implement the behavior methods used in late second and third grade, at home.

Developing the best program for your child is the most important thing you can accomplish each school year. The right program not only means that your child will be making progress, it also means avoiding disasters that can set him back. Although the process has gotten somewhat easier for us now that we know the steps, know the school district players, and now that we have a clearer understanding as to what is needed for Jack, it is never a given.

SCHOOL

 *Strategies*

• Do SUFFICIENT PRE-WORK TO UNDERSTAND YOUR CHILD'S PRIORITIES AND NEEDS. Begin the school placement process each year by meeting with each of the private therapists and doctors who treat your child. Ask them to provide a written recap of your child's progress and current needs. Think through goals for your child's private therapy and the corresponding school-based therapy. Using input from team members, outline what you think the major academic, behavioral, therapeutic and social goals are for the coming year. Develop a memo that consolidates the progress reports, current functioning, and your child's needs and goals for the next year, based upon your team's input. Distribute the memo for your team to review and comment upon before you share it with the school-based team.

• THIS IS NOT THE PLACE TO LEARN ON THE JOB. Find the special education PTA in your school district and the parents in your local community that have slightly older children with similar profiles. Ask these folks to please educate you on your town's special education process.

• BE PREPARED FOR THE IEP MEETING. There are many good publications written to educate parents about the process school systems use to develop plans of education for special needs children. Whatever your hot issues are for a particular meeting, make sure that you have talked to people who have gone through similar experiences. They will be a wealth of knowledge and suggestions.

• CONSIDER HAVING SOMEONE ON CALL WHO IS VERSED IN THE FEDERAL AND STATE SPECIAL EDUCATION LEGISLATION. We have retained a lawyer in our state who has extensive experience in both litigating cases involving school districts and special education children, and writing the statutes for the state that dictate what school districts must provide for children with special needs. The attorney's entire practice is devoted to special needs children (he has been through the system himself, having a child with special needs). Each year he reviews Jack's academic needs with me, reviews what the district must provide, and advises us on how to work with the department of special education.

• Don't be afraid to bring in an appropriate liaison to your IEP meeting.

I usually review what the goals and issues of a meeting with the department of special education will be, and then determine who, if anyone, I would like to bring to the meeting.

I once brought a parent advocate, a woman who had been through the system with a child of her own and understood the laws, the players at the school district level, and how the system works, to an IEP meeting that I thought might get intense. While she had been very helpful to many people that I know, for us, her style was too confrontational. I ended up spending my energy trying to keep this woman from alienating the school team and destroying the relationship that I had worked hard to develop. If you do choose to bring in an outside advocate, be careful that her style is one that you are comfortable with and that she knows your perspective and what results you want for your child.

• A good relationship with the department of special education and your counterparts is not to be taken lightly—work hard to develop and protect it.

I am always surprised by the overtly adversarial stance that many parents take with the department of special education. The old saying about attracting more bees with honey than with vinegar makes tremendous sense here. Not only does my good relationship make meetings more than bearable, there have been countless times that my counterpart at the department has made extra effort to accommodate our needs.

- **PROVIDE THE SCHOOL WITH IMPORTANT DOCUMENTS THAT GIVE A CURRENT SNAPSHOT OF THE CHILD.**

You may want to note in the margins any changes or accomplishments that you've seen since the evaluation was done. If an evaluation is more than a year old, I ask the therapist or doctor to provide a brief summary letter that outlines current functioning, goals accomplished, and goals that we are working on.

- **PROVIDE EXAMPLES OF RECENT ACADEMIC WORK.**

I always have a few educational workbooks on hand for long car rides or nights when Jack can't get to sleep. I save samples of these and use them to show the school what independent work he is currently capable of. If a child is going from one program to another, you can ask the current teacher to save a sample of his work from each of the academic areas and use that as a work sampler.

- **GIVE A LIST OF EMERGENCY PHONE NUMBERS INCLUDING ALL DOCTORS, DENTISTS, THERAPISTS AND AT LEAST THREE FRIENDS OR FAMILY MEMBERS WHO CAN BE CALLED IN CASE OF AN EMERGENCY.**

Since it seems that people are rarely at home during the day, be sure to provide cell phone numbers, and pagers.

- **LEAVE A MEDICAL AUTHORIZATION FORM FOR DECISION MAKING IN CASE YOU CAN'T BE REACHED.**

Provide a short letter with the date that states you have given all decision-making authority for medical care, as well as any other important decision, to whomever you select. Be sure to give a copy of the authorization form and emergency numbers to more than one person at the school. It is amazing to see how frantic things become in an emergency. I usually give a copy to the teacher, the secretary in the main office, and the administration contact person.

A Different Kind
Of School
Finding the Right School Program

Sometimes a public school is not a good fit. Second grade fell apart for Jack, and Jack fell apart to a point of no return. It took a psychiatric hospital stay of eighteen weeks for Jack to be ready to return to school. When he was ready, the team working with us recommended that Jack attend a school with a more intensive behavior management program than any of our town's six elementary schools could provide. One of the team members suggested that we look at both therapeutic day schools and boarding facilities. A boarding facility would be the most dramatic and intense situation for Jack, since such facilities often have children with severe disorders. We all agreed that looking at this alternative would be a last resort. If we found absolutely nothing suitable within a forty-five minute driving distance, we'd have to consider sending Jack, who was only seven, away from home.

Although the board of education was responsible for finding an appropriate outplacement setting for Jack, I was a management consultant, and so wanted to do my own research as well. Other parents of special needs children told me that this was absolutely necessary as the department would come up with whatever solution would be least costly to the district. Despite the rocky kindergarten and second grade experiences, I trusted and respected the members of my school-based team and believed they would help us find what was best for Jack. I did believe that the school district worked within certain parameters but I also knew that they could unknowingly recommend a program that had even a remote chance of repeating our disaster of second grade. It would have been in no one's best interest to go through that experience again.

John and I hired an education placement consultant to ferret out any special needs classes in the surrounding counties that Jack could attend as a reciprocal student. These would have been hard to find on my own. I found and visited all appropriate special education schools within an hour commute of our town. In total, I visited seven private special needs schools and three public school programs.

Either I have uncanny timing, or there are more poor programs out there than any one would suspect. The first program that I visited was a special education school forty minutes from our house. The school serves children with social and emotional needs as well as learning disabilities. John and I had looked at the school a few years earlier, on the heels of the disastrous kindergarten year. At that time, we had walked from class to class in stunned silence as we observed children with a wide array of profound disabilities. We didn't see a single peer for Jack. On that chilled November morning, at the height of the pagers and phones ringing each day for me to come collect Jack from kindergarten, we had turned to each other outside the school doors and vowed, "No way."

Yet, here I was again, two years after a sudden breakdown and hospitalization. Maybe Jack belonged in the school that we once thought he was too high functioning for. Burying my pride and opening my mind to the possible benefits of a school program with such strong behavior management, I revisited the special school.

The director of the lower school went through Jack's paperwork. The report from the hospital spared none of the lows that we had hit while he was there.

I felt like a visitor on Point-Counterpoint. For every bad incident reported in the hospital notes, I gave the version of what I felt was really going on. "Kitten noises," the hospital said. "Jack's attempt to be cute and appeal to the staff that he was just getting to know," I assumed.

"Overly affectionate," the hospital said. "An inappropriate way of handling the anxiety of being among strangers," I replied. The worst moment came when I made the mistake of telling this school director that my counterpart at the department for special education in my district felt Jack might be too high functioning for their particular program. I thought that I was providing just another data point to help all of us make the best decision. It was not exactly taken in that vein.

The director said, "Animal noises? Inappropriate affection? Thank goodness all of our students are not as high functioning as this."

"Okay," I thought, "Maybe this will work out. Maybe I am in denial." We went on to the tour.

The director and I walked into the lower school building and were met head on by a young boy running through the halls in soiled underwear. On his tail was a young teacher wagging her finger in the way that I thought went out of style in the 1960s and saying, "You are a BAD boy. Don't you dare do that again!" She then pushed him down the hall.

I was unable to contain my heartsickness for this poor child, who, of course, had no control over his behavior. I turned to the director and said, "Is this acceptable to you?" She responded, "Of course not," and excused herself to deal with the crisis. This incident, plus the fact that I still had not seen anyone who seemed similar to Jack, made me once again cross the school off our list.

Next on my list was a private school in the next county. This school was set in a beautiful old mansion on one hundred and twenty acres. It was a school long on tradition and reputation. I had high hopes for the visit. I pulled up to the federal masterpiece, charmed by its tranquil setting. Hopping out of the car, I caught a scent of winter evergreen. A sign, I hoped, of new beginnings. I pushed open the heavy wrought iron gates and swung the car into the City of Oz.

I was not disappointed as I opened the old oak doors to the sounds of a student orchestra. As I paused to listen to the upbeat swing music and take in the energy of the students gathered on stage, I realized that this was the first time I had seen special needs students having a spontaneous good time together. How uplifting! How hopeful!

I continued down the hall to the admissions director's office. Poking my head into the door which indicated her jurisdiction, I was greeted by a cacophony of coughs. I know it wasn't her fault that she was in the last stages of a five-week virus, but it sure puts a dent in an interview when every sentence is punctuated by hacks. What's more, have you ever tried to understand someone who is talking with a mouthful of Luden's wild cherry cough drops?

The woman's twenty-year history as admissions director was evident. She was well versed in the school's behavior management approaches and curriculum. She could respond to my questions even with her talking ability curtailed by her illness. I began to get that feeling of comfort that usually accompanies a cup of hot cocoa at the end of the day. Bingo! *This* must be the answer to our search.

On with the tour. The director indicated that I should put on my coat as we were heading to the building next door. History told me that when someone says, "Building next door," we are about to head to the real behind-the-scenes adventure. Such was the case.

We ducked out a side door to the one-story structure that was the lower school. The director chatted casually as we walked along corridors, pausing so that I could observe a class in progress. My stomach butterflies started fluttering at the first stop, the recreation room. It was all room and no recreation.

In that dilapidated and somehow woeful room, the only sign of something that could be recreated with was an old piano, standing in a corner. I was told that this room was transformed into a game room, gym room and assembly center (not at the same time of course). Each room we poked into had a similar quality. I couldn't figure out where the structure of the class was.

We were almost finished with the tour when we stopped into the youngest class, first grade. Two students and two teachers were just finishing free time. It was not until we had shut the door and begun to walk down the hall that I heard it: the screams of a child and the angry retort of a teacher. Intrigued, I turned back and peered through the slotted blinds of the classroom window. There, I saw a teacher pushing a child into a time-out chair and heard her yelling at him, "And you'll stay here until I tell you not to." She turned her head and began berating the child to the other teacher. By this time, the admissions director had retraced her steps and was watching with me as the scene unfolded. Unable to watch any longer, I backed away.

All I could think of was that some set of parents and department of special education were paying tens of thousands of dollars and putting their trust in a school of supposed experts. This so-called behavior management couldn't possibly be teaching the young child self-control or supporting his self-image.

I turned to the admissions director and said, "Is that acceptable to you?"

She said, not slowing a step, "I didn't say we were perfect did I?"

The past three months had done nothing to increase my patience. Exasperated, I thanked her kindly and said that I thought this school was perhaps not the right place for Jack. Two down, how many more to go?

It took seven more visits and seven more disappointments until I found what we were looking for. And, as Auntie Em said, it was in our own backyard.

We still had not found a program for Jack when, out of the complete blue, Cooperative Education Services (CES), a consortium school for special education that serves all the districts in our county, called my contact at the department of special education. They let her know about a new class in their therapeutic day program that would be starting soon. The class would consist of a maximum of seven students, all high functioning with internal behavior (regulatory) issues. Since the majority of the classes at this consortium were composed of children with external behavior issues (such as conduct disorder) this class was somewhat of an anomaly for the school. Furthermore, it would be for children at or around age seven. Did she have any candidates?

In a matter of days I was sitting across from the program director, Dr. French, not believing my good luck. Here was a man who got it. Here was a man who was undaunted by my story. He anticipated questions, had stories that made sense, and was eager to learn about Jack. The classroom did not disappoint me. Dr.

French explained the school's approach to behavior management. The program was run by professionals who had the benefit of fourteen years experience in special education. They also had the foresight to work closely with a consultant who was invaluable in helping the consortium pull together a workable program for children of all abilities. The program's reputation was well earned.

Our school district, Dr. Jackson (Jack's psychiatrist), our speech therapist, and John and I looked closer at the CES option. My counterpart at the board of education went with me to visit CES. The team decided that CES was the right next step for Jack.

A little bit of success is a dangerous thing. It opens up the door to the question, "How much further can we go on the path that we are on?" Spurred by Margaret, our baby sitter, who has consistently asked that we try Jack without drugs, we asked Dr. Jackson to consider forgoing the psychiatric drugs the next day, the first day of school. After all, Jack had been taken off all drugs just a week earlier when he developed a body rash that ultimately turned out to be scarlet fever. Dr. Jackson agreed with the idea but suggested that Jack should only spend an hour or two at the new school, to get acclimated. Finally, Jack was ready to return to school.

We arrived at school and waited in the lobby for the teacher to appear. Jack was able to tell me during the forty-five minute drive that he was, in fact, kind of scared (he was afraid the teachers would boss him around). I promised him that this school was unlike any of the others that we had looked at. It would be perfect for him. This was not an oversell. The moment the teacher walked into the lobby and assured Jack that his brand-new lightning shoes would be fine to wear in school, she won his approval. Jack followed her to the classroom, where he was the first to arrive. By the time I finished handing over emergency forms, Jack had settled into his desk.

One of the treats of being a parent of a special education child is that the ordinary events of life, like holding a child's hand to cross a street or sharing a conversation, are poignant beyond words. Today was no exception. After a brief meeting, Dr. French suggested that I peek in the window to see how Jack was doing. There

Jack was, head bent over his work in what was clearly concentration, seated calmly. I will have this image etched in my mind forever.

I suggested that I pick Jack up after an hour and Dr. French said, "Only one hour? No way. We'd at least like to enjoy him until lunchtime." This was the first bit of calm that I'd felt in almost a year. When I returned at 11:45, I found a child who had bought into the Reward Systems and Levels hook, line and sinker. He had earned 85 of a possible 100 points. He was practically smitten.

The thrill of a successful day one made me putty in Jack's hands. By the end of our after-school errands, Jack had gotten a small bag of McDonald's fries, an extra half an hour beyond bed time, and the promise of an immediate game of Monopoly when we got home. This success system was exhausting me but boy was it worth it!

One of the toughest things about a child like Jack and a rational, planner person like his mom, is that there is no predictability and no pattern to Jack's behavior. The last four years had taught me that. So, when I heard Jack's first day of school was successful I didn't lean back and breathe easy. I did appreciate the success of the moment. I knew that even though this day had been easy, there was no telling what tomorrow might bring. This here-and-now orientation is a life lesson that I have always held dear. It's easy to enjoy the good days, but getting comfortable with the uncertainty, the possibility of crisis, the edge that might be too near, now that takes a lot of talking to yourself. Appreciate the moment.

Jack made it through the first two weeks of his new school beautifully. And what was amazing was that it was without any psychiatric medications. Unbelievable! Not for a minute did I think that no medication was the right way to go for Jack, long-term. But I couldn't believe he had even made it for a little while, without what I thought was a lifeline.

Jack had been at CES for three weeks when it was time for spring break. I had set up a meeting with Dr. French to get some feedback before the children left on holiday. Dr. French sat back in his chair with a small smile playing around his mouth.

"So you want to know what we think after fifteen days at CES?" he asked me. After I confirmed that I did indeed, Dr. French continued. "Our psychiatrist, our social worker, Jack's teacher and I have taken a look at Jack. And we've come to the same conclusion. We see a child with very intense ADHD who has an Asperger quality to him, who is so smart and persistent that he needs very, very strong limits and structure."

Of course he went on to say that their observation of Jack had been short and time would tell, but this was their initial impression.

And so, in just three weeks, we had stabilized Jack. He was secure and excited about school. I felt like we were on the road to recovery. Though, as in all recoveries, we knew where the breaks were, and how easily they could be broken again.

Outplacement

 *Strategies*

• GET A COPY OF THE BOOK, *The Porter Sargeant Directory of Schools for Exceptional Children.*
This book reviews every special needs school in the United States.

• MEET WITH YOUR DEPARTMENT OF SPECIAL EDUCATION COORDINATOR AND LAY OUT THE PARAMETERS FOR THE TYPE OF PROGRAM THAT YOUR CHILD NEEDS.
If your coordinator is not knowledgeable about programs in nearby school districts (that have reciprocity with your district), have him introduce you to the person in his office who is knowledgeable. There may be some very good programs in neighboring districts that your child can participate in.

• TALK TO OTHER PARENTS WITH CHILDREN IN OUTPLACEMENT SETTINGS.
By asking around and working through organizations like the special education committee of the local PTA, you will be able to find parents who have children in outplacement settings. These parents can give you firsthand information on schools and programs.

• IF THERE IS A SPECIAL EDUCATION SCHOOL THAT SERVES A DIFFERENT POPULATION THAN YOUR CHILD BUT HAS A GOOD REPUTATION, TALK TO THE ADMISSIONS DIRECTOR TO SEE IF SHE KNOWS OF ANY PROGRAMS SERVING CHILDREN LIKE YOURS.
Admissions directors are often very knowledgeable about other special needs schools and can provide you with some names.

• VISIT THE SCHOOLS.
This is a must. You have to see in person, in session, the school and the specific classroom that your child would be part of.

• CONSIDER TAKING ALONG ONE OF THE PROFESSIONALS ON YOUR TEAM, OR THE DEPARTMENT OF SPECIAL EDUCATION COORDINATOR, TO LOOK AT PROGRAMS. Once you narrow down some options, you may want a professional to go with you to observe and evaluate the school in order to gauge its appropriateness for your child. Who you bring depends on who you think can best evaluate the program and help you determine the best fit for your child.

• TALK TO YOUR PSYCHIATRIST, PSYCHOLOGIST, AND ANY THERAPISTS THAT YOUR CHILD SEES PRIVATELY. Since these people know your child extremely well and are familiar with the special needs schools in your area, they will be able to give you good guidance. You may even want one of them to come along to observe a classroom when you are getting close to a final decision.

III. NAVIGATING EVERDAY LIFE IN AND OUT OF THE HOME

THE NUTS AND BOLTS OF DAILY LIFE

WE DON'T WANT ANY SUMMERTIME BLUES

TO THE GRAND CANYON AND BEYOND

WHAT'S GOING ON WITH THE
OTHER KIDS IN THE FAMILY

FISHING AND OTHER PASSIONS

HOLIDAY HURDLES

KEEPING THE PARTY IN BIRTHDAY PARTY

GROCERY SHOPPING AND OTHER
POTENTIALLY EMBARRASSING SITUATIONS

The Nuts and Bolts
of Daily Life
From Getting Dressed
to Getting to Bed, Reasonably

Our daily home life is set up in a way so that Jack is no longer running the show or setting the tenor of the house. It took creativity, patience and a strong backbone. It might have been easier in the short run to ignore the child who ignored my direction. But in the long run, I would not have been doing him any favors. A looser approach would have only reinforced Jack's natural inclination to operate out of his own agenda.

Although I did as much as I could to create a structured environment, it was not perfect. Sarah had needs, I was working part-time, and I had outside obligations. Eventually, I learned to take the pressure off myself and let go of some concept of what the ideal home was supposed to be like. I set small, specific goals that would help our home function a little bit better and would help Jack learn how to be part of a family. In the beginning, we chose just one piece of a daily routine and worked hard on it until Jack demonstrated that he could follow it regularly, with a reasonable number of prompts. This took years.

When Jack was three years old my husband and daughter carried out a plan we had made to spend the New Year skiing in Colorado. The trip came on the heels of Jack's first psychological evaluation. He was 2½ years old and had just been labeled ADHD. Jack was oppositional and hyperactive. He followed no one's rules but his own. I knew that he could not manage a ski trip but I thought he would be fine spending the New Year with my sister, her husband and two children, who lived outside of Boston.

So John and Sarah headed to Colorado and Jack and I made the four hour car ride without incident to the Boston area. Jack and his cousins got ready for bed. Jack asked if he might have a juice box. My sister, Wendy, had given the boys their final treats and had specifically said that there would be no more trips to the kitchen. Jack persevered with his need for a juice box and did not relent.

I had just finished reading a book on behavior called *1-2-3 Magic*. The basic theory is that you count to three and the child knows that if he doesn't follow the rule by three there will be a consequence. The best consequences are those that are natural and relate to the incident. In my naiveté, I thought I needed to break Jack, and had begun to use this approach.

I looked at Jack, told him the No More Juice Box rule one more time and explained what the consequence would be if he was not in bed by the count of three. The consequence was that we would not be able to stay at my sister's house if he didn't follow the rule. I must have been tired myself because that consequence certainly had no relationship to the incident. I now know that Jack was probably very anxious staying at a new place and that a juice box was his way of comforting himself (since at home he usually had a drink before bed). But on that particular New Year's Eve I didn't understand what psychological things might be going on inside of Jack. Needless to say, we landed back in the car and ushered in the year with James Taylor on the long stretch of I-95 back to Connecticut.

It took us a few years to figure out which of Jack's behaviors stemmed from manipulation and were controllable, and which ones were due to an inability to cooperate. As Jack got older, we had to go through the same process over and over, asking ourselves, "Is this manipulation, or is this something that cannot be controlled?"

I think Jack also wonders about what he can't control because just last week he asked me, out of the blue, "Do you think I'm going to make some stupid mistakes when I'm a teenager?" I told him that everyone makes stupid mistakes in their lives; the important thing is to try to do the right thing, but if we make an error we need to learn from it and not repeat it. Getting on a behavior management program that can help Jack control his impulses and do the right thing has been a key part of his growth.

1-2-3 Magic is just one behavior management approach of many. It is actually one of the simpler ones. For many children, a predictable system with consistent consequences may be enough. But for others, the behavior system may need to be more stringent.

A behavior management system will do several things. First, it can take the emotion out of discipline. Instead of Mom or Dad being the bad guy, it's the system. Second, having something predictable in place seems to settle everyone. Knowing what will happen each time a certain behavior occurs will eventually extinguish the behavior or show you that a more stringent approach is needed. Third, knowing what is expected of the special needs child can help you fine-tune discipline in the other children in the family. Being so precise and conscientious in certain behaviors with Jack has raised our consciousness with Sarah.

We have used different systems at different times to help Jack follow the structure of home life and to take on responsibilities as a member of the family. Here is a brief description of approaches that we've tried.

The Picture Pocket Method

Our occupational therapist suggested the Picture Pocket Method for Jack when he was three years old. Jack had significant sensory integration deficits, which interfered with even the easiest organizing and planning activities. The concept behind the method is that when you break a task down into finite steps the child can learn the sequence.

We took a large poster board and cut and glued twelve felt squares to make pockets on it. Four squares were in each row. The squares corresponded to an activity that Jack needed to accomplish. For example, the first square dealt with getting dressed. I had taken photographs (with Jack posing) of each step of this process: 1) clothes in the drawer, 2) taking clothes out, 3) laying them on the bed, and, 4) putting each article of clothing on, one by one. These photos were placed in order in the felt pockets. In the morning Jack took out the set and as he did each step he put the photo back in the pocket. We used this system for getting dressed, making the bed, eating a meal, taking a bath, and going to bed. For a week or two Jack loved the routine of taking a photo out, doing what it showed, and then putting it in the back of the pocket holder. However, this routine got old fast. Perhaps other children will sustain an interest in the process or be motivated by a reward when all the steps are followed. For Jack, the Picture Pocket Method was a good jumpstart but not sustainable.

The Point Sheet System

The premise of the Point Sheet is to reward (and therefore encourage) positive behaviors and penalize (and hopefully extinguish) negative behaviors. There are lots of different methods for developing point sheets (also called goal charts) but the one that was most effective for Jack was identical to the one he used at his therapeutic day school. Here's how the system worked. The day was divided into three time periods: 1) 8 a.m.-11 a.m. 2) 11 a.m.-4 p.m. 3) p.m.-8:30 p.m. Jack began each time period with 100 points. He could earn bonus points for identified positive behaviors and lose points for identified negative behaviors. Each positive or negative behavior had a specific number of points lost or gained. At the end of each time period Jack would earn a privilege if he had maintained a certain number of points. At the end of the day we would total his points and keep a weekly total. When he achieved what would equal eighty percent of the total possible number of points per week for three consecutive weeks, Jack met his goal of moving towards a new level. Reaching a new level meant that he had achieved a certain group of behaviors for a specified period of time; new privileges came with each level. An example of the Point Sheet is provided in Appendix V, The Point Sheet System.

I think the fact that this system was used at school (so he was very familiar with it) had a lot to do with its effectiveness for Jack. We used the chart for seven months and Jack moved up two behavior levels. When he consistently followed the requirements of the chart, we were able to pull back from its use.

There are lots and lots of behavior plans out there. Your psychologist and psychiatrist can help you determine which system is best for your child and your family. Some behavior programs are implemented by trained consultants that come into your home.

You are an important part of selecting what behavior management system to use. You know your child. You know what motivates him and what sustains his interest, what will be seen as fun and what will be a bore. Go with what fits your philosophy and your gut. Remember, the burden falls on you to follow the plan. Don't institute a plan that is too complicated for you to follow. All this does is send a message to your child that you're not really serious about changing his behavior.

Behavior management has been the key to cracking one of Jack's greatest stumbling blocks, his self-agenda. When Jack was in pre-school and even through kindergarten, his psychologist believed that we should put as few demands as possible on him. Jack had a short fuse at that point. He would frequently run out of the house and hide when something was asked of him that he did not like or could not handle. So, from age three to six, Jack did pretty much as he wished. It was not until Jack was hospitalized (which you will read about later) and forced to participate in an extremely tight behavior management system that his self-agenda was broken.

I have come to appreciate that unless a child can: 1) tune in, 2) process what you are saying, and 3) cooperate, nothing can be accomplished. The child who is able to do these three things has laid the foundation for all other growth. The time and energy it takes to get a system in place to help your child accomplish these three things will pay off hugely in the end.

Tuning in (step 1) is something we work on constantly with Jack. Since he tends to hyper-focus on whatever he is doing, getting his attention is not easy. Establishing a reciprocal gaze, one of the first parts of tuning in, is not easy for Jack. Without eye contact, it is very hard to listen to another person. Unless we constantly remind Jack to give us eye contact, it gets lost.

Processing is a complex business. It can be part of the reason why a child is not following directions. In part of Jack's diagnostic testing, a speech therapist determined that Jack had a deficit in processing information. Jack could take in information but had trouble making sense of it, and he could only manage limited bits of information at one time. Jack still has trouble with information overload. He has a hard time discriminating what information he should listen to and what is background noise. Too much information given all at once can become a jumble. We have learned to simplify directions and to only give one or two directives at a time. Understanding how Jack processes information and determining the best way to give him directions played an important part in gaining his cooperation.

In the early years, if we were in a crowded setting and Jack was getting overloaded by the noise around him, I would quickly write on a piece of paper what I needed him to do. My sister, an occupational therapist, and I once spent a trip to the circus writing on slips of paper and handing them to Jack: "Stay in your seat," "Don't touch the lady in front of you." It was an effective way to break through the overload.

If there were an easy fix for getting a child to follow directions, many of our lives would be significantly improved. I have spent hours just watching Jack and trying to figure out why some days he will follow a direction with just a couple of prompts while on other days we battle for hours until he complies. Although it wasn't an easy fix, we found the biggest change was when we put a behavior management plan in place. We followed the plan to the letter, setting up the environment in a way that worked with Jack's limitations and instituting a program that had clear goals.

With all my talk about behavior plans you may think we have gotten more and more rigid as time goes on. Actually, my goal is to achieve a level of functioning that allows me to remove the crutch of a behavioral system. Even when Jack was very young, I had a premonition that, at some point, Jack would have the knowledge and ability to just flat out refuse to follow a system. Working towards a special toy or extra television time might be motivating when you are five, but I had a sense that these carrots would not be enough eventually. We had to get Jack to a point where he would be able to carry out his daily living functions because they were completely ingrained in him, or, where he would be self-motivated to do so, because he knew and believed that it was the right way to behave.

Things are actually more relaxed at our house nowadays. Once Jack was regularly achieving a high level on our daily home Point Sheet, we set a target for completing the program. If he reached a certain number of points for seven days, John and I told him we would no longer use the Point Sheet. He reached his target and we set the Point Sheet aside. For awhile, if Jack was not responding to requests all I had to do is say that I would be taking points away and he would comply. He and I both knew there was no Point Sheet in play; the prompt must have just been enough to let him know that I was serious.

When I say that things are relaxed I don't mean that they are loose. I run the house with deliberateness. Jack knows that everyday the same requirements are made of him, for example, in the morning to make his bed, get dressed and brush his teeth. If he comes down to breakfast and one of these isn't done I say to myself, "Okay he's a kid. As long as he gets ready in sufficient time that's acceptable." To Jack I say, "What are your plans for making your bed, getting dressed and brushing your teeth since that should have been done already?" If he is making significant gains or under pressure in other areas, such as social skills at school, or has new academic demands, I back off even more from the daily living expectations, until he has the new demands under control. It is a constant game of observation and balance.

Daily Living Skills

Morning is one of the most hectic periods of the day at our house. Actually, John, Sarah and I are quite organized with regular morning routines that has us showered, dressed and generally picked up after ourselves before we race out the door for the day. If mornings were up to us, we would be on time and on top of schedule. But mornings include Jack. And that's a whole different kettle of fish.

Jack has had sleep problems since birth, so when we talk about morning we have to look at what's happened the night before. And the night before is often a very, very long night. It would not be unusual for Jack to get to bed just before or just after midnight, which means that wake up time for school comes much too early. When Jack was young, I used to let him sleep in (okay I admit it, I loved the peace and quiet of getting Sarah ready for school without Jack the Whirlwind) and drive him to school late, but as he gets older this sends to wrong message to him. Now, regardless of what time Jack has gotten to bed the night before, I wake him up for school. He is Mr. Grouchasaurus in the morning. If waking Jack up is difficult, getting him to cooperate with the morning routine is near impossible. The impossibility begins with getting dressed and ends with getting his backpack and other gear.

Any semblance of calm, peace and order that I have achieved with Sarah in the morning is in grave jeopardy once Jack is awake. It takes every ounce of energy to try and get Jack out the door without losing my temper, keeping him in a good emotional place, and having at least a tooth or two brushed. Here are a few ideas, to try and keep down morning commotion.

MORNING

⭐ *Strategies*

• BREAK DOWN THE MORNING ROUTINE INTO SPECIFIC STEPS.

In the beginning, we kept it very simple. Here is how Jack learned to dress himself. Each night as I put Jack to bed, I would nonchalantly put his clothes out for the next day while talking to him. I didn't make a big deal about it but I made sure he noticed what I was doing. I picked clothes that were easy to put on and felt good (like elastic waist pants versus zip fly and button). Once Jack accomplished the first step, I added a second: put socks and shoes on. I continued to add onto the routine until Jack was dressing himself completely. It is easy for Jack to get out of the habit. I reinforce routines regularly so that these little patterns of daily care stay in place.

• GET AS MUCH READY AS POSSIBLE THE NIGHT BEFORE.

The most obvious is to have baths or showers taken in the evening and to help the children get their clothes out for the morning. I sometimes set the breakfast table and have the menu in mind. While all of this takes a little extra energy at the end of the day, it makes for a much more relaxed morning.

• PRAISE YOUR CHILD FOR EACH LITTLE ACCOMPLISHMENT.

Although putting on clothes or brushing teeth may not seem like a big deal, it is a really big deal for some children. Make sure you let your child know how great a step he has taken when he has mastered even the smallest part of his routine.

• YOU MIGHT THINK ABOUT REWARDING A DEFINED ACCOMPLISHMENT.

Jack can now watch a few minutes of cartoons before school if he has made his bed, gotten himself dressed, brushed his teeth and hair and eaten breakfast. The danger of something like this is that the child gets obsessed with the reward and cannot transition to the next thing that is required of him.

• STAGGER THE MORNING ROUTINE OF THE OTHER SIBLINGS SO THAT YOU CAN GIVE EACH CHILD AS MUCH INDIVIDUAL ASSISTANCE AS MAY BE REQUIRED.

In our house, Sarah starts school thirty minutes before Jack's bus arrives so I am able to get her going and have a quiet breakfast with her before Jack is up and needs attention.

• SET A PLEASANT AND RELAXING TONE TO THE MORNING.

I have classical or spiritual music playing softly in the morning. This backdrop sets a soothing tone to the day and gives the children a little exposure to some wonderful musical genres. For some children, even the softest of music will be too much stimulation. You will need to decide if this strategy is an asset to, or a strain on, your household.

• GIVE YOURSELF FIVE MINUTES TO GATHER YOUR THOUGHTS AND CENTER YOURSELF.

On the mornings that I am on top of my game, I get up extra early and read a bit of the Bible or inspirational reading. A very wise Jesuit once suggested that I begin the day having a cup of coffee with the Lord. For me, it is a tough discipline to keep in place but a good one that I find really makes a difference in my attitude when I manage to do it.

MEALTIMES

Mealtimes are one of the toughest periods of the day for us. For a taste of mealtime at our house, I bet that you can easily imagine a one year-old who, when placed in his highchair, slithers down inside the chair and onto the floor—no interest in eating for him. When I tried to tighten the safety belt in the high chair, he would scream. If anyone wanted to have any peace at dinner, we had to release Jack and let him scamper away.

As Jack got older, the situation got no better. First, it took us at least thirty minutes to assemble at the dinner table. By the time I got Jack to the table the food was cold and everyone else was angry by having to wait so long. If Jack did make it to the table, he played with his food, and was up and down so often that you could get dizzy.

Part of his issue was that he was on Ritalin—notorious for loss of appetite. The other piece was the "H" of ADHD, hyperactivity. Jack just couldn't slow his engine and manage all of the interactions that took place during a dinner hour. The psychologist suggested that we not focus on this area initially. We were dealing with so many off behaviors that neither John nor I had the energy to tackle this particularly exhausting one. So, for a period of time, dinner was without Jack.

Eventually, Jack would get hungry and take the dish of dinner food that I had left in the refrigerator for him. Often, he would bring his dinner to the edge of the bathtub and pick at it while he was bathing. Of course this is completely inappropriate behavior but, in his two's and three's, we let mealtime go.

Once we had therapies underway and medicine to help manage his hyperactivity, I began to work with the mealtime problem. Besides not having an appetite at regular mealtimes and having difficulty sitting still, Jack had very little language. Having a conversation during mealtime wouldn't work for Jack.

The first few months on the dinner goal (when Jack could finally sit), we used the Picture Pocket Chart that just showed: 1) coming to the table, and, 2) sitting down. I kept a timer on the table and Jack's first goal was to sit for one minute until the timer rang. During this minute I kept the conversation to brief, three-word phrases and just tried to make it a relaxing moment—something that he might think was pleasurable. When Jack could sit for three minutes I knew we'd need something to focus on if he was going to stay at the table. It needed to be interesting, visual and concrete.

I found just the thing at a teacher's supply store. A company called Trend Company puts out a number of picture decks. The one that I initially used with both children is called Situation Cards. Each card has a situation drawn on the front. The back of the card asks a question and provides three possible answers to select from. Here's an example:

> At lunchtime, a friend has forgotten his lunch and asks you to share
> your apple. What do you do?
> a. Tell him next time maybe he won't forget and keep the apple.
> b. Pretend you didn't hear him.
> c. Give him half of your apple.

Each card than provides an answer and explanations as to why that answer shows the correct behavior. Both children enjoyed the cards and learned some good moral and social lessons. I was constantly on the lookout for interesting, simple games that we could do during dinner to keep Jack's attention. Dinnertime became a positive experience for both children. As Jack continued to improve in his communication skills and focus, I was able to move away from the visual prompts.

It is a good idea to keep a card game with you when you take the children out to a restaurant. Just in case the dinner gets drawn out, or your child is having a fidgety time, the cards come in handy to keep his mind occupied and his body in his seat.

Since my ultimate goal is for Jack to be able to sit through dinner showing appropriate mealtime behavior and to be able to participate in a conversation, removing the visual prompts was an important intermediate step. For the next three years I turned to a book called *Yearly Devotions for Kids*. This book has a short story about a family for each day of the year. The story is related to a Bible verse and has a lesson. We went through the book twice and have only recently moved to a new dinnertime device. I have begun reading a book titled *Classics to Read Aloud.* These are excerpts from—you guessed it—classical books. The children get to learn about some literature that they may not otherwise come across, and the stories offer conversation starters. Our dinners don't last more than fifteen minutes, so I usually read for the first eight or nine minutes and then conversation just takes a natural course.

When we moved through the different dinnertime scenarios we were always on a behavior plan. With the Point System, points could be lost for inappropriate behavior such as silliness, getting out of your seat too many times, or interrupting another speaker. Although we don't use the point system anymore, we are still working on mealtime goals and have natural consequences for unacceptable manners.

I have found that just having a behavior management system may not be motivating in and of itself. Yes, you might get the desired behavior but it can feel like the military if you don't add an element of fun or interest. We have gone through very dark periods where it doesn't feel like there is much to smile about, let alone have fun with. But I guarantee, the more that you can use creativity and keep a good attitude, the brighter things will look.

MEALTIME

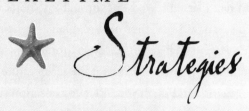 *Strategies*

- **START WITH REASONABLE EXPECTATIONS.**
A child who can't sit for ten minutes certainly can't sit for a thirty minute meal.

- **USE PROPS.**
If your child has limited language abilities, use visual devices and games to get the "conversation" going.

- **SERVE FOOD THAT IS "KID FRIENDLY."**
This is not the place to try out any fancy menus.

- **HAVE FUN.**
Don't make dinnertime a game of rules.

- **KEEP A REGULAR ROUTINE.**
Saying Grace, putting a napkin on a lap, and waiting until everyone is served to begin eating keeps order and is just plain, old good manners.

PERSONAL HYGIENE

There are two issues here and both have always been very difficult for Jack. The first is the nightly bath. There is not even a question in our house regarding showers—Jack flatly refuses to take a shower. For years he would fight me about getting in the bathtub, claiming that he hated water. Strangely enough, once in the water, it was equally difficult to get him out of it. In fact, one night he was in the bath so long that I went in to check on him (he was six at the time). There was Jack, completely engrossed in a book that had slipped so far down that it was in the water and disintegrating around him as he read it. I have tried lots of different strategies and various ones have worked at various times. Like many things, discovering what works is largely a matter of trying to get into your child's head to see what obstacles are preventing compliance.

Recently, at age nine, Jack has again been very resistant to bathing. Now that he is able to communicate well, I've tried harder to get into his mindset and figure out why he won't cooperate with a request. He claims that baths are too relaxing for him. That if he gets in them he has a hard time getting out—and then he'll use up time for what he really wants to do. We solved this by agreeing that I would just come in after five minutes and drain the water. I know that it seems incredibly cinchy but that's what we've been doing and it's working—for now.

The second hygiene issue that we struggle with is the everyday, throughout-the-day hygiene, washing up and brushing teeth in the morning, and remembering to wash after using the bathroom and before meals. Although it is tiring, I find the best approach to get these things ingrained is to remind, remind, remind. For example, every single time I catch Jack coming out of the bathroom I ask, "Did you remember to flush and wash your hands?" With enough reminders, even the slowest of learners will make this task a habit.

Hygiene

★ Strategies

• **Discuss the health implications of not taking a bath.**
Once Jack was able to understand the dangers of germs and bacteria, staying clean made more sense to him. For some children, obsessing about cleanliness can become an issue so I didn't dwell too much on this argument. Very simply, I reviewed what happens when dirt and grime stay on the body, stressing the possibility of bacteria and viruses. Not wanting to be sick, Jack would often get into the bathtub as the perceived lesser of two evils.

• **Make bath time fun.**
Nothing was more exciting to me than discovering Crazy Foam, Mr. Bubbles and Bathtub Paints. Though this can become a costly option if used daily, the promise of fun time at bath time made it very easy to get Jack into the tub.

• **Bath time might be part of your behavior program.**
"Taking a bath with only one prompt" was a specific evening goal on Jack's Point Sheet. Once it became part of his routine, it was a much smaller issue. Still, for much longer than what it would take with a typical child, I assisted Jack during his bath, scrubbing him while he played. At some point I realized that he was getting clean, but I was doing him a disservice. I wasn't teaching Jack to be responsible for his own hygiene. Now, I only run the bathwater and throw a bar of soap into the water with the reminder that soap is what removes grime—not water alone. Though Jack is probably not as clean as when I was helping him, he is doing it himself.

• **Make sure soap and hand towels are available in every bathroom and easily accessible to children.**

• FIND NEW WAYS TO GET THE MESSAGE ACROSS.

You do want to make sure the message is heard but you don't want to be a broken record so that everyone tunes you out. Sometimes, I surprise the children and have a little sign taped on the mirror that serves to help them. I am always on the lookout for clever personal care items and have been known to surprise the children with soaps that have little animals in them (Jack succeeds in using the entire bar in one bath just to get to the prize), fun bath mitts and rubber duckies (always a good staple). I've even suggested that they put on swimsuits and goggles and have filled the tub up to the brim for them. A little creativity can go a long way and turn a dreaded chore into fun for all.

• IF YOUR CHILD HAS BATHROOM HANG-UPS, ALWAYS REMIND HIM TO GO TO THE BATHROOM BEFORE YOU LEAVE HOME.

To this day, I watch Jack hop around from one foot to another, lie on his tummy (anywhere, anytime), and wiggle, to try to avoid using an unfamiliar bathroom. In a worst case scenario, I'll pull off the road and let Jack run behind a tree. Although this probably sounds pretty bad, it sure beats having a child trying to hold it in for several hours, making everyone nervous around him.

BEDTIME

Before we realized that Jack suffered from a real sleep disorder, we just thought that he was a difficult child when it came to bedtime. I read various books on sleep disorders (*Sleep Better!* By V. Mark Durand is a good one) and tried the different strategies suggested. I truly believe that getting children into a pattern at bedtime makes for the easiest bedtime transition. But in our house, it was—and remains—a challenge. Every evening at the end of dinner I announce that I expect people to be in bed by 8:30 p.m. I remind them that if they want me to read to them they must be in bed by 8:00. I tell them all desserts and last minute snacks must be ingested before 8:00 p.m. as well. They hear the same tale night after night. It is not new news. However, at 8:00 p.m., I have children with a host of schemes and last minute projects.

I, in turn, become The Nagger. Part of the problem is that John does not get home from work most evenings until after 10 p.m. Having two children to one adult is definitely not good odds at bedtime. Since Sarah needs more sleep and can be counted on to stay in bed until she falls asleep, I usually begin getting her to bed first. Jack, being less cooperative and having a sleeping problem, takes much more time and focus.

Though it may seem next to impossible, try to keep a routine as closely as you can. Begin with teeth brushing and putting on pajamas and end with reading together for a designated period of time or whatever other activity sets a calm tone. Even if you can't get your child to sleep by an ideal time, training him to stay in his room and in his bed is a good first step—and will allow you to get the rest that you need.

BEDTIME

 Strategies

• SET UP A BEDTIME ROUTINE AND STICK TO IT.

The younger your child is when you set up a routine, the easier it will be for him to accept that the routine is the routine, and the greater the chance is that you will not be challenged on it. Baths are known to be great relaxers. You might want to start with the bath, brushing teeth and reading with the child for thirty or forty-five minutes each night. Having a cuddly reading time to look forward to at bedtime might be an incentive. It is also a wonderful way to get some of the classics and other good books into the hands and heart of your child.

• SET A TONE THAT IS MELLOW IN THE HOUSE.

Make sure there is no loud music or television on; think about playing classical music as the children get ready for bed.

• CONSIDER HAVING A CASSETTE IN EACH CHILD'S ROOM WITH CHOICES OF SOFT SLEEP-INDUCING MUSIC.

Jack went through a stage where he would listen to books on tape until he fell asleep. Meditation tapes for kids and classical music tapes are other soothing options. Your local library and children's book or toy stores will have options for you to try. Some nights, I come in and turn on a tape of classical music or soft spiritual tunes while Jack is asleep.

• IN THE CASES OF POSSIBLE REAL SLEEP DISORDERS, ASK YOUR DOCTOR ABOUT BENADRYL OR OTHER MEDICATIONS.

At one time, Jack was taking Clonidin as a sleep-inducer. Since Ritalin is a stimulant, if it is taken late in the day this medication can make it very difficult to wind down for sleep. Eventually, we learned that 25 mg. of Benadryl would also wind Jack down so that he could fall asleep. However, after a year or so,

Benadryl didn't seem to take affect any longer. Your doctor may try a mild antidepressant to help your child relax and get to sleep.

• MAKE SURE THERE ARE NO DISTRACTERS IN THE BEDROOM.
Probably obvious, but toys and electronic devices (e.g. Gameboy or a television) will not help children learn how to fall asleep naturally.

After School and
Extra Curricular Activities

First things first. I notice that with Jack, having food in his system affects his behavior. Unfortunately, Jack doesn't eat lunch at school most days (remember, Ritalin causes a loss of appetite). So, the minute he gets off the bus I have a snack ready. Snacks such as cut up cubes of cheese, a protein bar, rice cakes with peanut butter, nuts or a piece of fruit usually hold him over until dinner.

For the first few years of school, private therapies took up all of Jack's after school time. With such a heavy therapy schedule, there was no question as to how we were spending time after school. Workbooks kept in the car occupied Jack as we drove from therapy to therapy. Once therapies were part of his school program and no longer an after school activity, we had to rethink the time spent between his arrival home from school and dinner.

I have finally learned that trying to talk Jack into an activity that I think would be good for him will not be successful if he has no interest in it. The only activities that have gone well after school are those that genuinely interest him. I have come to appreciate that school is emotionally draining for Jack. He needs a lot of time to unwind when he gets home.

Many children don't get enough down time or free time. The Huckleberry Finn kind of time where you go outside and play around, inventing things and exploring the neighborhood. Jack has learned more social skills from hanging around Julien, the thirteen year old "big brother" who comes over weekly, and through casual play dates, than anywhere else. However, even this type of down time needs to be structured.

AFTER SCHOOL
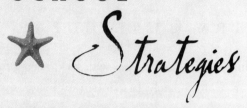
Strategies

• REMEMBER THAT SCHOOL IS A TREMENDOUS DRAIN ON EMOTIONAL ENERGY.
Some children need to just hang out after school. Learn to respect that need.
Jack needs time to recharge his emotional batteries. He is a much happier and
cooperative child when he has a chance to unwind.

• EVEN AFTER SCHOOL NEEDS TO HAVE SOME SENSE OF ORDER TO IT.
Children should know what they are doing after school, before they even leave
for the day.

• DON'T TRY TO MAKE YOUR CHILD BE SOMEONE THAT HE'S NOT.
You've had your childhood—give your child the opportunity to carve his own.

Hang Around the House Time

When Jack was under six years old, free time at home was one of the most stress-filled times of our day. Jack had no interest in toys, games or television and no interest in peers; he just wanted to be on the go. He also had no regard for safety.

Since Jack didn't seek out other children to play with, his only limitation was his own imagination. He loved to be outdoors where he could be free. Combine this with absolutely no safety limits and you've got quite a setup for disaster. As much as I tried to keep a good eye on Jack, he was very fast. He would take off on his bike with no memory of road rules and no recall of what boundaries I had set. I am embarrassed to tell you the number of times that I had to hop in the car and circle the neighborhood with the window down, yelling his name.

As Jack has gotten a little older he has become much more interested in having friends and having them over to play. On one hand, this is fantastic because it allows him to practice his social skills. On the other hand, it is more work for me. There is no way that I can have a child over and not be in the same room, or at least in the next room to the boys.

Jack had a little boy from summer camp to our house just last week. Shortly into the play date, I heard absolutely no noise coming from the family room, where they had gone. I peeked in, only to find Jack playing Gameboy and the guest peering over his shoulder. Luckily, I was available and used the situation to talk to both boys about what is and isn't a good activity at a play date.

FREETIME

 *Strategies*

• TEACHING YOUR CHILD HOW TO ENJOY FREE TIME IN HEALTHY WAYS IS A LIFELONG LESSON.

You have a certain amount of control over what free time choices are available—use it.

• REMEMBER—JUNK IN, JUNK OUT.

Just say "No" to too many passive activities (like electronics games).

• HAVE OPTIONS AVAILABLE SO THAT THEY ARE EASY FOR THE CHILD TO FIND.

At the Montessori school, shelves are everywhere; activities are laid out one by one on the shelves. I use this same concept. Rather than store things in big containers, I lay them out on a counter or bookshelves so that the children can easily make a selection.

• YOUR CHILD'S FREE TIME WILL BE WORK TIME FOR YOU.

You need to be supervising, even if it's at a distance (such as the next room) so that you can intervene, if necessary.

It is funny how the little routines of a day—getting ready for the day, mealtime, bath time and bed time—can be completed quickly and easily. And yet, for some children these are major battle grounds. Think of each of these daily hotspots as an opportunity. You are not only teaching your children critical life skills to one day function on their own, you are also modeling for them what it means to live together as a family.

• TOGETHER WITH YOUR CHILD, DETERMINE A REASONABLE AMOUNT OF TIME WHERE HE CAN FOCUS ON HIS HOMEWORK, UNINTERRUPTED.

Set up a plan where your child does his homework for a certain period of time and then takes a short break. Make sure the break is timed and is no longer than five minutes or it will be hard for him to get back to his work.

HOMEWORK

There are many different philosophies about homework. One approach is to have children sit down and do their homework as soon as they get home from school. The argument here is that children are still in a school mode so it should be easy to focus on academics. Another line of thinking argues that children need to let off some steam and re-energize before they can tackle more academics. Here, children are allowed some free time before being asked to buckle down. Sometimes, it's not easy to hold to any kind of routine, with after school or after dinner activities. For special needs children, as well as typical children, the most important aspect of homework is to set up healthy study skills. Study skills that are established when children are young are most likely the ones that they will fall back on in middle school, high school and college. I am even willing to bet that how someone approaches his job is similar to how he approached his school work. Work skills are probably closer to study skills than one would suspect.

Our two children have completely different study habits. Sarah falls in the camp of getting homework done as soon as she walks in the front door. She prefers the feeling of getting it out of the way.

Jack, on the other hand, never makes it from the school bus stop to the front door. Jack has a routine. The school bus lets Jack off at the end of our long driveway, which passes over a stream. He steps off of the bus and flings his backpack on the ground on his way to the stream, where fishing pole and tackle box await. There he plays, checking in on the snapping turtle that holes up under the bridge. Even if I meet Jack at the bus stop, he is hot, exhausted and worn out from the long bus ride. This is not a good time for sitting down with homework.

Jack and I have gone through our share of homework battles. Our afternoons disintegrated until I let Jack establish his own homework routine. I kept reminding him that homework was waiting. Jack's anxiety and emotions rose and we accomplished nothing. It wasn't until we worked out an agreement where Jack was free to play for the first hour that he was home, and began homework no later than 5:30 p.m., that homework time did not mean stress time. The more I learned how Jack studied best, the more I could help him.

No matter how much you try to structure homework time, sometimes it is an endless battle to get your child to cooperate. There are a few things that you could try if you get to this point. First, talk to your child's teacher or the special services coordinator at the school. Perhaps a teacher's aide or teacher can work with your child after school to get homework completed. A teacher might be able to understand what gets in the way of homework. Is the work too difficult for the child to complete on his own? Are attention issues preventing him from concentrating? Once you figure out what the stumbling blocks are, you can devise strategies to remove them.

Another idea is to bring a tutor to your home to assist your child with homework. For several years, a marvelous teacher, who had taught Sarah for three years at the Montessori school, worked with Jack. Mrs. Brent used subject material that she knew Jack would find interesting as a means to get him to write. She set up a learning and working environment that Jack was ready and eager to work in. She had an organized approach, calm demeanor, and kind spirit.

One year, fourth grade, we hired a teacher, Mrs. Cleery, who was to come to our home three days a week to supervise Jack's homework. She planned to focus on developing organizational skills with Jack. At the first visit, Mrs. Cleery came armed with science and nature books. She knew that these were subjects that interested Jack. The visit had lasted a whole of seven minutes when I heard the old "Mmmooooommmmmyyyyy!!!!" I raced towards the cry to find Mrs. Cleery at the work table and Jack at the computer. "Have her leave, Mom," Jack said to me in a loud and slightly annoyed voice. "I could have been done by now. She's messing me up!"

Later that day I talked to one of our babysitters who used to teach Jack. She and I decided that the tutoring idea was overkill. The fact of the matter is, Jack doesn't have any learning issues. He can whip off homework in no time at all.

He is even fairly well organized about it. He may need someone to help him as work gets harder but right now, he does not need a tutor.

One final note. Your child's homework is not your homework. It is not your responsibility. You have already been to school. You are there to support, guide and coach. But you cannot do your child's homework for him. That will not be in his best interest, in the long run. Leave the consequences for incomplete homework to your child's teacher and the school-based team. Share with the school-based team your observations: when the homework is being completed and the effort and focus being put into it. With your additional input, your child's teacher will be in a good position to deal with the homework dragon.

Homework

★ *Strategies*

- Help your child keep his workspace organized.

If you can dedicate a desk or workspace for a child to do homework, or at least keep homework supplies, you will help him develop organization skills. We converted an attic to a study space. Here, each child has a desk and supplies. They have a large work table for big projects, and counters that they can use to lay out work-in-progress. We outfitted a nearby closet with floor to ceiling bookshelves. The books are organized and available for easy access. I cull the bookshelves on a regular basis, giving away books that the children have outgrown and adding new books to the selection.

- Teach your child to do his best work.

I love to tell the children the story about how my mother would not allow any erasing on homework assignments. If we made a mistake, we were expected to redo the entire page. Although I'm not as strict with our children, if an assignment is really messy, it has to be redone.

- When your child has a project with a due date that is more than a few days away, have him write down intermediate deadlines on a calendar, to be sure that the assignment is completed on schedule.

Teaching children how to break down large projects into manageable components is a skill that will be help them enormously later in life.

- Absolutely no electronics (television, Gameboy, telephone) until homework is completed and reviewed by Mom.

Once a child gets locked into a program, it is very difficult to get him to refocus.

• TELEVISION AND HOMEWORK DON'T MIX.

Many children insist that they can do their homework while watching television. All you have to do is try to write a letter while watching a show and you'll see how difficult the homework/television combination is. From time to time I have gotten lax with Jack and given in to his convincing pleas that homework and television go together. It takes him three times as long to complete his homework and the quality of the work is definitely lower.

CHORES

When Jack was at the height of his negative behaviors, we concentrated on a few basics of life and let everything else slide, including chores. Though overwhelmed, I still had a nagging sense that if I let Jack off scott free to live in the house on his own terms, I really wasn't looking out for his best interests. I agree with those child psychologists and educators who believe children need to have regular responsibilities at home. These responsibilities give children a sense of being valued.

Although I didn't add all that pressure to Jack or me when he was five, six, and seven, I did insist that he make an effort to clean up his toys. This meant that I needed to be cleaning right there beside him. With a child as distractible and self-propelled as Jack, even now I often can't send him off to do a chore (or even to get himself ready) alone. A trip to make his bed can become a forty-five minute odyssey—but that's only because he's been sidetracked by something else that's caught his eye. If I stay by Jack's side as the assistant, I can keep him focused and offer the most judicious way to get boring chores accomplished.

I often weave in stories about when I was young for the children, reminding them that my daily chores were a lot more time-consuming than theirs. These stories, and beginning with small steps like cleaning up toys, set up expectations that as the children became older, more chores would be required.

We have gone back and forth in the relationship of chores to allowance. Personally, I like the idea of an allowance. With an allowance, if you want something, you save up for it. I was spending a lot more spare change and teaching no lesson when being asked while we were out, "Can I have this, that or the other thing?"

I am not of the camp that you get an allowance just for being part of the family. I don't want the kids to get the impression that later in life they will earn a salary without doing anything. In our family, each child gets an allowance equal to his age. During the week, each time his bed doesn't get made or the table chore is not done, there is a $0.50 deduction from his allowance.

$\mathcal{S}$*trategies* FOR
HOUSEHOLD CHORES

• CONSISTENCY IS IMPORTANT.

Whatever you decide to do for the chores request, stick with it.

• MAKE SURE THAT THE CHORES ARE APPROPRIATE FOR THE AGE.

• BE REASONABLE WITH YOUR EXPECTATIONS. KIDS ARE KIDS.

• EXPECT TO BE AN ACTIVE BYSTANDER.

Depending upon the child, you may need to be right next to him, coaching him as he does his work or in the same room, prompting as needed. Don't enable him but do provide support.

• GIVE FREQUENT PRAISE.

Everyone loves to be acknowledged for good deeds.

• MAKE CHORES FUN.

Hide a quarter in a room that is supposed to be being cleaned up and see if it is found. It adds a little bit of fun to the task.

THE NUTS AND BOLTS
OF DAILY LIFE

TV, Gameboy, Nintendo, Computer Games and Other Addictive Toys

We limit television in our house so most of the time it never rules. On days when there is a tricky schedule, when a babysitter is in charge, or when I am caught up in household chores, the limitation mysteriously moves in Jack's favor. Still, knowing how easily Jack gets hooked, I try to toe the line in this area.

When Jack was in second grade, the birth of Gameboy and introduction of Pokemon were the catalysts for a near obsession in our house. Jack spent all of his after school time in eager anticipation of the 4:00 Pokemon cartoon. He followed the show with a phone call to a friend to discuss the episode and then moved on to a Pokemon Gameboy game after dinner, winding down with a Pokemon collector's magazine in bed. Jack's Pokemon fixation was maddening. Trying to interrupt a Pokemon game or change the topic of discussion away from Pokemon was an invitation to trouble. I felt hostage to a gang of cartoon characters—many of whom weren't very nice.

I do admit, when Jack was absorbed with Gameboy or a television program, it made my job at the moment easy. He was occupied, content and not moving at his usual breakneck pace. Jack's psychologist contended that a certain amount of zoning out was probably a good thing for Jack. Since interacting with others was so exhausting, Gameboy and television served as rebound time.

Still, I hate watching kids aimlessly, passively watching television. Jack was very influenced by what he watched and spent time thinking about it. He even recited phrases and retold sketches that he had seen on television. Because of this, we were very, very careful to monitor his program selections. He was allowed to watch precious few sitcoms, and mostly old-fashioned ones like "I Love Lucy" or "The Wonder Years." No violent or ill-mannered animated cartoons were permitted. The only movies that he was allowed to watch at age nine were those rated G, and occasionally, PG.

Strategies FOR ELECTRONIC GAMES

• MONITOR WHAT YOUR CHILDREN WATCH.

Particularly for children with little natural social sense, exposure to inappropriate language, behavior and social circumstances can leave a lasting impression.

• LIMIT THE AMOUNT OF TIME THAT YOUR CHILD SPENDS WITH ELECTRONIC GAMES AND TELEVISION.

• BE SELECTIVE WITH WHAT SOFTWARE PROGRAM YOUR CHILD USES—MANY OF THEM ARE FILLED WITH VIOLENCE.

• IT NEVER HURTS TO "LOSE" THE GAMEBOY TEMPORARILY OR TIE THE USE OF IT TO A BEHAVIOR MANAGEMENT PROGRAM.

HAIRCUTS

When Jack was two and three years old, a haircut was a complete disaster. Jack could not stand the entire sensory experience. He hated the itchy feeling of the hair falling on him, having scissors clipping near his head was annoying, and staying like a statue was nearly impossible. We've tried many different strategies and what worked (or worked the best that it could) depended, in large part, upon the hair stylist and Jack's mood that day.

The first essential ingredient was the hair stylist. It took a cut on the ear for us to recognize the importance of having someone very patient and understanding to cut Jack's hair.

Jack's haircuts involved a lot of stopping and starting, so the stylist always allowed for extra time during Jack's appointment. This kept her from feeling frazzled. Going to the same stylist regularly was critical. Helen was extremely soft-spoken and mellow. There was a separate room within the salon for private cuts—this is where Jack got his haircut. The private room meant that Jack had less external stimuli to negotiate and didn't bother the other clients if he was up and down from his seat. I *always* made sure that we had a hand-held game or some kind of amusement with us. This is one of the few times that I didn't complain about his use of Gameboy. As long as his head stayed still, he could play the game while his hair was being cut.

I still get a lot of complaints from Jack when haircut day rolls around. Sometimes, we get there and it's clear that it's not going to work so we just re-schedule. Recently, Jack reminded me how awful the loose hair on his neck felt after it was cut. We brainstormed together and came up with the idea that Jack would wear one shirt to get his haircut and bring an extra shirt that he could change into after the haircut. We are also thinking about having a hairstylist come to our house for the dreaded haircut.

HAIRCUT

★ *Strategies*

(THAT YOU CAN APPLY TO OTHER HOT SPOTS)

• ASK FRIENDS WITH SPECIAL NEEDS CHILDREN WHAT STYLISTS HAVE HAD
SUCCESS WITH CUTTING THEIR CHILDREN'S HAIR.

• KEEP YOUR CHILD OCCUPIED WHILE THE HAIRCUT IS GOING ON.

• BE PREPARED THAT SOME DAYS JUST WON'T WORK AND THAT YOU WILL HAVE
TO RESCHEDULE.

• SEE IF YOU CAN FIND SOMEONE WHO WILL COME INTO THE HOME IF YOU
THINK THAT THIS WILL CUT DOWN ON THE STRESS.

THE NUTS AND BOLTS
OF DAILY LIFE

WE DON'T WANT ANY SUMMERTIME BLUES
Setting Up a Successful Summer Plan

The most difficult thing about planning Jack's summers is that I don't know where he will be, behaviorally and emotionally, by then. If I select a camp in the fall, it may be too high functioning or too low functioning for Jack by the time summer rolls around. It is a real catch-22, because if I wait until February or March, I will have a better handle on what sort of place will be best for Jack, but most likely no space will be available. The years that I waited a little longer I ended up knowing what would be perfect, but was unable to get Jack into the program. Then I was left scrambling to find something and that something usually wasn't quite the right program.

It is equally tough to make the right call between a typical camp and a special needs camp. We've had all sorts of experiences. One year we thought a regular camp would work and it did, but another year a regular camp did not work. Similarly, one year we tried a special needs camp and it worked, yet another time a special needs camp was a disaster. We have finally approached the problem by applying Jack to camps of different types. Then, in May (or whenever the final cutoff date is for withdrawal), we reassess Jack's functioning level and make a final determination.

After we select a camp, I educate the camp on how best to work with Jack. I prepare a presentation that overviews Jack's disorder and explains how the disorder affects his behavior. I also send recent and relevant reports, being careful not to overwhelm the camp office with paperwork.

The key here is to provide information that is practical and useful. I like to send this information in advance so that the camp director has a chance to share it with Jack's counselors before camp begins. If there will be an aide specifically for Jack, I try to set up a classroom visit for the aide while school is still in session so that he or she can see the behavior management program in action.

In the early years, we hiccupped our way through local camps. We tried the YMCA camp at age four, but Jack spent most of the day by himself, catching butterflies, digging for worms and trolling for seashells. At age five and six, we tried an all-around day camp for typical children. The program consisted of outdoor games, swimming, golf, tennis and arts and crafts. Because Jack had only a mild interest in sports he was completely distracted. He would be in the ready position on the tennis court one minute, and off tracking down a wandering butterfly the next.

When the children were toddlers, I happened upon a nature-based camp, Farm & Wilderness, in Vermont. Much of the day was spent caring for animals, working in the nature barn, enjoying the lake and learning about our environment. One of the keys to getting Jack to move from his self-absorption to a larger platform was to use his areas of interest as a springboard. This camp was perfect since Jack was a nature nut.

From age three, when Jack joined the youngest campers in the Butterfly group, this two-week experience was the highlight of his entire year. Every year, it amazed me to see Jack visibly relax as we crossed the state line into Vermont. The slower pace, green open spaces, and emphasis on nature fit him perfectly. Although his issues didn't disappear, the structure and activities of Farm & Wilderness matched Jack's interests; so staying focused wasn't as great a concern as it was in some other summer programs.

Although Farm & Wilderness was the perfect camp for Jack from the point that what they did matched what Jack loved, each year was a little dicey. Because Jack had a very tough time making transitions, staying with the Butterflies was difficult for him.

At two and three years old, everyone looks a little bit disheveled. But by age four, other kids had begun to pull themselves together. Jack stood out as the Lone Ranger. This particular summer there were times when Jack flat out refused to join his group for an activity. At the end of the two week term, the camp director and I decided that Jack must have an aide with him the following year.

The next summer, I went back and forth with the director, trying to decide if we should bring a teacher's aide from home with us, or use an extra camp counselor as Jack's aide. Someone from home would be very familiar with how to work with Jack but wouldn't be knowledgeable about the camp. A camp counselor would know the ropes of the camp but wouldn't know Jack. The director had identified a high-school girl whom she thought would be a good match for Jack. I wasn't able to find anyone to come up to Vermont with us, so the decision was made.

It did not take long to see that while Jack's aide was a wonderful person, she did not have the skill to re-direct and maintain control over Jack's very powerful self-agenda. Over the next two weeks, my blood pressure rose as I read the daily entries in the communication book that the aide and I used. I read entries like, "Jack spent most of the day at the lake catching newts. He would not participate in the activities of his unit," and, "Although Jack did play with some other children, it was only when they came to the lake where he could show them the best newt-catching spots."

Other years we had a day or two where I would be paged and would have to pick up Jack, when he'd run away from his unit. Although we didn't have these problems since he had his own aide, he never joined his unit except when they came down to the lake for their swim period.

The lack of participation didn't faze Jack in the least. In his mind, he was having the same fabulous experience that he always did at Farm & Wilderness. He was caring for pigs, collecting eggs from hens, playing with bunnies and had an extensive newt collection. What could be better?

At the end of the two weeks the director sat down with me to say that unfortunately, Jack would be unable to return the following summer. It was too confusing to other campers to see a child who was allowed to set his own agenda. Each day, the campers asked the same question: "Why doesn't Jack have to stay with us?"

I broke the news to Jack as best I could. I knew it would break his heart.

"What?" he replied incredulously. "I stayed at the lake because I had an aide and she said it was okay. If she had made me stay with the group, I would have stayed with the group." I'm not convinced that Jack would have really relinquished his own desires to follow the group, but it is interesting that he clearly felt that he was in charge of the aide.

When a summer does not go particularly well, there is a greater likelihood that the beginning of the year will follow suit and be rocky. Sure enough, the school year following this particular summer was kindergarten, and it was rough. If you have not had the smoothness that you had hoped for in the summer, be extra careful when school begins. Work with the school from day one to get your child back on track.

The summer between first and second grade marked a change in direction so subtle that none of us saw its impact until too late. First grade had gone so well that we had all assumed we were on a positive track. We were not keeping an eye out for patterns of change.

We hired Sheila, who had been one of the teacher's aides in Jack's first grade classroom. Although Jack did not seem to be particularly bonded to Sheila, she was available and eager to accompany Jack to the town day camp and to a two-week program at the maritime aquarium, which was going to replace the Farm & Wilderness experience. Unfortunately, Sheila did not let us in on how far Jack was really sliding—and he did slide—over the course of the summer. We only got the true gist a year later when he returned to the maritime aquarium camp. Then we heard about Jack's non-compliance and lack of participation the previous summer.

The summer between second and third grade, we hired a different teacher's aide, Jamie, who had worked very well with Jack during the school year. Jack was going to spend most of the summer in the extended school program at his therapeutic day school. Jamie would be at the summer school program as well. At the end of the eight week summer school program, Jamie was to accompany Jack to the same two-week maritime aquarium camp he had attended the previous summer. Jamie and the head teacher at his school set up a Point Sheet to use at the aquarium that was similar to what Jack used at school. The difference in how well Jack did at the maritime aquarium was dramatic. Even the director of the camp remarked that Jamie's system, and her rapport with Jack, were quite impressive.

The summer between third and fourth grade we decided to have Jack attend a special needs camp. The day camp was for children with ADD, ADHD, PDD and LD. The camp used a similar behavior management program to the one that Jack's school used. Jack had had a terrific school year and was getting close to transitioning out of the therapeutic day school to a less restrictive environment.

Without a good communication flow with the camp counselor or aide, I'm pretty much in the dark any given summer. With Jack, I rarely get any feedback about what goes on at school or camp. But this particular summer, I got little vignettes. Jack had stories to tell. And the stories were upsetting. He would talk about kids hitting each other and saying words that he didn't know. "What's a crutch, what's a vinegar?" he'd ask, not understanding that this was not misuse of a word that he knew, but a mispronunciation of a word that he shouldn't know. I also had to explain what sex was, as kids were talking about it. When I asked where the counselors were, Jack would say, "They didn't see what was going on."

Jack had sorted out the kids in his camp into friends, dorks, losers and plain, old, really mean kids. I had never heard him be so judgmental. He was rarely aggressive with others in language or actions unless he was feeling unsafe or threatened. Jack had worked hard at school in learning how to problem-solve with words, rather than run away or use his hands. This held true during the first two weeks at camp, where his communication log said things like, "Jack is a good example to the others," and, "Jack had a great day."

Despite Jack's perception of mean kids, Mr. Social began to emerge. He would walk in the door from a full day of camp asking, "Could so-and-so (another camper) come over?" Thrilled that Jack finally had an interest in making friends, I agreed every time. When I met some of the campers, things began to fall into place. One boy, Mack, interspersed his language with foul words. He was also aggressive towards Jack. To Jack's credit, at the end of the play date, when I suggested that the boy wasn't such a good match for Jack, he said, "I agree. Mack's out, we'll try Sam next."

Sam came over and, while discussing what movie we might go to see, he informed me that his parents allowed him to see a movie of any rating. Excuse me? "Yes," he explained, "they feel that I'm mature enough to handle it." This twelve-year-old boy had lost his biological mother when he was five years old. In just ten minutes with him I could see the emotional issues. No way should the boy have had to negotiate the violence, sexuality, and language of R-rated movies. After the play date, Jack and I agreed maybe that didn't work either.

The next camper to come over was a fellow who had true Asperger's Syndrome. Jack's focused interest was transportation, particularly trains. After a little verbal back and forth, I came into the kitchen to hear what they were discussing. Jack started to tell me a joke while Jack said, "Don't do it, don't do it, don't do it." The joke was so vulgar and inappropriate that it took me a minute to stop him—I thought that I must have been misinterpreting what he was saying. Another one off the list.

I'm not suggesting that Jack was not without flaws or that every camper had a problem. But a few bad apples can spoil a bunch. And sure enough, by the end of the camp experience, the counselor told me that Jack resorted to using his hands sometimes (an act of self-defense Jack claimed, when the bullies were bugging him). I talked this over with Jack, who was convinced that he wouldn't have used his hands if there weren't so many rough kids to contend with. Who knows?

There are a number of ways that you can find the right summer program for your child. Your child's school and the board of education will know of programs. Talk to parents with special needs children, ask support groups and national organizations targeted to your child's disorder, and search the internet, using search words such as "summer camp + special needs." If you find you are not turning up viable summer placements you may want to hire an educational specialist. I worked with a summer camp consultant the summer between second and third grade. She introduced me to several summer camps that I had not heard of. She knew the camp directors at each camp and presented Jack to them in a more objective way than I was able to.

Strategies FOR FINDING THE RIGHT SUMMER PLACEMENT

• WORK WITH THE SCHOOL-BASED TEAM AND YOUR PROFESSIONAL TEAM TO ARTICULATE GOALS FOR YOUR CHILD'S SUMMER EXPERIENCE.

Remember, summer is nearly one quarter of the year—don't look at it as down time or as just getting by until school begins again. This is a good opportunity to work on goals in new settings and reinforce what has been accomplished during the school year.

• WITH INPUT FROM YOUR PROFESSIONAL TEAM AND SCHOOL STAFF, DETERMINE THE LEVEL OF SPECIAL NEEDS ORIENTATION THAT YOUR CHILD REQUIRES.

Would your child do best in a typical camp, a camp that has experience with special needs or a total special needs camp?

• WHEN LOOKING AT SUMMER OPTIONS, YOU MIGHT WANT TO CONSIDER AN EXTENDED SCHOOL YEAR OPTION.

According to section 300.309 of IDEA, a school must provide extended school services if your child's IEP team determines these are necessary. If you and the team decide that this is the best option for your child, you will determine a program specifically for the summer time period.

• START THE PROCESS EARLY TO FIND THE RIGHT SUMMER CAMP FOR YOUR CHILD.

Whatever track you take to find a summer placement, be sure that you start the process early and be as thorough as possible—come June you will appreciate your hard efforts.

- IF A CAMP IS NOT EXCLUSIVELY FOR SPECIAL NEEDS CHILDREN, MAKE SURE IT IS WELL STRUCTURED, WITH ACTIVITIES APPROPRIATE TO YOUR CHILD'S ABILITIES AND INTERESTS.

Structure is one of the key requirements for many children with special needs.

- IF THE CAMP IS FOR SPECIAL NEEDS CHILDREN, BE SURE THE STAFF IS QUALIFIED AND TRAINED.

In particular, if the camp serves children with significant emotional and social needs, be sure that the supervision is very strong and that the counselors have ample experience in the field.

- MAKE SURE THE ACTIVITIES OF THE CAMP MATCH THE INTERESTS OF YOUR CHILD.

It's not enough to find a camp that has the right structure and support for your child if he isn't interested in what the camp has to offer. When Jack was six, he was enrolled in a program at the local YWCA that welcomed special needs students and provided trained aides to shadow them. Despite all of their accommodations, Jack was just not interested in the program content. This began as non-participation in camp activities and deteriorated into a situation where the aide was trailing Jack as he wandered about.

- IF NECESSARY, SET UP A BEHAVIORAL CHART THAT THE CAMP CAN IMPLEMENT.

Ideally, this will be a system that is already familiar to your child. For example, if your child is on a behavioral system during the school year, try to adapt this situation to the camp. When children have trouble with transitions or are easily frazzled by new environments, having something familiar to them that can help keep them centered will be very valuable.

- IF AN AIDE IS NEEDED, THE RIGHT AIDE CAN MAKE OR BREAK THE SUCCESS OF YOUR CHILD'S EXPERIENCE.

If you have a child who is complicated, it is best to have someone as the summer aide who has already worked with him.

- SET UP A PROCESS FOR DAILY COMMUNICATION WITH YOUR CHILD'S AIDE.

The only way that you will know if the camp experience is working, is through communication with the people who are working with your child. A daily communication journal can help you reinforce goals and discuss issues that happen at camp with your child, and give the camp strategies to solve issues that arise.

• KEEP YOUR EXPECTATIONS FOR SUMMER PROGRESS REASONABLE AND BE PATIENT WITH YOURSELVES AND YOUR CHILD.

Summer can often be a trying time even for parents of typical children. The combined excitement and ease of this non-scheduled time of year can lead to not enough sleep (due to later bedtimes) and mischievousness (that often stems from lots of free-time). A special needs child craves structure and often adapts poorly to change or new situations. It may take you a few years to sort out what kind of camp best suits your child.

To The Grand Canyon
And Beyond
How To Have a Good Summer Vacation

When I was growing up we took one big vacation a year. I remember trips to Cape Cod, Plymouth Rock, Williamsburg, Amish Country, Hershey Park, Disney World and Washington, D.C. With my high energy level and John's imagination, I always thought that our family would go on frequent explorations. But vacations, I learned, must have several key ingredients to be successful. Why is it that I always learn these lessons the hard way?

When Jack was four years old, we met dear friends with their eight and six year old daughters in Florida. We were staying at a hotel that was a little bit removed from the hub-bub of Disney World. This was a good place for Jack, given his sensory issues. It had a very well run children's activity program and babysitting service.

The first evening, we enjoyed a swim, fed the children and brought them to the evening children's program with the idea that the adults would have dinner in one of the hotel restaurants. We had not even gotten through the salad course when the telephone rang. It was the director of the children's program. Jack had been reaching for some crayons and had fallen, cutting his eyebrow. Off Jack and I went to the local hospital. Four hours later, Jack was stitched up and I was exhausted.

It was a sign of things to come. Jack had a knack for getting lost at Disney World. One minute he'd be by my side (since he was unwilling to hold my hand; standing next to me was the best that I could do), and the next minute he was gone. Do you know how scary that is when hundreds of people are around you in every direction?

Jack got lost once while he was watching a street band, once when he was talking to the oldest street cleaner employed by Disney, and once when he was looking in a gift shop. His wandering made it tough for one family to remain sane, never mind navigating two families through the crowds. As much as I wanted Jack and the rest of the family to be able to enjoy the company of friends, I realized that it was too much to worry about for all of us.

It took two more vacations to crystallize for me what worked and wouldn't work for family vacations.

I had already learned that I couldn't travel more than five hours with Jack. Long flights and car rides were exhausting for me, even though I went well equipped with games and activity books. When Jack was five we decided to go on a ski vacation, since we were hoping to develop skiing into a family activity. I had selected this particular ski resort because it was easy to get to and fit my five hour travel time rule.

The hotel we were staying in seemed perfect. Ski in, ski out, with a big marshmallow pit and roast at the ski base. Not thinking about Jack's sensory overload and ADHD issues, we signed him up for ski school on the first day. Equipped with a pager connected to the children's ski school, John and I went off to ski, worry free. We were just heading off the slopes for a late lunch when the pager went off.

I arrived at a cafeteria filled with more than two hundred children and deafening noise. Jack was in a side room with two instructors holding him down. He had tried to escape out of a side window. Sarah was crying hysterically; the instructors had dragged her in to help with her brother (what were they thinking?) and Jack had kicked her.

The problem, it seemed, was chocolate milk. At the time, I was trying Jack on a wheat free, gluten free, sugar and chocolate free diet and had indicated this on the sign-in sheet. While every other child received chocolate milk for lunch, Jack was handed white milk. He asked the instructors to call me to see if he could have a special treat of chocolate milk, since he knew that occasionally I relaxed the restriction. But the lunch staff kept pointing to the sign-in sheet, saying that it was clear to them what my wishes were. The noise of the room and staff's reluctance to call me were too much for Jack. Into fight mode he went. Luckily, we managed to get Jack back on track and from that point on had him with private ski instructors. I learned several big lessons in a painful way.

Since Jack and Sarah have different school vacation schedules, I can sometimes plan a trip with just one of them and tailor it exclusively to their interests. When Jack was in second grade, we planned a mother-son trip to Scottsdale, the Grand Canyon, and Sedona, Arizona.

The day before our trip, I thought about the amount of traveling that we would be doing and panicked. Jack made out like a bandit as I worked the Route 1 corridor in search of the Gameboy and Pokemon cartridge that he had been begging me for, for months. Jack is persistent and does not give up when he wants something. It took me five stores until I found a place that had a Gameboy in stock.

The first test as to Jack's emotional health came less than twenty minutes after leaving home. Reaching into his backpack for the Gameboy, he discovered that he had left it at home, where he had been playing with it just minutes before leaving. For a minute it looked like meltdown time. I thought about using the situation as an opportunity to teach a lesson. Here was a natural consequence for not taking care of his toys. But I knew Jack's fragility and tolerance level. It was enough of a lesson that he would not have it for the plane trip. So, I helped him solve the problem. We asked Suzanne, our reliable babysitter, to please go to the house and send it overnight so that Jack would have it for the rest of the trip. With a solution in sight, Jack pulled himself together and turned his attention to a pint size Monopoly game that we had bought for the trip as well. Off we went, without incident or commotion, arriving in Phoenix five hours later.

We gathered our bags and went off to rent the bright red car that would be our mission control center for the week. Minutes later we were in Scottsdale, where we would stay in a hotel that had a huge waterslide. I had learned from the ski trip that Jack needed a small, safe environment where there is something to do to regroup. The pool, with its waterslide and sand beach, would do the trick.

I think the tone of the trip was set as we unpacked. Unlike Sarah, who learned how to pack her suitcase at age five, Jack (at age seven) usually ignores me when I suggested that he help me pack. But for this trip Jack was motivated to see the Grand Canyon and had actually packed himself. When we arrived at the hotel room, I was amazed to see that he listened as I taught him my tricks for getting organized when you are on vacation: unpack your luggage right away, get your toiletries out and set up, and visit the concierge to plan your next few days if you haven't a schedule already set.

I watched incredulously as Jack mimicked me, taking clothes out of a suitcase, hand pressing them and putting them away. I let him take the lead deciding whose clothes would go where and was surprised to see how he liked this role and took it seriously. We were just about to leave the room when he discovered the patio of our sixth floor room. "Look, Mom," he said, "We can sleep out under the stars!" Immediately, I voiced favor for his idea. Although sleeping out on deck chairs wasn't my idea of a good night's sleep, I have learned to be flexible as well. If this was his idea of a tiptop vacation, I could go for it.

Two things about this vacation stand out in my mind: How well Jack related to other people (including authority figures), and his zest for life.

On most holidays, Jack would become so engrossed with the regional wildlife that he forgot about the people around him. This was certainly true the summer when my entire family gathered to celebrate my mother's sixty-fifth birthday in Florida. While the other eight cousins were busy getting reacquainted and joining in the many kid activities offered at the hotel, Jack stayed behind, obsessed with catching lizards. He only interacted with the cousins to the extent that they joined him in lizard hunting. In a place like Arizona, where I knew wildlife would be close at hand, I expected the same. I was in for a surprise.

With the decision to sleep under the stars and the discovery that this was a first experience for both of us, Jack and I started a list of things that we had never done before. We each delighted in seeing the list grow. This was the adventuresome Jack that I loved.

I have this theory. In our town (or maybe it's in our day and age) families operate at treadmill pace, from activity to activity. Many of our friends take their children to two team sports a night, after a full day of school. Life becomes, "How many activities is *your* child doing?" It creates a rhythm to the home that is not exactly relaxing. Although with Jack it was therapies that we were running to rather than team sports, these had the same exhausting impact on him. I was curious to see what Jack would be like in a place like Arizona, where we would have a schedule, but not the constant juggling of two children, racing to too many therapists, and the lack of daily mental and physical space to just wander the land, observe nature, and be free.

At dinner the first night I set up a team scenario with Jack. I gave him the leading role. He was to select no more than two activities a day. I introduced him to the concierge and helped him select a number of advertisements for local attractions. Although each day would appear to be structured to Jack, I made sure that the demands upon him would be kept low.

I worked hard during non-school times to keep as close as possible to the behavioral concepts and management plan that were being used at school. If I allowed this vacation time to just be free there would be a risk that old behaviors would re-emerge and new gains would be lost. It would definitely be harder for Jack to transition back to the school behavior program.

At this point in time, Jack was using a daily goal sheet very successfully at school. I wanted to keep the concept of the daily goal sheet while on vacation. I would use small gifts found on the trip as prizes. This was very motivating since Jack was a sucker for anything to do with animals. At one of the first pit stops we made he eyed a gigantic tarantula in a blob of Plexiglas and immediately claimed it as a prize he'd like to work towards. A few minutes later, Jack was the potential owner of this thingamajig.

In addition to the goal sheet, I wanted to keep the concept of a set schedule. To do this, I made Jack our daily timekeeper. He was the timekeeper and must watch how much time we had between activities. If he wanted to do something like go swimming and asked how long he could go, I turned the question back to him, if I thought there was a chance that he would give a reasonable solution. "How long do you think would be good?" I'd ask him. When he began to give me consistently reasonable answers I went to step two. "Why do you think that is reasonable?" I'd add. I was surprised at the responses, sensible and always honest.

I have to say that I don't know when I've had five days of such pure fun. We tried so many things that had been on my wish list for a long time: kayaking, hiking down the Grand Canyon, hiking at sunrise in the red mountains of Sedona, closing down a honky tonk cowboy town, fly fishing and, of course, sleeping under the stars. What was so nice was that during these activities we weren't fighting wills, battling behaviors and moving in friction. Except for one or two disasters, where I had not carefully prepared a guide or completely checked out group dynamics, everything went smoothly.

I can't say enough for the importance of pre-planning trips, to the point of talking to guides and people with whom your child will be relating. In Arizona, I had several phone conversations with Jim, the fly fisherman, who was to take us out to Oak Creek Canyon to spend a morning learning the beginning steps of fly fishing.

This activity was risky. I knew that fly fishing required great patience and that Jim was reluctant to take Jack on. He rarely took on children less than ten years old and then, only when children were exceptionally mature. After I explained that Jack had ADHD and he said, "So is he mature?" I knew that Jim had no idea what Jack was like. Yet, I pressed on because I had a feeling that Jack would take to fly fishing, considering how many hours we logged bait fishing.

I spent long phone conversations explaining what Jack might be like and how he might behave upon meeting Jim. I also gave Jim a few broad-brush hints as to how to work with Jack, such as, "Be firm but be fun." Although I believe the advance conversations were helpful, what was ultimately the key was Jim's own natural style. He was a combination of no nonsense and quick wit which is the golden combination for Jack. I would not have believed the level of cooperation and change in behavior that occurred in Jack had I not seen it myself. Jim told Jack to stand still and stop wiggling when he was showing him something and boom! All the wiggles that we had been told were part of a sensory integration issue dissolved.

One of the great things about fly fishing (and fishing in general) is that you can find a lot of axioms of life. "When you're fishing, I can't hear you if you aren't facing me because the wind will take your words away, so look at me when you are asking a question, Jack," Jim said in the first few minutes we were at the creek. That reasoning made sense to Jack. So he made eye contact with Jim when he asked his million and one questions.

Jack learned a roll cast and basic cast, fished off rocks and bank, and earned the top score in all the goals that we had set for the day. While I sat on a rock watching the creek roll by and listening to the sounds of nature, it struck me— we don't always give children credit for what they can accomplish. It is easy to fall into a pattern and assume that the way it has been is the way that it will always be. So, one of the great lessons of this trip was that some of what I had always assumed as neurologically impossible for Jack to achieve might be a conditioned response, or a response to a challenging environment. Certainly, the demands that Jim placed on Jack while fly fishing, as well as the demands on self-control that were necessary in order to hike the narrow trail of Grand Canyon, kayak as a part of a group of ten people, eat in nice restaurants, attend a children's camp program, drive ten hours in one day, and change hotels three times were high. And Jack handled most of them with flying colors.

The second greatest surprise of our trip was seeing how social Jack had become with peers and how generally well he related to them. With the hottest game at the moment in his hip pocket, he could engage children almost instantaneously. He had an appropriate and inviting opening line, and more times than not the child he approached also had a Gameboy so that they could share games and compare programs.

As I watched Jack during the week, I noticed something that I have not been able to put my finger on before. We always knew that the environment could determine how Jack behaved, but most of the time we limited this to the size of a space or a noise level. I now saw that the behaviors of other children were a determining factor in how Jack would behave. A camp program of quiet, focused children led Jack in the same direction. A jeep ride with a high spirited, playful child brought out the overly silly, wild side in Jack. In short, he could sink to the lowest or rise to the highest denominator of the group. This was important learning for camp groupings, extra curricular programs or future vacations.

Five days later, with over fifteen hundred miles logged on air and land, I felt that we had made some important strides, together and individually. Of course it had helped that I could schedule the time and craft a program to suit Jack's needs without having to worry about anyone else.

When I plan trips, I think about the interest of each person in the family as well as what the family dynamics are like at that point in time. For John, we build in ample time to hang out since that is a luxury that he never gets. With Sarah, I make sure that the spot chosen has lots of children her age and that there is a good selection of sports. For Jack, I look for places that have good nature activities.

Our most successful family vacations are the ones that fit everyone's interests and that give Jack freedom within a safe setting. One of our all-time winners is on an island in the South, which is only three miles long. We are able to rent a home, which negates the need for dragging children out for meals—a major benefit for a child who does not eat meals at regular times. The children can rent bikes and pedal to the dock for crabbing and fishing. There is nightly bingo for the family, a children's activities program and a nature program. Gentle southern nannies are there year after year to help with the children. There is a nice beach and an array of water activities. This is a vacation that works.

$\mathcal{S}$trategies FOR SUCCESSFUL VACATIONS

• Pick a vacation spot that has the sorts of activities that your children enjoy.

Interested children are happy children.

• Look at the setting through the sensory capabilities of your child.

Managing the environment will be the first hurdle for them to overcome.

• Gauge the wandering factor.

If your child is too young or unable to go from place to place on his own, you may want a place that's not too big. This includes the number of overall rooms in a hotel, size of the place, and proximity to major roads. The bigger the place and the busier its location, the easier to lose a child.

• Do you want to bring an extra pair of hands along?

A babysitter, high school student, or relative who is good with your children can be a huge help. What you give up in privacy, you may gain in peace of mind.

• Bring board games and busy activities to do in down time.

If we are going to be somewhere for any length of time I ship a box ahead. Generally included are favorite board games, cards, a family puzzle, Legos and other manipulatives, art projects and a few books.

If you are traveling by plane:

• Request the bulkhead seat.

In the early years, Jack would spend the entire trip with toys spread out on the floor, and he with them. Later, the extra leg room was still helpful for wiggly children.

• IF YOU CAN'T GET THE BULKHEAD SEAT, SIT AS FAR FORWARD AS POSSIBLE.
When it is time to exit the plane, it's far easier than trying to hop over seats racing after the child who has dodged between passengers' legs.

• REQUEST A KID'S MEAL.
It will make mealtime less of an issue.

• STOCK UP ON SMALL GAMES, CARDS, BOOKS OR WORKBOOKS TO KEEP CHILDREN BUSY.
I try to select things that they can play with a child that they might meet on the plane, or that we can do together. Stuffed animals and toys might be cute but they don't entertain for very long.

• ON SHORT FLIGHTS, BOARD THE PLANE AS EARLY AS POSSIBLE.
You might explain to the gate agent that you have an exceptional child. It might take a bit of work to get your child settled and this will be easier to do when there are fewer people around to negotiate.

• ON LONG FLIGHTS, BOARD THE PLANE AT THE FINAL CALL.
Use the last few minutes for a bathroom break and encourage your child to walk around to try to use up as much energy as possible.

• IF YOU USE MEDICINE FOR BEHAVIOR, TRY TO TIME IT TO COINCIDE WITH YOUR TRAVEL TIME.

• THINK ABOUT YOUR CHILD'S BEST TIME AND SCHEDULE TRAVEL TIME TO COINCIDE WITH THAT TIME.
Early morning flights always work best for us because everyone is well rested, fresh, and usually in a good mood.

IF YOU ARE TRAVELING BY CAR:

• MAKE SURE YOU HAVE PLENTY TO KEEP CHILDREN BUSY.
Books on tape are always good for a couple of hours.

- PLAN ON REGULAR BREAKS.

Let the children stretch their legs, get a drink or snack, and wash up. Be mindful of what they are selecting for food and drink. You may get more energy than you wish if they are choosing sugary drinks and snacks.

- GIVE EACH CHILD A MAP MARKED WITH THE ROUTE SO THEY CAN FOLLOW ALONG.

- PICK UP SOME FAMILY TRAVEL GAMES.

We love Car Bingo and the Brain Teasers questions.

What's Going on with the Other Kids in the Family?
How To Help Siblings Cope

There is no way around the fact that your other children will, in some way, be affected by the child with special needs. If birth order and number of children in a family influence the development of each child's personality, certainly the way a child with special needs interacts with his siblings is going to impact those siblings. Sometimes you see the affect right away, other times you see it in later years.

When Jack was very young he went through a period of poking Sarah when she didn't go along with his wishes. For a few months (despite our work trying to get Jack to stop his aggressive behavior), Sarah tolerated Jack's jabs and became our little psychologist, also trying to teach him not to hit. Eventually though, our daughter got sick of Jack's behavior and began giving him a taste of his own medicine. Today, nearly eight years later, if Sarah does something not so nice to Jack, she's likely to say, "Well, he used to hit me!" It takes a long time for transgressions, endured for a long time, to be forgiven and forgotten.

As the children get older and as Jack's social skills continue to improve, their overall relationship is improving. Their best moments are when we are at home and they get a spontaneous idea to entertain us. Plays and shows are top on the list. Most difficult is when one child has a play date at our house. Then, the usual balance is off, the child without the play date wants to join in, and more often than not that child is excluded.

It is difficult to see which of Sarah and Jack's ups and downs are typical sibling behavior and which are due to Jack's social limitations. In a home with all typical children we would let them work out their own differences. In Jack's younger years (five, six and seven), ages at which a child can begin to negotiate, we *had* to get involved when things heated up. Although Sarah was ready and willing to negotiate, Jack would not hesitate to hit Sarah or do something that was out of the realm of acceptable behavior.

I don't think outsiders have any idea of the minute-to-minute pressure Sarah is under, having a sibling with extremely low social skills. Besides having to endure a lot of unwarranted physical bumps, Sarah doesn't get to enjoy the daily companionship of a sibling. Yes, there are moments of connectedness, but on the whole, Jack is buried in his fishing, Pokemon, or some other obsession that is solo and silent.

For a long time, we used Saturdays as a day where Ken and I could focus on Sarah. Margaret, our babysitter, was with Jack on Saturdays so it was easy to have Sarah with one or both of us. On the days that Margaret was not babysitting, each of us took a child. What we did was never as important as the fact that we were giving Sarah our complete attention. With Ken, Sarah would go to her morning sports activity (where he was often an assistant coach), then have lunch and do errands. When Sarah was with me, I would plug into her latest area of interest. One summer, I took the opportunity, when we were driving down to Baltimore to a soccer camp, to stop at The Winterthur Museum, since Sarah had recently expressed an interest in architecture.

Having one-on-one time gives us a chance to give Sarah some focused attention on things that she enjoys, and can give her a chance to have her say. So often, Jack has difficulty waiting to speak and will interrupt Sarah as she is trying to explain something to me. While I chide and correct him, he will just barrel forward, forcing Sarah to stop her conversation and wait until he is finished. Although we have explained to Sarah repeatedly that Jack is unable to control his impulsivity, this is nevertheless frustrating (and probably hard to understand) for a child who is only slightly older. When we are alone with Sarah, she has the space to talk without interruption and we have the peace of mind to really listen (another difficult thing when you have a child in the background who is demanding attention).

Like it or not, the majority of attention in our house centers on Jack. In the early years, this was due to the need for constant damage control. In the later years, we were no longer containing problems, but we were busy trying to draw Jack out of himself to interact with us. This took a lot of energy and focused attention. The heightened attention on Jack took its toll on Sarah. We hoped that by spending time on Saturdays with Sarah, we were doing something to tip the scales back into balance.

It is always very confusing to Sarah to have two sets of rules at work in our house, one for Jack and one for her. Unfortunately, there is no way around this situation. Some things that a typical child should do no matter what are just not possible for Jack. For example, Jack could not get himself to sleep at night. Not only could he not get to sleep, but he always became hungry, right at bedtime. I learned that it was far better to let him stay up an extra hour and give him a bedtime snack than to argue about why 8:00 p.m. was the bedtime and why he couldn't eat after dinner. Of course, this didn't sit well with Sarah, who abided by my rule that there was no eating just before bed and that 8:00 p.m. was bedtime.

The rules may be different for each child, but, we are very, very careful to give Sarah extra privileges—and to let her know that these privileges are extended to her when she is able to show us responsible behavior.

Sarah's feelings about having a special needs brother are buried deep. We see them come out not only by what she says but also by her behaviors. During rough periods with Jack, there is a certain edginess to Sarah—she too, is affected by the stress. The more you can get a sibling to talk about her frustrations and feelings, the less likely you are to see the anger, frustration and disappointment express itself in actions. I try to take a few minutes when Sarah goes to sleep, just to sit on her bed and talk about whatever she wants to talk about. Many nights, the name of her brother never comes up. But there are other times when, all in a gush, she brings up some incident of the day and we are able to discuss it.

Each summer and during the school year, we have made sure that we have a couple of older girls who can spend time with Sarah, like a big sister would. We try to find girls who have similar interests and are good role models for Sarah. It is very important to us that Sarah knows and feels that we are keeping her needs and interests at heart.

Sarah is a very independent soul and was eager to experience sleep-away camp at the age of seven. Though in our neck of the woods many people look to the eastern seaboard and the New England mountains for children's camps, Sarah's godmother loved a camp in the Ozark Mountains, which is the oldest Christian camp in the country. Kanakuk-Kanakomo is a Christian sports camp; there is an equal emphasis on Bible study and worship and sportsmanship through teamwork. Kanakuk is probably the single most important experience in Sarah's life. We both seem to count the days until the camp session begins. When Sarah is at camp, I know that she is part of a family and a community—sharing bedtime talks, activities and meals in a happy companionship that she does not often have at home.

SIBLING COPING

 *Strategies*

- **GIVE TYPICAL CHILDREN THEIR OWN TIME WITH YOU.**
One-on-one time lets the typical child know that they are as valued as the one who may be getting the bulk of your time and attention.

- **BE DELIBERATE IN EXTENDING SPECIAL PRIVILEGES TO THE TYPICAL CHILDREN, WHEN DESERVED.**
They learn soon enough that life isn't fair, getting stuck with extra chores or an overall harder line to toe than their special needs sibling. Let them also feel the privileges for being responsible and dependable.

- **TAKE THE TIME TO TALK WITH SIBLINGS ABOUT THEIR FEELINGS.**
There are lots of feelings that need to be expressed; don't just assume that everyone else in the family is fine.

- **DON'T HESITATE TO BRING IN A "TALKING DOCTOR" (PSYCHOLOGIST), IF THINGS GET ROUGH WITH SIBLINGS.**
For a couple of years, Sarah was so stressed out and affected by Jack that we had her meet with a psychologist once a week, to talk about her feelings. I think this time gave Sarah another indication that we were very concerned about her and her feelings, and that although we couldn't change the way things were at home, we could give her support in dealing with them. Sarah knows that John and I regularly meet with someone to help us deal with our unusually stressful circumstances. We want her to feel that it is completely okay to get extra help with feelings, when she needs it.

- **TRY TO FIND A BIG BROTHER OR SISTER MENTOR OR SPECIAL BABYSITTER FOR THE OTHER SIBLINGS.**
The extra attention and role modeling will do them a world of good.

• LOOK FOR LOCAL PROGRAMS TO HELP SIBLINGS COPE WITH THEIR SPECIAL NEEDS BROTHER OR SISTER.

The Junior League and the organization serving the special needs population in our community both offer get-togethers twice a year for siblings of special needs children. The get-togethers are organized by age group (of the siblings). The purposes of the gatherings are to provide a forum for sharing experiences, to help children realize that they are not alone in their situation, and to make connections of support. Whether the siblings in your family find this helpful or not will be a very individual thing.

• IF SIBLINGS CAN HANDLE THE INDEPENDENCE, ENCOURAGE THEM TO SPEND SOME TIME AT A SLEEP-AWAY CAMP IN THE SUMMER.

Everyone needs a break from the child who is demanding. Let siblings be in a place where they are just themselves.

FISHING AND OTHER PASSIONS
Helping Your Child Find Hobbies and Interests

When we were able to incorporate Jack's therapies into his school program and eliminate outside sessions, a whole new world opened. I was tempted—and actually attempted—to schedule various after school activities for Jack. I chose these with input from Jack's psychologist and therapists, with an eye for accomplishing some of Jack's behavioral goals.

Karate was one of the selected activities. The particular karate we chose advocated a philosophy of respect for others, respect for yourself, and self-control. These seemed like perfect goals for a child like Jack. The teacher was fun, kept excellent control of the class and had great patience with Jack. While I loved the self-discipline and control that the sport instilled in Jack, we found that it required more obedience and conformity than he was capable of. We eventually dropped it.

There have been a number of activities that seemed, on paper, like they would be a perfect fit for Jack, but did not work out as planned. It is important for you, as a parent, to be supportive of what your child is doing but maintain your perspective. Remember, it is your child's activity. All of us have seen the parent who has gone from enthusiastic to overenthusiastic and controlling. Except with the most complacent child, no amount of convincing will turn around a child who is not interested. We have found that a child who is happy with what he is doing is happier in general.

When the children were very young, I taught them how to play chess. I was using board games as a structured way to work with Jack on turn taking and following directions. Jack loved the game and supplemented our games with the software, Chessmaster 5000. By the time he was eight, Jack was good enough to be accepted into an after school program, Chess for Tournament Players. Luckily, the teacher who led the class was an extremely entertaining and patient person.

At the first class, I stayed in the classroom, sitting in the back, in case I was needed. It took less than twenty minutes for me to put down my paperwork and laugh along with the class as I listened to Rich's brilliant chess games, peppered with phrases like, "Time to say, HELLO PRETTY LADY!" and, "Here comes HELLO MUDDA, HELLO FADDA!" Jack was crazy about Rich as well as about learning chess at a whole new level. What began as an experiment to see if he could handle an after school class with typical kids grew to include participation in local tournaments, private lessons, chess games with peers, and eventually, the national chess championships in Dallas, Texas. What an enormous jolt to Jack's self-esteem. Not only was he doing fairly well in terms of competing, he was part of a real, live team, just like his sister. If you can find something that your child likes and that he can develop proficiency in, it can be a great release and a great boost to his morale.

Strategies FOR DEVELOPING OUTSIDE INTERESTS

• TIE ACTIVITIES INTO YOUR CHILD'S AREA OF INTEREST.
Working off of an interest or passion can give you a pathway to work on goals. Jack has always had a passion for animals. One winter, he attended a Saturday series at the local Audubon center. Not only did Jack build an incredible knowledge base, the class gave him an opportunity to work on his social skills with other peers.

• A TEACHER OR COACH WHO CLICKS WITH YOUR CHILD IS A KEY TO SUCCESS.

• TRY TO FIND A FRIEND TO SHARE YOUR CHILD'S INTEREST.
As Jack has gotten older, I find that if we can encourage one of his friends to join in the same activity, Jack has yet another incentive to hold to his commitment.

• EXPOSE YOUR CHILD TO HOBBIES THAT DRAW UPON HIS STRENGTHS.
Jack wasn't into sports. He had always declined or quit a sports team. It wasn't until we began practicing baseball, and I complimented him again and again, that he had the confidence to then see if he could cut it on a team. I knew that he had some natural talent and had worked with him to get it to a level that I thought boys his age would be playing at. For a few weeks, Jack hung in and did a good job of being part of the team. Unfortunately, he couldn't see the point of spending half of his time on drills and eventually quit.

• THINK ABOUT SPORTS WHICH ARE STRUCTURED AND MORE INDIVIDUALIZED.
Your child can begin sports like horseback riding, swimming, and squash solo, and later on, incorporate them into a team activity.

HOLIDAY HURDLES
How To Set Up Successful Holiday Celebrations

As a child, I loved holidays. My memories of holidays begin in a home filled to the brim with kind relatives, eager to hear our latest piano accomplishment and patiently watch the newest and coolest dance steps. The biggest dilemma my siblings and I faced was how we could get out of doing all of the holiday dishes. In an Italian-influenced household, where Christmas dinner consisted of seven courses and could be four hours long, we had a sure shot for dishpan hands. We finally figured out a strategy to avoid dish duty. We would trade this loathsome task for the promise of putting on a play during the dessert hour. Try it sometime and see if doesn't get you out of kitchen work.

Special occasions often put Jack in a new setting and a new situation. Unfamiliarity—with a place, a situation and with people—can confuse the rules of conduct and behavior that Jack has mastered. With a little advance planning, Jack now looks forward to most special days, rather than dreading them. Holidays and special occasions, such as a day spent in a new city, attending an arts event, or going to a ballgame, are successful when we organize them carefully and have contingency plans.

Just getting into holiday clothes—pants with a real waistband, a belt and a button-down shirt—is a struggle for Jack. I go back and forth in my mind as to whether I should let him dress comfortably but inappropriately for where we are going, or if I should make sure he is dressed correctly and run the risk that his sensory bells may start chiming, possibly with behavior ramifications.

As in everything with Jack, I try to understand what issues are getting in the way of his cooperation. In the case of holiday clothes, I make sure that pants are not itchy (fabrics that are blends rather than pure wool or stiff cottons fit the bill here) and that shirts are not too stiff. Whenever possible, Jack wears a sweater over his shirt so if he takes a shirttail out (a frequent occurrence) he doesn't look too sloppy. For warmer weather we look for shirts that are meant to be worn outside of pants. Although wardrobe is one of the least important things to worry about, it is a good example of how to find a creative solution for your child. And though it may be completely unimportant to your child, the old saying, "First impressions are lasting impressions" does have some truth to it. Sad to say but true, the disruptive child who looks pressed and starched is forgiven a bit more than the child who is ill-behaved and looks a mess.

Anytime we have a special event in the family, I mentally walk through the day. I think about what the setting will be like, what will be required of Jack, and possible occurrences which could set off a not-so-great response in him. By thinking about the day, you can anticipate and head-off many difficulties.

Take a situation where your family is seated in a restaurant or club for a holiday dinner. If you have a child like Jack, with sensory and attention difficulties, you probably already know what I am talking about. The center of a restaurant is the worst place for Jack. I find that a table against a wall is good, close to a door in case we need to make a quick escape is even better. A seat near the windows or a door leading to outside could be too tempting for Jack so we try to avoid these settings. Just thinking through the physical setting and requesting a table that will best suit the needs of your child can get the day off to a good start.

It is not unusual for my husband and me to drive separately to an event. This is part of our repertoire of emergency plans. Though it is sad that we can't travel as a family we've learned that it is far worse to have to quickly gather our troops and head out, should a storm suddenly rise in Jack. With two cars, Sarah and one parent can stay to enjoy the remainder of an event if Jack needs to leave.

As Jack has gotten healthier it is rare that we have to actually leave an event. Instead, I scout around a place as soon as we arrive to look for a few quiet spaces that Jack can go, should he need to pull himself together. It is probably best to find a manager when you get to a place, briefly describe your situation (there is no need to overly alarm him), and ask where he would like your child to go, should he need to take a break. I have found managers to be more than willing to help me create back-up plans, and they often appreciate my respectful attitude toward the other guests.

When Jack was seven years old we went to a family reunion picnic at a distant cousin's farm. There were nearly one hundred relatives, of whom Jack knew only a handful. This was the period when he was obsessed with Pokemon; I had told him that all rules were off and he could use his Gameboy as much as he wanted for the day. I knew that for the rest of our family to get good visiting time in, Jack would need to be occupied. I also knew that at that stage he wasn't likely to voluntarily meet people he had never seen before.

All was well for the first two hours of the party. Jack even managed to look up and say "hello" to a few people to whom I introduced him. Then came the hayride.

We joined a group of people and got ready for a ride around the farm. Jack was up and down, all over the wagon, jumping from side to side trying to spot different animals. This was a tough situation. I had no escape hatch. We muddled through it, amidst my apologies to the other newfound relatives.

About an hour after the ride, John and I decided that it was time to take the tribe home. I had just seen Jack fifteen minutes earlier. I looked around the picnic grounds but he was nowhere to be seen. The search began. We went to neighboring farms, in and out of the different animal buildings on my cousin's property and all around the land. No Jack anywhere.

Finally, just when I thought we'd have to tell the cousins that we needed their help for a manhunt, we spotted him. Big as life, there he was, in the middle of the horse cart, rounding the bend from a second hay ride. This was one of those situations where, although I had planned the best I could, I simply could not have foreseen everything that might happen. Fortunately, the only thing that was injured that day was our departure timetable.

One summer day we attended a minor league baseball game with another family. I went over with Jack what the day would be like a couple of days in advance of the game. At age eight, Jack was able to tell me that he didn't think he could sit through the whole game. I called ahead to the ballpark and learned different places we could go and things we could do when Jack needed to take a break. The ballpark actually had a playground, which we frequented every few innings. I probably would not have come across it, had I not talked to them in advance.

This year we had an afternoon of gingerbread house making with the cousins. I've had other gingerbread house making parties. They are usually a candy free-for-all. More candy is consumed or smashed into carpets than lands on the houses. It's a nightmare.

But this year Sarah took my preparation approach into her own hands. First, we found a bakery that made the houses—undecorated of course—for a reasonable price. No more sides falling and roofs caving in. The structures were solid. At every child's place Sarah organized piles of assorted candy. That eliminated the reaching, grabbing and jockeying for the same pieces.

When Jack and the cousins came to the table all was in place. Sarah had arranged little cups of frosting and a knife at each place, along with assorted candies and the gingerbread form.

We had so much fun. Each child had a unique approach to his creation. Jack's was the pared down, single color approach. Two lines of green gumdrops defined the grass. Straight lines of stick gum acted as roof shingles. He made a cobblestone path out of M & Ms. He may not have stayed focused as long as the other children but he was certainly part of the group. All from a little advance thinking. Praise you, Sarah!

Although your fairytale vision of what holidays and special family occasions should be may not be possible given your unique situation, you can still have a wonderful time. Once we figured out how to plan for and set up situations that would work for Jack, we were able to relax and enjoy the day. One final thought—if you feel in your gut that the day will just be too much for your child to manage, consider not attending. You know what your child's capability is at any point in time. There is no sense in testing a limit if you have a sense that the chances of success are pretty low. But don't sit home and stew about your loss. Send the rest of the family (if they wish to go) and plan an outing for that day that you know your child can manage. You will be giving him the message that he is still capable and can enjoy life.

HOLIDAY AND SPECIAL EVENTS *Strategies*

• Review the day's itinerary with your child several times before the big day arrives.

You don't ever want to introduce an element of surprise to exceptional children. When children are younger, just talking to them about what will occur on that day is about all that they can manage. For children who are slightly older and have begun the process of introspection, you can ask them what sounds like it might be difficult for them and together, brainstorm different strategies. As Jack gets older, he is able to tell me what he can and can't handle.

• Check out the acoustics of the place, particularly if there is to be live music or entertainment.

If you have a child who is sensitive to sound you will not want to be too near any sort of loud, live entertainment, like a band. On the other hand, sitting up close to a show that is on the quiet side, such as a magic show, can help hold your child's attention. Again, a little pre-work will help you determine the best place for your group to sit.

• Be aware of the tactile stresses that a child might experience if he is wearing party clothes.

Clothes that don't feel right will have behavioral ramifications.

• If your child is on medication to assist with behaviors, time the dose so that he is fully covered during the time that you will be at the event.

Jack's medications are not effective after 3:00 p.m. Since we use them primarily to assist with focus and attention, I hold off on the first dose of medication so that it becomes effective about thirty minutes before we arrive at our destination. As his medication only has a 3½ hour efficacy, I want to be sure that it's operating when we need it.

• BE CONSCIOUS OF WHO YOUR CHILD IS SITTING NEXT TO AT AN EVENT OR MEAL.

John or I usually sit next to Jack to help him maintain appropriate behavior. Since he enjoys being with other children, we make sure that a child (one who is on the calmer and quieter side) is seated near him as well. Think about the seating arrangement ahead of time.

• ALWAYS HAVE A CONTINGENCY PLAN IN PLACE.

"Exit, Stage Left" is a trick that you'll do well to use when there is no other way to deal with a situation that is bombing out.

• GET IN THE GRAMMY GOODY BAG HABIT.

My mother always brings little grab bags of things to keep the grandchildren busy when we go out to a restaurant. We both keep an eye out for travel toys, Legos or other put-together toys, workbooks and reading books that might be on sale or particularly clever. I keep a hiding place in the house for these things. I pull them out when we have to go on a long trip and to special events which require Jack to sit for a long period of time, such as a holiday meal. Sometimes I round up a board game or two that he can play with another child. Something like Trouble, which doesn't have too many loose pieces, works particularly well.

• THINK THROUGH HOW LONG YOU THINK YOUR CHILD CAN COMFORTABLY ENJOY THE EVENT.

When we go to a relative's house for a holiday, I think through what the plans for the day are and consider what amount of time I think Jack can handle the event. For example, last year we went to my sister's for Thanksgiving dinner. There were going to be six children and seven adults—the maximum commotion that Jack can handle. Dinner was to be served at five o'clock. I planned our day so that we arrived at Wendy's house at 4:00. This would give Jack some time to enjoy his cousins' company, but not enough time to get too revved up.

• LET PEOPLE WHOM YOU WILL BE WITH KNOW THAT YOU MAY HAVE TO LEAVE QUICKLY.

At my sister's Thanksgiving dinner, I knew that we were probably okay with Jack for about 3½ hours. I let her know in advance of the holiday that there was a chance we would have to leave right on the heels of dessert. Preparing others for what could occur will save misunderstandings and hurt feelings—particularly with all the work that goes into holiday preparations or a birthday party.

• IF YOU HAVE A LONG DISTANCE TO TRAVEL, PLAN THE TRIP SO THAT THERE IS TIME FOR A BREAK BEFORE THE EVENT.

For Thanksgiving, we gave ourselves enough time so we could stop at the hotel, let the children unwind (even suggesting—and having them accept—the idea of taking a relaxing bath) and change clothes. After that we proceeded to my sister's home. Just forty minutes of downtime calmed them and gave them a renewed perspective.

KEEPING THE PARTY IN BIRTHDAY PARTY
Creating Birthday Parties That Work

When I was growing up family traditions were a natural part of the rhythm of a year. We had certain ways that we celebrated each holiday, birthday, and even how we spent every Sunday. We never thought about our family habits as tradition or talked about the importance of them—they were just part of the way our family operated.

I've spent a lot of time thinking through what activities and traditions I want to be a part of our family's life together. When I first began thinking about this, I started by defining what values and elements of a family were important to John and me. Once I analyzed what was important, I began creating experiences where those values would be put into play.

When it comes to birthdays, we have several traditions in our home. We set aside an afternoon or evening and go to a special event. The person's birthday evening calls for their favorite meal, and often includes Grammy. But, more important than what we do is the tone of the celebration. All of the traditions focus on one goal—to make the birthday person feel particularly loved and appreciated. In this tremendously fast paced world it is more important than ever to take the time to celebrate life—and what better day than on a birthday. Marking someone's birthday says, in essence, that the person *matters*. In the case of children who may rarely get that feedback, it is more important than ever that their birthday be remembered.

It has taken me successes and near disasters to figure out what makes for a successful celebration for Jack. I am almost embarrassed to admit that it took us four tries until we had a celebration that was fun for Jack and not emotionally wrenching for me. There seem to be two fundamental questions that need to be answered before you can plan a child's—and not just a special needs child's—party.

Does your child enjoy many people around, or is he a small group person (maybe even a one-on-one person)? When Jack was four years old we had a party at an inside adventure park. Not only did Jack need to negotiate his ten guests, he also had to filter through the noise and commotion of the place. In order to hold himself together Jack spent much of the birthday party in the bathroom, where it was quiet.

What does your child like to do? When Jack turned eight years old we celebrated with a party at a small bowling alley. By then, we had figured out the size thing and were feeling comfortable that the party would be a hit—after all, we were the only people in a six lane spot. Unfortunately, I forgot what Jack's interests were at that time. It was clear to me while we were warming up that bowling was not Jack's thing. He couldn't have been less interested in seeing how many pins a little ball could knock down. So, although the guests had great fun with an afternoon of bowling, Jack spent most of the time wandering around.

For many years, I really couldn't include Jack in the planning of the celebration, beyond his selection of a party theme. His ideas about what would work (i.e., what he could handle) and what would be best for him didn't match up. So, I planned the party, making sure that Jack knew what we would be doing and walking him through some basic party manners. As he got older, I was able to spend more time teaching Jack about what a good host would do (and not do). We covered the basics of making guests feel at home, treating friends equally, and, if we were going to open presents, making sure to react to each present with the same enthusiasm.

This last year, when Jack turned nine, we sat down together and planned the party, a pool party at our home. This was the first time Jack had the ability to think through what he could handle, and what his two guests could manage. It as a great jolt to his self-esteem to take on the responsibility for his party.

You do not want a party for your child to become a free-for-all with children running all over. You do want everyone to have fun and to be relaxed. I have found that if I let Jack and his friends get too excited they go into an overdrive mode that is very hard to manage. I plan a party that is structured from the first person greeted to the last person leaving. I like to have too many activities ready to go if needed, rather than run the risk of running out of things to do, which leads to children running free.

For years, as Jack's birthday party approached I'd develop a fair share of anxiety. You shouldn't have to do the same. With a little planning and a "less is more" philosophy (at least until you have the experience and confidence that your child can handle, and wants, more and bigger), the day can be a wonderful celebration for the whole family.

Once you figure out what kind of setting would be best, the maximum number of guests, and the kind of activities that your child would enjoy, you can plan a party. For Jack, I now know that fewer guests are best, the setting should be quiet, and the activity we do should tie into his latest interests. Our most successful party was the pool party. We invited two friends from school over to our home for an hour of swimming and a birthday lunch. The party lasted two hours. The party was successful for several reasons. First, it was in a space that Jack was comfortable with. Second, he was with friends that he was extremely close to. And third, he was doing something that he enjoyed.

PARTY

Strategies

- **INVITE ONLY THE CHILDREN WITH WHOM YOUR CHILD IS EXTREMELY COMFORTABLE.**

This is not the time to invite people over that you would like your child to get to know better. Birthday celebrations often rev up the easily revved up child and bring on heightened emotions. Why bring a new child into a situation where your child may not be exhibiting his best qualities? Keep your own anxiety level down and invite only those children that are already good friends with your child.

- **KEEP THE PARTY TO A REASONABLE TIME FRAME; IN FACT, ERR ON THE SIDE OF A SHORTER (VERSUS LONGER) EVENT.**

Particularly if you are having a party with a number of special needs children, you can't be sure how the party will develop. I have seen the birthday child totally fall apart, children getting so wound up that the day became a free-for-all. I find that a shorter party is more than enough time for Jack to feel that he has celebrated his special day with friends, but not enough time for the party to get out of control.

- **INVITE PARENTS OF YOUR CHILD'S GUESTS TO STAY.**

You may not know your child's friends all that well or be familiar enough with their special needs to be able to intervene, should you need to. I feel a much greater comfort if the parents of other special needs children stay at the party. Plus, since our parties tend to be under two hours, it doesn't make sense for parents to leave and come back. It takes just a little extra effort to have drinks and perhaps extra food for the adults, and it may prove to be invaluable.

• THINK THROUGH THE GUEST LIST CAREFULLY.

For a few years, Jack invited both friends from his special education class and children with no special needs. In retrospect, this wasn't such a great idea. The typical kids didn't know the special needs kids and weren't used to some of their behaviors. From the perspective of the special needs children, when a number of them would get together their behaviors would frequently become elevated. Nowadays, if there are a couple of typical children that Jack would like to celebrate his birthday with, I arrange this separately from the party with his special needs friends.

• INCLUDE YOUR CHILD IN THE PLANNING OF THE PARTY, TO THE EXTENT THAT HE IS ABLE TO PARTICIPATE.

This has become lots of fun as a family activity and a good conversation starter for dinners that can last weeks!

• THE PARTY SHOULD HAVE STRUCTURE TO IT, WITH A BEGINNING, MIDDLE AND END.

Don't leave anything to chance. Better to have too many things to do planned and ready to do, rather than too few.

Grocery Shopping and Other Potentially Embarrassing Places
Navigating Your Child Through Public Spaces

I don't go anywhere without my disaster-control radar operating. With one ear tuned in for any changes in Jack's emotional state, I am usually able to anticipate what could become an intolerable situation and head it off before it occurs.

Of course, this is not always possible. Like the time our whole family needed to be interviewed. This meeting took place in a noisy dining room, where many families were eating Sunday lunch. It didn't take long before the noise and commotion put Jack under—literally. One minute we were shaking hands and sharing introductions, the next we were trying to conduct a friendly conversation and act as if nothing were awry while Jack huddled under the table. Obviously, it was impossible to put my exit strategy in play, so I quickly explained to the people whom we had just met that Jack had a hard time with over-stimulating environments and used this under-the-table strategy as a coping mechanism.

When Jack was five years old, the under-the-table move didn't seem all that offbeat to outsiders. It gave Jack the security and quiet that he needed and allowed our family to stay and finish the interview. When Jack was seven, this table stint didn't play so well; we needed new strategies to replace the old ones. We are constantly reassessing what works and what does not and making changes along the way.

I remember when Jack was 2½ and nothing was going right. We had just withdrawn Jack from his Montessori school and were about to start a psychological evaluation. I decided to try to keep some semblance of my daily routine, which started with an exercise class. My idea was to de-stress and then figure out some activities that Jack and I could do together, working around the evaluation appointments.

The exercise studio had a babysitting room with arts and crafts. Jack was accustomed to this room since he often came with me on Saturdays. The morning started off well enough, meaning that both children got dressed without needing too many prompts and joined me for a quick breakfast. We drove Sarah to school.

Jack and I arrived in plenty of time to get him settled in the babysitting room before the 8 a.m. class. Although my stomach was rolling in anticipation of our first appointment with the psychologist a few hours later, I managed to concentrate and get through almost all of the class.

That is, until the door creaked open.

I knew before the receptionist beckoned to me that I was the one who would be summoned. The trouble, of course, was Jack. Jack had been busily coloring in one of the books when the babysitter informed him that each child could only color three pictures in that particular book. Jack simply couldn't accept the limit. He was on a coloring roll and roll he must. So, after the babysitter repeated her warning to no avail, she removed the book from my of-the-moment artist. He warned her that if she didn't return it he would take action. When she didn't, he wet his pants.

I wish that I could report that a level-headed, thoughtful discussion between my son and me about accepting limits and appropriate behavior took place. Nothing could be further from the truth. I was so mad! Here we were, not two hours into the new routine and things were out of control. Not only was I mad, I was scared. Here was a new behavior. Jack had crossed a new line.

The truth of the matter was, while I was mad at Jack, I was furious with myself. What was I thinking? The child was fragile and unable to cope in a group setting, and although he might not have understood exactly the ramifications of being removed from a school, he certainly couldn't be feeling good about himself. So why did I start the next day out by putting him in an environment where new demands were placed on him? Why didn't I just create a nurturing space at home, letting him nest a little while we got through the evaluation process? This was my first lesson in not putting Jack in situations that might be beyond what he could manage.

Now that Jack is almost nine, I have begun to talk with him about the fact that he is made wonderfully, but also made differently than many others. I talk about the fact that he and I are going to have to work creatively and work hard to help him learn what sometimes comes naturally to others. Our current topics are focusing, not being too silly, and learning how to be a good friend. I always make sure that I start the conversation by telling Jack how lucky we are to have him in our family and how special he is to me. I end by assuring him that everything is going to be just fine. As our conversations grow in frequency and length, it is easier for me to reason with him, so if we need to escape a situation we can do so (usually) by my whispering to Jack that the circumstances are probably very difficult for him and that's okay, so why don't we just leave and do something else.

This sort of planning and contingency planning is critical for successful ventures with Jack. The way I think about planning for disaster is using the old Venn diagram. According to the diagram, there are two major settings: the internal environment (the home) and the external environment (public settings). There are strategies that are unique to each place but there is also a common set of strategies that apply regardless to where you are.

Strategies for Assessing Appropriateness of an Activity

Wherever we are, I keep a mental checklist of the requirements for a setting to be manageable for Jack, along with a mental list of the things that could set him off. I build this list from Jack's current behaviors and his general stability level. I ask myself questions like:

- How able is Jack to make transitions?
- How flexible is Jack to changes in routine and changes to the schedule?
- How is Jack's anxiety level?
- How large an environment can Jack handle at the given time (number of people, general noise level, and size of space)?
- How is Jack's safety awareness and sense of boundaries?

I try not to be a slave to a schedule. While I want as much consistency and structure as possible, I find that what is achievable during one period may not be achievable in the next one.

Going to church is a perfect example of this in our family. At the beginning of each church school year, I provide the church schoolteachers with a letter which briefly describes Jack's disorder and outlines strategies to guide the teachers' interactions with him. (You will find an example in Appendix I, Letters.)

Some years I was able to attend the full service; the teachers rarely needed me to stay to provide additional support for Jack during Sunday school. In second grade, Jack couldn't participate in Sunday school at all. His behavior was too disruptive and silly. He would hide under a sofa if he didn't get to sit next to a friend that he adored. After a few weeks of such behavior, my husband and I decided that the best strategy would be for him to stay home with Jack and I would give him a Bible lesson when I returned from church. In the meantime, Sarah and I could attend church without worrying that, at any moment, Jack would go over the line from difficult to disruptive.

Jack was able to return to church in third grade. Each Sunday morning, I gauged his temperament and decided if we would go straight to Sunday school, go to the first part of the church service and then Sunday school, or have a Bible lesson at home.

A few weeks ago we decided to go for the entire church morning. When it was time to go to the front of the church for the children's message, Jack went up. This was unusual for Jack. He had not gone to sit on the steps and listen to the minister's lesson for months. But this particular morning he spotted a friend and off he went, racing to the front. As the minister started to deliver his message, Jack lifted his shirt and lowered his head into it, rotating the shirt around his body as he did so. I held my breath and waited to see what he would do.

He was adjusting the shirt so that he could look out an armhole. As he did, the minister asked a question of the children. No one raised his or her hand but Jack. He was called upon and gave a very reasonable response—speaking through the armhole. Eventually, the shirt was put back on correctly.

As we walked out of the service a friend of mine stopped and mentioned how good Jack's answer was.

"Yes," I said, "but what was he doing with the shirt?"

"Oh, that's just Jack," my friend replied.

How comforting my friend's response was. It was not disapproval, but acceptance of who Jack was, along with a compliment. One of the most important things I now know to do for my family and myself is to try to go only to places where we are okay if Jack does something unusual. For this reason, church is a wonderful place. People know us and know Jack. Because of where we are, people are accepting and encouraging. Many a time, the church teachers have found some little uplifting story to tell me about Jack. Although I am sure that there are a lot of stories that are not so positive, the teachers look for the good that is in Jack.

The key for us is FLEXIBILITY. Don't latch onto one idea of what the family should do or should be. Having a vision for your family that is not realistic given the uniqueness of your situation puts unfair demands on everyone, and particularly on the child who is trying his best to hang on.

When deciding what events we should attend with Jack, I go through my mental checklist to decide if the situation is too challenging for him on that particular day. If I decide that the outing should work, I still don't sit back comfortably, assuming that all will go as it should. I think through a contingency plan, just in case. This might mean that I have games to occupy Jack, a book, an escape vehicle, or whatever makes sense.

A few summers ago, Jack was having a fairly good experience at our club's camp program. Although every day wasn't perfect, the teacher's aide who accompanied him was quite good at reading Jack, and could divert a problem by skipping a particular activity to take a short regrouping break or leaving for the day. Jack was comfortable with the layout of the club and the camp staff understood his special needs.

One lazy Sunday we were enjoying a family day by the club pool when my husband, in a moment of optimism and encouragement, suggested that we stay for the family buffet dinner. Jack was on Ritalin at the time. We knew he would rebound shortly after dinner but we thought he could make it through the meal. We decided to give it a go.

We had not been seated for more than a minute when Jack began running around the dining room. He seemed to be propelled by an energy outside of himself. John and I took a quick look at each other, and praised Above for our foresight to have taken two cars. I convinced Jack to leave instantly by promising a much better meal at McDonald's.

While no one likes to think of themselves as having to resort to bribes, these are in my bag of tricks. I use them when absolutely necessary. I will use a bribe without hesitating when we are in a public place and I sense that a situation could be extremely embarrassing for both Jack and the family.

It is important that I preserve the public dignity of Sarah, who as a pre-teen is becoming exceedingly concerned with how she presents herself in public. Just as important is Jack's own dignity. For me, bribes are a response to the age-old utilitarian philosophy of the greatest good for the greatest number.

A few weeks ago, in the midst of nine days of straight rain, I suggested an early evening movie. Sarah's first response was, "Can a friend come?" Although I acquiesced, she couldn't turn anyone up in the midst of summer with only ten minutes advance warning. Sarah would have gone along no problem until Jack, at the last minute, stuffed a Pokemon animal under his shirt. Not a small one.

There we were walking down the main street of town, Jack looking pregnant and Sarah trailing behind saying, "This is SOOOO embarrassing!" I'm not sure which one was more embarrassing. I was sure however, that in the last dog days of summer there was no way that we would meet up with any of Sarah's friends, and finally convinced her to not bail out.

But, wouldn't you know it, we bumped smack into Sarah's friend's sister and her mother, who were also going to the movie. Sarah's angst was escalating. Meanwhile, I kept muttering under my breath, "Don't make a big deal of it and it will go away." Luckily, Sarah held it together. The younger girl was more interested in wooing Sarah to sit in her row and no harm came of it. Just be prepared for anything and try to keep small things—unusual as they may be—small.

We had another incident at the movies. Sarah was at sleep-away camp and Jack and I went to a PG-rated movie. At that time, PG movies were a little above Jack, socially. He recognized this fact and stuck to G-rated movies, but this particular night none were playing. Jack agreed to go see the movie with the condition that if he didn't like it we would leave. The storyline began with a man who was an image consultant poking fun around his career. Well, to a nine year old, what's that all about? Within five minutes Jack leaned over and said, "I know you want to see this movie so may I have some money to get a snack? Can I get popcorn, candy or both?" I told him one or the other and off he went. I was sure he had his Gameboy shoved in his pocket and I would find him sitting on the floor lobby playing it.

After a few minutes, Jack came back, claiming that the $6.00 wasn't quite enough. He was already talking so loudly that I didn't want to prolong the conversation. Plus, I was curious to see what kind of decisions he would make. I handed over $10.00 more and off he went.

Jack soon returned with the largest tub of popcorn you can imagine, a super-duper sized Pepsi, a bottle of water, and a pack of sour patch candies in his pocket. Jack leaned over and said in a voice that the whole theatre could hear, "Here, Mom, just chill on your diet." He knows that I'm always watching what I eat. "The popcorn and candy is to share. The soda is for you." Bless his heart! I will remember that night forever.

PUBLIC EYE

★ *Strategies*

• ALWAYS TRAVEL WITH THINGS TO DO TO FILL IN DOWN TIME OR MOMENTS OF BOREDOM. Jack often has the greatest difficulty with periods of waiting or in-between activities. With an inability to just be, watching life float past, Jack is apt to resort to silly or hyper behavior to fill a space of time. I usually bring a couple of workbooks, a handheld computer game such as Connect Four, and a deck of cards. Old Maid, or the new version, Old Bachelor, Fish or any of the newer games are great choices. If you have other children, be sure to remind them to bring something to keep themselves busy, or pack a few things for these children as well. It is important to try to keep things even since siblings hear life isn't fair often enough.

• PREPARE YOUR CHILD FOR THE ACTIVITY.
This adage is found in many books on special needs children and it's a good one. While I am settling Jack into bed I often talk to him about what is going on the following day—as long as it is something that he will see as a treat and not something that will produce worries. Keep it short and descriptive, avoiding "don't do" and "you'll need to." Describe what you'll be doing, including what the setting will be like.

For example, if you are going to a baseball game you might want to briefly describe the stadium in positive terms such as, "The stadium is in a circle with the ball team in the center. We will be sitting about half way up the rows so we will be looking slightly down on the team". Don't say something like, "It is a great, big stadium and there will be hundreds of people there." This can set off any number of anxieties in the child, such as fear of large spaces or fear of crowds. The next morning, remind your child (as well as the other children) what you will be doing for the day. Then give all of them a goal of three positive behaviors. If we were going to that baseball game I might say, "We have three goals today: 1) To stay safe, meaning staying with Dad or me at all times, 2) To be a good friend to your sister, meaning to share popcorn or sit nicely in your seat next to her, and, 3) To not talk non-stop to strangers seated next to you."

• TAKE WIGGLE BREAKS, AS NEEDED.
At this point, we might brainstorm together how to safely take a break when Jack has had enough with the game or of sitting still. In the case of the ballgame, I might suggest that we find a space where he can run around, or ask the ticket taker for an area that might be free of people where we can take a break. I also might tuck a soft ball or something in my pocket so that we'll have something to do. Give him some options. After all, he's not just a dog that can be run on a leash.

• DON'T ASSUME WHAT COULD BE HANDLED LAST WEEK CAN BE HANDLED THIS WEEK.
Just because your child can sit quietly in church one week doesn't mean he can do it the next. Try to tune into your child's mood and adjust your expectations accordingly.

• CHOOSE YOUR SEAT CAREFULLY.
Wherever you go, think about where you are sitting. Make sure the sound, activity and general feel of your seats will work for your child. For a long time, I thought sitting in the back of the church would be best for Jack (and the other congregants, in case we needed to make a quick escape). However, when I tried (just for the heck of it), sitting right up front, I found that Jack could concentrate better and was more interested in what was taking place. In general, as long as the noise is not too loud for Jack, up front is more engaging.

• BRING A BUDDY.
If possible, bring a babysitter or an older child along with you so that if your child needs a break, there is someone (other than you) who can help him take it.

• ALWAYS, ALWAYS HAVE AN EXIT STRATEGY.
Having a way to get out of a sticky situation can save face for you, your family and your child.

IV. SURVIVING A CRISIS— HITTING BOTTOM AND BACK AGAIN

FALLING APART AT A STOP SIGN

FROM THE HOSPITAL WAITING ROOM

Falling Apart at a Stop Sign
When You Have A Crisis

Jack was returning to the same school for second grade that he had attended the previous year. Being able to greet familiar faces and spaces was a huge relief for a child with anxiety. Maybe he finally belonged somewhere.

The school year began with vaguer goals and a fuzzier picture of what the program would be like, since the school was feeling confident from their success with Jack in first grade. So, although the place was known, everything else was not. This uncertainty wasn't good for a kid like Jack. Jack had recently begun talking to me about why he was in the self-contained classroom instead of the regular mainstream classroom. I explained that he needed a little more learning to follow directions. The goal of making it full-time to the regular class seemed to motivate Jack to try to improve his cooperation abilities.

Jack and I were talking about this goal as we walked up the front path to join the other families on the lawn of the old-fashioned neighborhood school. The school year officially began with the raising of the American flag and the school band playing the national anthem. Maybe this was the land of endless opportunities—and miracles.

For someone with limited social skills, Jack had an amazing ability to read certain aspects of a situation. He could easily spot the adults that were comfortable with him and could help him. He could also gauge which ones were nervous and as a result, would not work with him in a calm, effective manner.

Jack's anxiety skyrocketed almost from day one of second grade. He began by making noises about his teacher in the special education class. He complained about her, focusing on her physical size (claiming that it scared him) and insisting that she was too rough with him when he didn't cooperate with something. We quickly saw the impact of the classroom issues: a marked increase in obsessive and perseverating behaviors, aggression and depression.

The strangest thing about second grade was the variability in Jack's behavior. Each day began with Jack attending the mainstream class, headed by the same teacher that he had had for his mainstream experience the previous year. The second grade class was different from first grade. There were twice as many students in second grade. Jack was in the setting for two hours versus the twenty minutes of first grade. That's a big leap in several directions.

With the assistance of an aide, Jack managed fairly well in the mainstream class. He adored the mainstream teacher, understood that this was an important bridge for him to cross, and liked the other children. Only towards the end of the mainstream experience did Jack become more distracted, impulsive and interruptive. We looked at this behavior and read ADHD. The solution? "More Ritalin," the doctor thought. Maybe the greater academic demands were taxing him and more Ritalin would increase focus and decrease impulsivity.

A pattern began to emerge and escalate: After a visit to the nurse for his second Ritalin dose of the day (at the end of the mainstream class), Jack began to act out in the self-contained classroom. His actions varied. One day he might just refuse to do any work and on another he might try to leave the building. By late September, he had weekly incidents that were unsafe and was physically aggressive towards his own property.

I began to take my pager with me everywhere. I actually developed a physical response when the pager went off, sweating, developing stomach cramps and beginning what would later in the day become a full-blown migraine.

The call was the same each time. The vice principal would say they were having a problem and perhaps I should come assist them. I would arrive at the teacher's lounge, now designated the Jack meltdown room, to find the head teacher sitting cross-legged with Jack on her lap (facing out) held in a restrictive lock that the school said was in compliance with some state law for restricting children who were physically out of control. Jack was frantic, like a caged animal. He had horrible sensory fears. One of his greatest fears, we had learned when he was in kindergarten, was being in a small space and being confined. The scene was overwhelming.

We never figured out what caused this rapid spiraling down in Jack. In hindsight, we concluded that there was a kindling effect that began the first period of the day.

The kindling experience (we suspected) went something like this. The first piece of kindling was the mainstream class, where Jack expended a tremendous effort to keep his behavior in line and accomplish the work. After a brief period in the homeroom class, Jack would go to lunch in a cafeteria of 150 children. Noise, confusion and non-structure meant that Jack, a child sensitive to noise and loud spaces, had to work hard to keep himself together. Twig two on the woodpile. Recess would prove to be equally difficult—no structure or rules, a large area and screaming children. Throw another twig—or maybe a log this time—on to the growing woodpile. Sometime soon after recess the fire would ignite.

What puzzled me was that Jack seemed unable to control himself in these incidents but when I arrived at the scene, he would calm down almost the second that we got into the car, and would be quite manageable the rest of the day. Was this controllable, calculated behavior or was it impulsive and beyond control? Did Jack have anxiety and worries circling around the self-contained class? How were the teachers interacting with him? I had recently seen several bruises on his arms—was something happening that I should know about?

Unfortunately, by the time we had sorted out what might be going on with the kindling concept, an incident took place that would set into motion an experience I hope never to repeat.

In early October, John and I were away for a rare, four day holiday. The children were left in the care of our Saturday babysitter, Margaret, and the housekeeper, Lea. The children had known and worked with Margaret for five years and Lea for one and one half years. We left emergency numbers in the school communication book and emergency names and numbers on the emergency cards at school.

Margaret was clearly on the tippy top of Jack's list of most important people. In fact, he had told me on numerous occasions that Margaret and I were tied for first place. This might bother some moms but I was actually thrilled that a child who had trouble connecting to others was so close to someone other than his mom. When I asked if perhaps I could be just a teeny, tiny bit higher on the list than Margaret, Jack said, "Mom, that's just the way I feel. I can't do anything to change my feelings. They're just there." Fine by me. It allowed me to take this unexpected holiday with little worry.

Jack did a great job the first three days, cooperating at home and, generally, at school. Since Margaret was in graduate school during the day, Lea picked Jack up from school for an appointment with his psychologist on the third day. Apparently, Jack did not want to leave what he was doing at school when Lea came to pick him up for the appointment. According to Lea, the teacher rather strongly encouraged Jack into the car (Jack said later that "pushed" was a better word).

While driving away Jack told Lea that he was going to leave the car and go back to school. I can't say that this was a new idea. Ever since school had started, Jack would threaten to leave the car if something struck him the wrong way. Truth be told, he had already opened the door once when we were driving.

We had battled over Jack's not wearing a seatbelt many times. I had tried everything on this one: car seats, pulling over to the side of the road, lectures about what happens in an accident, even bringing Jack to the police station to discuss with a policeman why seat belts are the law. In the back of my mind, I wondered if the threats would ever turn to reality. I now had my answer.

When Lea stopped at a stop sign a few blocks away from school, Jack did as he had threatened and jumped out of the car. He ran back to school and hid under the teacher's desk in his room. At one point he yelled out to the teacher, "I bet you don't know where I am!"

The teacher was surprised to see Jack back in the room. She quickly got his favorite aide, who began to read to him while they waited for Lea to park and catch up. All stations had been alerted and the principal called the psychologist to let her know what had happened.

The psychologist asked that Jack be taken to his pediatrician to make sure he was okay. It was decided that someone should go with Lea to the doctor to ensure that Jack wouldn't jump out again. Jack said, "Please don't have Mrs. Hart (his teacher) go with me." However, because of insurance issues, the school determined that Mrs. Hart would be the one to go. Anxious and agitated, Jack lost control in the car and tried to jump out again.

Although they were just as close to the doctor's office as to the hospital emergency room, Mrs. Hart told Lea to go to the hospital. The emergency room had been forewarned and Jack was greeted by strangers grabbing him, holding him, restraining him to a bed and injecting him with Risperdal.

Why wasn't I paged? Why weren't any of my friends on the emergency list called? Why wasn't Margaret contacted? At no time during this incident was I paged, despite that fact that I had my pager, had left the hotel number and indicated exactly where I would be at the hotel.

The pediatrician's office finally called me at 3:15 p.m. to tell me briefly, "Jack didn't want to go to the psychologist so he had jumped out of the car but he's fine. They are bringing him here to the office and he is fine."

Based upon that information, I did not worry, and thus was surprised and shocked when I received a message from the vice principal and was told Jack was at the hospital. Luckily, Margaret had been called when the decision to admit Jack to the hospital's psychiatric ward required her signature. Margaret disagreed with the admission plan and was at the hospital within thirty minutes.

Jack was a mess when Margaret arrived. Margaret insisted that she take him home. At home, Jack was calm and safe but extremely upset. He continued to talk about how they (the hospital) hurt him and he slept poorly.

When John and I arrived the next day on the first flight back, we found a little boy who was a ghost of who he was when we left. For the next three days I kept him out of school. He talked to no one, cried intermittently and obsessed about what had happened to him. I hugged him and hugged him and hugged him. No response.

Twenty days later, Jack had not recovered. He had lost all interest in activities and only wanted to watch television or sleep. His expression was less than a blank slate. He returned to school but was aggressive in the self-contained classroom and apathetic in the mainstream class, where he had been so proud to belong just weeks before. Jack had been badly damaged.

Unfortunately, things never righted themselves.

So there we were in second grade with everything crumbling. We patched together a band-aid school day. Jack attended the mainstream class for two hours, since he seemed to be holding it together there, and then I picked him up at 11:00 a.m. All of a sudden, there I was sort of home schooling Jack.

I asked the teacher for worksheets and set up a deal with Jack that went like this: We'd stop at McDonald's for an early lunch and then head to the town's Audubon center. Jack thinks that he will be an animal scientist when he grows up, so what better place for his desk to be than in a bird watching room? I explained to the nature center a bit about what we were dealing with (leaving out the goriest details that might scare them off) and asked if we could work quietly in the bird room for a few hours each day. They were completely supportive and generous with their time and space. I laid out a sheet that said:

2 pages Math= 10 minute nature walk.

We then worked together and at the completion of each subject Jack received his payoff. Jack and I teamed up like this for the remainder of October and through November. I kept a behavior log with me each day. Do you know that Jack didn't have one single meltdown the entire time that we held our woodland school?

This was one of those periods when I kept my blinders on and didn't think too much about the craziness of what we were doing. I took leave from all outside activities, and luckily, had someone to whom I could hand my part-time work assignment. But this was no way to live and it didn't accomplish the social goals that were the top priority in Jack's IEP. It was a moment just to catch our breath and figure out what to do next.

CRISIS

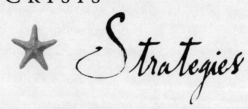

Strategies

- **HAVE A CRISIS PLAN IN PLACE—FOR THE JUST-IN-CASE SCENARIO.**
I have since learned that many communities have general crisis plans developed in the event that a child becomes seriously unsafe or is in an unsafe situation. Know the key players who will implement crisis plans and take a bit of time to familiarize them with your child. A one-page letter that tells your child's diagnosis, medications, key doctors and therapists, emergency numbers and what behaviors they might run into (and how to manage them) might be helpful.

- **KEEP A DIARY OF WHAT IS HAPPENING.**
 I began a diary at the onset of the crisis. So much was swirling around in my head that I couldn't think clearly. I thought it would be helpful to keep notes that the doctors and I could later review to help decipher what was taking place.

- **GET THERAPY FOR YOURSELF AND FOR WHOMEVER ELSE NEEDS IT IN THE FAMILY.**
Getting through a crisis is gut wrenching. Don't say that you don't have time to have someone help you through this period. It's a necessity.

- **GET ENOUGH SLEEP.**
An exhausted mom or dad is good to no one.

- **SIMPLIFY YOUR LIFE.**
Now, more than ever, you need to reduce your load to bare minimum.

- **IF YOU CAN POSSIBLY AFFORD IT, GET EXTRA HELP.**
You will be spending a lot of time at school and with doctors, trying to figure out what to do next. An extra pair of hands will really come in handy.

- **REMAIN COMMITTED AS A COUPLE.**
Now is not the time to start pecking at each other. Close the hatches, bear down and keep your eyes on the real dragon at hand.

From the Hospital
Waiting Room
If Your Child Is Hospitalized

Two months after Jack's hopping out of the car, we still couldn't get him back on track with any kind of regularity. In and out of school, Jack seemed more angry and remote than ever. Dr. Jackson began to think that something was horribly changing in Jack's neurology.

With things getting no better, Dr. Jackson raised for our consideration admitting Jack to the university hospital that he was connected to. He meant in the in-patient pediatric psychiatric unit. He asked that we just think about it—no decisions yet.

Another few weeks passed. It was mid-December and we were at a complete standstill. I was losing hope and Jack was losing time. None of us could tease out what variable might be pushing Jack over the edge. Was it an adverse reaction to the Risperdal that was introduced in the hospital and then continued in order to take the edge off Jack's anger? Was something happening at school? Was Lyme disease, something that Jack had recently tested positive for, somehow exacerbating his symptoms? Or, worst-case scenario, had something dramatically changed in Jack's neurology or biochemical balance? No one could answer these questions.

By this time, John and I couldn't think of another solution to break the cycle. I called Dr. Jackson to seriously discuss the hospitalization choices. We wanted to get Jack in a safe place with a knowledgeable staff where, in essence, we could take a fresh look at him.

Several options were presented to us. We looked at each treatment center's reputation for working with children in our son's age group, its distance from our home, and what we could expect in insurance coverage. We ultimately selected the teaching hospital that had an in-patient children's psychiatric unit and a partial hospitalization program (a school program with therapies and medical supervision). The facility had a very good reputation, it was within reasonable daily driving distance, our psychiatrist was on the teaching staff, and he had previously had good experience with the unit.

With the decision made, I went to the bed and bath store and bought a cheerful comforter and sheets for Jack's hospital room. I didn't want anything from home brought to the hospital as I feared it would later have a negative association for Jack. With cozy flannel comforter and sheets, a few stuffed animals and a duffel bag of clothes, pajamas and toiletries, we were ready to go.

On December 16th, John and I took Jack to the hospital. On the way, I explained, in unemotional and simple terms, that we needed to have Jack looked at twenty-four hours a day in a medical setting to try and determine what medicines were effective and not effective. Jack accepted my explanation with little complaint. Even so, we walked into the facility with hearts that were filled with fear, guilt and choking sadness.

The following italicized excerpts are from the diary that I kept while Jack was in the hospital.

December 16th
Today we took Jack to the hospital on the advice of Dr. Jackson. It just seems that we cannot break the cycle of out-of-control incidents and mounting anger. I have cried for the entire week—this on the heels of visiting the unit and seeing the strict behavior program that they use. It goes like this: the time-out chair to the quiet room (a closet sized padded room) to physical restraining.

When we got there Jack was scared and hardly spoke. It took less than half an hour after we arrived before Jack had his first encounter with the padded room. John and I were being interviewed as Jack was led to his room. Apparently, he laid down in the hall on his suitcase and wouldn't continue. Although given many prompts, he wouldn't move.

Unable to sit on the time-out chair, Jack was put in the quiet room. Since it was his first day, I was called for and allowed to go in to the quiet room. I tried to reassure Jack and was able to get him pulled together. Unfortunately, this incident was followed by a second when John and I were finishing up the intake interview. Jack had bolted from the evening group meeting to go lie down on his bed. Skipping a meeting was not allowed. By the time we arrived after this incident, Jack was again in the isolation room, beside himself.

John nearly pulled Jack out of the program then and there. The doctors instructed us to go to the window of the cell, remain emotionless and say some words of love and encouragement, telling Jack that we would be leaving but would return in the morning. I was shaken. As if a puppet, I lifted a hand and weakly waved from the outside world. I am still haunted by Jack's shivering look and aching voice as he screamed to me from the quiet room, "Mommy, take me out of this place!" There he was, trembling and cold, no clothes on in a room no bigger than a broom closet. I tried to keep a smile on my face and told him not to worry, I would be back tomorrow and to please sit quietly on the bench in the quiet room so that he could get out quickly.

The hospital Fellow assigned to Jack's case lost no time in taking action. He pulled us into a side room and told us that sometimes Ritalin could have a side effect of bizarre and out-of-control behavior. They were going to stop Ritalin—my lifeline—immediately. Questions were swirling in John and my minds as we left— not the least of which was, "How would the doctor know so quickly, within forty-five minutes of Jack's arrival and virtually no time spent with him, that Ritalin was at the root of our problems? How did he know this was not just a child that had claustrophobia or was scared out of his wits?"

It all seemed too fast and decisive for a child who had eluded us for so long.

Months later, out of the blue, Jack told me what was behind this incident.

"Mommy," Jack asked, "Remember when I had that problem at the hospital for not putting my suitcase away?" I was packing a suitcase in readiness to pick Sarah up at summer camp six months to the day after his hospitalization. I told him of course I remembered and asked him what that was all about.

"I told them," he said quite earnestly, "that I needed my mom to help me put my clothes away."

Jack then said, "I could never go anywhere and not have you help me set myself up. Not Daddy or anybody can do that. I need you. And the hospital wouldn't listen to me."

Aaaahhh. The anxiety of a new place. Why didn't the hospital staff read this as scared, anxious, and frightened?

December 17th
Today, a family meeting with the social worker was held and went well until he asked a question that Sarah wanted to answer and he told her "No, let your brother answer." Since seventy-five percent of the meeting had focused on Jack, Sarah did not like this answer. She ignored the rest of the meeting.

Between that vignette and the dynamic of Jack calling John by his first name, the social worker recommended some family counseling to help us work as a unit, rather than the divide and conquer (one parent-one child) line-up that we were operating under.

The family assessment over, the next day brought an analysis of John and me as a couple. After three hours of intensive discussion, the social worker was satisfied and pleased with what he heard was happening at home. Because we are blessed with a very strong social support group, financial health, and a good marriage (having endured some very rocky roads), he saw this piece as less of an issue for Jack than perhaps the medicines and the school situation. I wish I knew what they were finding in the hour-long simulated school observation. I wrote myself a note to remember to ask on Monday.

December 18th, Morning Visit

Whenever I go to a place for the first time, I try to fix my impressions of it in my mind very clearly. Experience has taught me that having this memory box of what something first feels like gives me perspective later, when things become too familiar and I'm unable to separate feelings from place. It is often these initial encounters that later give me guidance and a road map to navigate sticky situations.

"What do you think they call this color blue?" was my initial thought as I walked into the hospital for the first time. Well, I didn't exactly waltz right in.

As you might expect (though I didn't, as it was my first experience in a psychiatric facility), the Child Center is a locked facility. Either a lack of available space dictated the center's location down an alley to an old brick building that looked like it could have been a cloister, or someone had the sensitivity in the early planning stages to seek out a location that would be rather private. At least you didn't have a host of strangers' eyes watching you walk into a building that announced your child had psychiatric problems.

I walked nervously through the front door (once it was buzzed open to let me in) and saw that awful color blue. Not a sky blue or robin's egg blue, but an intense, non-relenting Gatorade blue. I've gotten to know this blue quite well since it is carried through the waiting area and staff offices. In the first weeks I used to think that the tension I felt in those few minutes waiting for visiting hours to begin was the uncertainty of what I would find when I opened the door to the ward. But even now, with history as my guide as to the low probability that I'll find Jack in a time-out or quiet room, I can't seem to relax as I flip through the same issue of Working Women *magazine that has obviously been in the magazine rack for some time. I think the cause of my tension is that color blue. I wonder why no one thought about color theory and mood effect when selecting the color scheme for a psychiatric facility.*

December 18th, Evening Visit

After watching the children and parents at visiting hour, I began to think differently about misbehavior. Any incident or misbehavior is an opportunity for teaching a child the right way. If we look at it like this, as an opening for education and growth, it takes the drama out of the moment and the emotion out of the event.

December 19th
Jack and I had fun playing a card game. Some of the other children wandered over. I can see that they are starting to get used to me and me to them. My prejudices about mental illness are beginning to slide away. I see the beauty in each of these children and my heart is beginning to really ache when one of them can't follow a direction and disintegrates into a behavior that lands him or her in the quiet room. Jack still seems dopey and lethargic and more than a little bit sad. He is beginning to ask when he can come home and saddens when I have to leave. This is painful.

December 21st
I wonder if doctors truly don't know what it feels like to be on the other side of the desk or if they just close off a piece of themselves for their own protection. The breezy way they convey major news never ceases to amaze me. It was like that the first time the doctor said "bipolar" to me. I was actually leaving the hospital for the day and Dr. Johnson, the hospital Fellow, stopped me to ask if we could chat for a few minutes. That is when he first told me that following a week of observation the team was beginning to see Jack not as Asperger's Syndrome but as being bipolar. I'd never heard of that term. Two bears? What could that possibly mean to me?

At the time, my mind was half on the dinner I would hastily prepare for Sarah when I got home. I was unprepared for an intense discussion and a proposed change in diagnosis. I wasn't ready to discuss what the diagnosis would mean for Jack and for the family until a day or two later, when the doctor asked if John and I could meet with the team. By that time, I had already gone on the internet and procured a number of basic articles and a couple of books on the topic. Some brief and painful details of how the medical staff had arrived at the diagnosis—the replay of the most troubling moments of Jack's stay at the hospital—had been given to me during the on-the-fly meeting by Dr. Johnson. The formal meeting, when we were emotionally steeled, was really a review of the hallway conversation.

December 22nd

It's fascinating to see what things make people feel that they are having a good Christmas. So many of our friends, family and acquaintances have said time and again during this particular holiday season, "It must be just awful having to spend Christmas like this." While there certainly is no getting around the fact that not having your little one home, especially the one who still believes in Santa Claus, is painful, there is also a poignancy to this Christmas that we have not experienced before.

Luckily, part of the expression of Jack's disorder is that he does not attach to people and places like others might. The traditions and rhythms of each holiday that many children (and adults) crave and use as defining anchors of the season pass unnoticed by Jack. He has rarely mentioned missing home although I know it hurts every time the end of my hospital visit draws near. Spending so many hours among children who are at the hospital because of environmental issues has put me in touch with a part of myself that has been dormant for too long. It reminds me of my days in high school when I used to go with other teens from our church to play with the inner city children. The faces are different and yet they are the same as the kids from the Saturday morning program.

All of these children are much more connected to the world than Jack. When I walk into the visiting room, Jack is certainly not the first to greet me. Four or five others will look up from their games or arts and crafts and greet me with an affectionate "hello!" or bound up from their chairs to grab a quick hug from me. It's these kids, the ones who have no visitors and are desperately trying to overcome the unfair situations that have been thrust upon them, who are bringing the meaning of Christmas to me this year.

Gone are the meaningless conversations of everyday life. Here, we slip into the timeless time of the board games that mask the real work of each of these children. And they do indeed call it work on the ward. What comes naturally to typical children—learning how to both make a friend and be a friend—is what absorbs these kids' time and energy. While typical children are busy balancing Christmas activities among their regular schedule, Christmas, for the children now at the hospital, is just a slightly brighter bulb on a string of lights.

FROM THE HOSPITAL
WAITING ROOM

At the ward it takes little effort to spread the message of Christmas. The kids are needy and their love freely given. I'm getting the message of the Christmas story in a real and moving way. As time passes at the hospital, I get to know each child. I have seen them laugh, joke, and get so angry that they no longer even look like themselves to me. Each of them is a precious gift.

Without the trappings of presents, decorating and endless holiday activities, I have decided to lead the family in reducing Christmas to its simplest components so that we can do the work that is often overlooked—uncovering the reason for the season. At home, we have left our treasured collection of ornaments in their cushioned boxes in favor of Sarah's homemade designs. The only other hint that Christmastime is here is in the dining room, where we have a nativity scene and advent calendar. Early shopping and wrapping and a pared down gift list has freed me from the holiday nights past where I'd wrap gifts and prepare gift tags until my eyes were bleary and hands well worn.

With so little focus at home on the stuff of Christmas, my friend, Virginia, and I have been able to orchestrate a visit by Sarah and her friends to the local nursing home. I'm not sure what the residents enjoyed more, three third grade girls belting out Silent Night on the recorder or the jolly ten inch Santa whose hips sway back and forth in time with a rocking holiday tune, courtesy of my upbeat friend and mother of the twins.

December 24th
Before I go to bed to wait for the birth of our Lord, I make a quick call to the hospital to see if Jack was affected by not being home for Christmas Eve. I am relieved to hear that he went to bed easily, but not before leaving a note outside his door that contained one single sentence: "Dear Santa, Please get me out of this place."

Christmas Day
We have managed to get a pass for Jack to return home for the day. Luckily, this is the first year that Sarah doesn't believe in Santa Claus. Although it is almost excruciatingly painful for her, Sarah manages to wait to open her gifts until Jack gets home at 10:30 a.m. (driven by John) so that together they can share the joy of Christmas morning. My mother (who has driven down this morning), Sarah and

I eagerly fling open the door when we hear the familiar crunching of the car as it makes its way up the long gravel driveway. Full of hope and anticipation, John opens Jack's door. Jack doesn't bolt for the three pairs of open arms hanging over the balcony of the stairs that lead to our back door. Instead, he re-enters one of the scenes that he probably misses the most—our backyard and the forest and stream that lie just beyond.

Busy crunching snow, gathering sticks and doing the same old messing around that usually keeps him entertained for hours, Jack only comes in after persistent calls to him and promises that Santa has indeed left many good gifts. Like a person entering an unfamiliar and unknown place for the first time, Jack is disoriented as he re-enters the real world. Santa has, as promised, left him a nice pile of presents, most of which are going to require the kind of assembly that Jack loves to do. A remote control construction set is supposed to be the big gift that Santa has selected for Jack. This system has all sorts of platforms, conveyors, trucks and things that move. Despite what Santa thinks, the mini-construction company does not capture Jack's fancy. In fact, nothing seems to.

Each gift is carefully opened but just as all the pieces are taken out and ready for assembly or play, wham! Some internal timer seems to go off and remind Jack that it is just the right time to move to the next gift. In his wake he leaves an extraordinary amount of paper, plastic pieces, and the rest of us, wondering how we will get through this day.

John, my mother and I had made a pact that we would keep the day very simple. With a sweeping decision I had brushed away my family's seven course tradition and opted for a simple meal, which my mother single-handedly prepared and brought for us. The three of us also agreed that we must be true to the methods of behavior management that the hospital had been using with good success. If Jack could not follow transitions he would have to receive a time-out after the appropriate prompts were given. This would be quite a challenge because Jack had never taken a time-out at home. But at this point of time at the hospital, Jack was following directions by the third prompt about sixty percent of the time—so we knew he could do it.

We were pleasantly surprised, although it was clear that he didn't think much of the new mom. "Why are you trying to be like staff? When will the old mom be back?" was heard repeatedly. Jack came to dinner as requested and followed directions during the day. But having Jack at the Christmas dinner table was like not having him at the table. Quiet and pensive, Jack ate his favorite Grammy's manicotti but not as much or with as great a zeal as you would expect from someone who has seen the typical fare of any hospital dining service across the nation.

I had managed to get wonderful seats to the Radio City Christmas spectacular in New York City. John and I decided that Sarah, my mother and I would enjoy the show and that John would hang out with Jack for the three remaining hours of his pass. Perhaps they would invite one of Jack's few friends and his dad, a good friend of ours, over. Since one of the by-products of Jack's decline this fall had been a rejection of John we thought that this time might begin to repair the relationship. Although there were no incidents to speak of, I returned home after a day of dancing Santas, ice skaters and the nativity re-creation to find a dejected father. Jack had interacted minimally with his friend and was operating in his own world even more than usual. So much for the first pass. Not a success, not a disaster, and not our Jack.

January 7th

There is a bench out in the waiting area. I call it the unloading bench. Since I log a lot of time on the bench between visits, other parents pass by me and some of them choose to unload their troubles on me. My observation and exchange with one mother still leaves me feeling chilled. It also points out to me how easily typical children, those blessed with no congenital psychological disability, can lose their psychological health. It reminds me to be conscious of what messages my interactions, tone of voice, and attitude with my own children may be conveying.

I had been sitting back to back with one mom, Mrs. Moss, and her daughter, Jennifer. Jack and I were playing Monopoly with another child; Jennifer and her mom where playing Sorry! Jennifer is a spunky six years old. She is one of those children that you look at and say to yourself, "Now, why would she be here?" I couldn't help overhearing them, or rather the mother, as they played the game. "You little cheater!" I heard her admonish Jennifer. And, as if that wasn't enough *she added, "I knew I shouldn't have bothered to come visit you." She continued to berate Jennifer and question her truthfulness as the game progressed.*

Shortly thereafter, the afternoon visiting hour ended, and I was waiting on the bench for an hour to pass and the next visiting hour to begin. Mrs. Moss came out, frenetic and frenzied. She stopped up short and asked me, "Do you know why my daughter is here? She tried to hang herself." Mrs. Moss had an attitude of "Can you believe that?" rather than of fright. "I knew I should have just kept my mouth shut and not said anything. Since she's been here, she wants nothing to do with her mother."

Well, it doesn't take a mental health professional to figure out why Jennifer might be reacting against her mother.

Now, I've watched Jennifer in other game situations and to be honest, she is a consistent cheater. But is belittling and yelling at the child the way to teach her honesty? Dr. Sawyer, Jack's psychologist, has a very effective strategy for dealing with situations like this. She says to the child in an unemotional, yet caring way, "I don't mind if you miscount your number of spaces with me, but if you play with other children they might not like this dishonesty and might quit the game." She rehearses and practices game situations, helping the child learn how to deal with the frustration of losing.

My philosophy is that any incident or misbehavior is an opportunity for teaching a child the right way. If we look at it like this, as an opening for education and growth, it takes the drama out of the moment and the emotion out of the event. What is that old story about Thomas Edison? Someone once asked Mr. Edison how he felt about the 2,000-plus experiments that he conducted which failed. Mr. Edison replied, "If I didn't have all of those failures I would have never invented the light bulb." How can you really enjoy success if you've never experienced failure?

January 21st
Are there guardian angels everywhere? Today's was Margaret. Margaret, our babysitter, came to visit Jack this afternoon. When she saw Jack, she noticed that his head and neck were trembling. Though we were upset that the staff hadn't noticed the trembling and it took one of us to get there and see it, they responded quickly.

Before tonight was over, the on-call doctor saw Jack and adjusted medicines several times. Apparently, one of the drugs they were trying on Jack has a joint stiffening side effect. An anti-stiffening medicine was given to Jack and his limb, finger, head and neck movement returned to normal.

January 22nd
Although the hospital's behavior management system has very effectively helped Jack eliminate the aggression and isolation that had been boiling to the point of eruption in October and November, new behaviors are emerging. In the place of uncontrollable reactions and no interactions we see silliness, inappropriate physical affection and hypersexuality. While some level of silliness is part of being a child, Jack is over the edge to the point of invading boundaries, unaware of others responses or feelings.

The hospital doctors took Jack off Ritalin after they witnessed his bizarre and severely wild behaviors in the quiet room the first day he was admitted to the program, but they would not consider removing the antipsychotic medication, Risperdal.[3] Jack was first given Risperdal in the emergency room that he was brought to during that infamous leaving the car episode. We wanted to get a baseline read of Jack's personality and behavior with no medication, but the doctors wouldn't listen to our request. They felt Jack needed the Risperdal since he continued to display disorganized thinking and said things that sometimes seemed to have no relation to what was happening at hand.

We were not sure why the medical staff cared if Jack became more manic (in their terms). After all, weren't they set up to observe, monitor and respond to behaviors in a controlled and safe environment? How can you get a clean starting point without removing all the drugs? Maybe the Risperdal was part of the problem. Jack continued to be treated by one antipsychotic or another for the first fifteen weeks of his stay at the facility.

During this time, I networked with parents who were well versed in special needs and connected with other parents. They introduced me to parents of bipolar children, since that was supposed to be what Jack had. I asked the

3. I don't mean to imply that Risperdal is not an effective medication. In our case, it might not have been the right choice. The medication is used only in this illustration to make a larger point

doctors at the hospital (as well as other parents) to provide me with bipolar-oriented sites on the internet that they had found to be useful. Although my knowledge of the internet was basic, I was able to find a parents' support group for bipolar children. This site was an incredible source of information and sharing. It was through this source, and confirmed by the doctors at the hospital, that I found two of the leading doctors in the United States for treating bipolar children.

What is overstepping your bounds as a parent and what is being proactive? With Jack making no progress at the hospital, I decided to share some key articles with the medical staff. John and I thought, "If we were told that Jack had cancer we would take him to Sloan Kettering. While the Child Center was a solid first step, why were we stopping here when there were doctors who dealt with bipolar children as their sub-specialty?" It was common sense. We began to press upon the hospital to seek out the doctors who specialized in pediatric bipolar disorder and suggested that we bring Jack to one of these doctors for a second opinion.

There is a risk in this strategy and one that we encountered almost immediately. The risk is that you alienate the team that you currently depend upon. Well, as John said, "If you want a friend, get a dog." My job was to make sure that the right path was being followed for Jack and that every stone was turned, until things began to fall into place. Beginning a search for the next layer of doctors made sense. If Jack was supposed to have bipolar disorder, it seemed that we should start by finding those doctors who are top in the field of bipolar disorder for pre-pubescent children.

Knowing that I probably wouldn't be ingratiating myself with the hospital staff, I nonetheless took it as my duty to begin sharing articles and information that I thought might be enlightening to Jack's case. Finally, John and I again brought up the idea of a second opinion, or consult, with doctors specializing in bipolar in children. I don't think that we would have pushed so hard to seek outside counsel if Jack had been responding to medications and progressing nicely on a treatment program.

Unfortunately, he was not progressing. In fact, Jack had never been so disorganized in his thinking, strange in his comments, and hazy overall. Except for the fact that he no longer seemed angry or aggressive, he was a bigger mess than ever.

The problem with bringing a child to an inpatient psychiatric center during a crisis is that the staff does not see your child as he truly is. They see a different person and use that impression as a jumping off point to begin sorting through diagnoses. What did this mean in practical terms for Jack? The hospital's first impression had been of an angry, out-of-control boy who could not follow directions. Jack had landed in the quiet room twice before we left that first evening. Only our desire to maintain some degree of privacy for Jack prevents me from relaying what went on in the quiet room. Let's just say that the doctors had seen enough to label his behavior "bizarre and primitive." How could we dig out from such a start?

John and I seemed to be alone in circling some fundamental questions:

1. Was the bizarre/primitive behavior that Jack displayed in his first days at the hospital a response to Ritalin, as the doctors suggested? If so, why had the child been so positively responsive to Ritalin up until the very day that he started second grade?

2. Was the bizarre and primitive behavior a response to being frightened of the center? Of being brought to a hospital where children were losing control left and right, where your parents were taken away within the first ten minutes of the visit, where you didn't know how long you would be in this unknown place, where you landed in a room no bigger than a closet that reminded you of a horrible experience in kindergarten? To be honest, I'm not so sure how I would behave under the circumstances. Maybe I, too, would tantrum and go over an emotional edge that I'd never gotten near before. This explanation never seemed to be one that the doctors would consider for even a minute.

3. Was the bizarre and primitive behavior exhibited at the hospital a reaction to one of the drugs that Jack had recently been put on? After

the car incident, Jack had been placed on an antipsychotic, Risperdal. When this seemed not to keep his aggression in place, our psychiatrist had added Zoloft. In total, Jack had come to the hospital with no less than six heavy-duty drugs bouncing around in his system over the past three months: Ritalin, Buspar (briefly introduced in September, then discontinued), Risperdal, Zoloft (discontinued the week before he entered the hospital), Desyrl, and Amoxicillin (used to treat his second round of Lyme disease). Why wasn't anyone looking at all these drugs and their potential interactions as a possible cause for Jack's digressed behavior?

These questions rose in our minds as we lay in bed night after night, me worn from the long trips to the hospital and John exhausted from juggling his always demanding job along with the added responsibility of picking up more care for Sarah, so that I could stay at the hospital longer. The more we circled these questions, the more we knew that we would never rest until someone answered them to our satisfaction.

We set up the appointment with one of the top psychiatrist's treating children with bipolar disorder. The first date available to see her was in three months.

January 24th
This is Sarah and what I have noticed is that Jack has a space problem with other people—they cannot go too close to him. My dad has seen that whenever he gets too close to Jack he pushes him out of the way or hits Daddy. I think that Jack needs to have a medicine like Ritalin but only softer.

I think this is a great experience for my brother and me but it is painful not seeing him every day. I think it is a great experience because my brother gets to see what other kids do and he gets to communicate with them and I think I'm having a great experience because I can see what it is like to be an only child.

January 28th (Anne's diary again)
When I was at Georgetown University as an undergraduate, I taught dance at an inner city elementary school in Anacostia. The children there might not have had

clothes that fit, a home with the essentials consistently provided to them, but they sure came suited up to dance every Thursday afternoon. We had no proper ballet equipment—no ballet barre or dance shoes. I never told them those things were needed. And so they learned to pirouette on their own, without the benefit of shoes that would help them grip the floor or a barre to break down these difficult dance moves.

Jack is just the opposite of these children. He is fortunate enough to have whatever therapists he needs and strong home supports, yet he has no internal balance and cannot maneuver through the dance steps of life. For him, spinning a phrase or just passing a conversation back and forth with someone would be a major accomplishment.

February 1st
The children at the center have well-articulated goals that they review with their assigned staff member throughout the day. Jack is working on following directions and not touching others (he's become a hugging fanatic). Children who are at the behavior management plan's lowest level, Try Harder, must show no aggression for twenty-four hours before they can move up the ladder. Once the children have reached their goals and have demonstrated them to the staff for twenty-four hours they can move to the next behavior level, Beginner. The Beginner level has added privileges, such as the opportunity to get a pass (i.e., leave the facility with an approved person for a period of time) and have a later bedtime.

Jack has finally made it on to the highest level, the Leader level. With this comes a host of special privileges, such as a later bedtime, having a tape recorder during personal time and posters on his wall.

For many years Jack had a horrible time trying to sleep at night. He slept only three to four hours per night in his baby years, despite my having read sleep books by specialists and having tried everything from regular schedules to holding the doorknob of his bedroom (only for a few minutes but I'm still embarrassed to admit it). We tried books and movies to relax him, along with many other techniques. For more than a year, book tapes seemed particularly helpful, as did workbooks.

Even if Jack didn't go to sleep with these, we at least had an hour break in what could otherwise be a very long evening. Not surprisingly, we gathered a library of *over fifty tapes. Out of this extensive group, a handful made the cut to go to the hospital for Jack to enjoy during personal time. Jack's new Leader level also opened up some new ways for us to spend time together. Seven weeks of playing board games had really pushed Jack and me to the height of boredom. Passes are more freely given at this level.*

February 2nd
Today was a similar "hit you in the stomach" experience as the one when Dr. Johnson told me so nonchalantly that he believed Jack had bipolar disorder. This time I received a call at home during dinner hour. Sarah playfully answered "Pizza Hut" and then handed the telephone to me.

The point of the call was simple enough. Dr. Johnson wanted me to know that the evaluation needed by the board of education to approve an out-of-district placement was complete.[4] In the course of the conversation, Dr. Johnson told me that the letter indicated Jack was one of the sickest children that the center had seen in some time. Somewhere inside of me was stubborn hope—hope that just wouldn't die. I guess it was from that spot that I said to the doctor, "But you don't really believe that do you?" Dr. Johnson assured me that he did mean this although he added that it didn't mean that Jack had the worst prognosis. While some children may have anger control problems and other issues which they act out, Jack seems to get the award for the most confused thinking process.

How do you resolve such news in your own head? Each time a new diagnosis is given or we complete a new experience, I redefine who I am in relation to my children.

First, it was coming to grips with being the parents of an ADHD child. This was long before ADHD became almost cool. Just five years ago, parents of children with ADHD were still being asked, "Do you think a change in his diet could help?" or, "Maybe he needs more discipline." Then it was thinking of myself as the parent of a child with Asperger's Syndrome who might be brilliant but would have narrowed interests and quite impaired social relationships.

Jack is very young to have already gone through so many diagnoses. Thinking

4. When the school district does not have an appropriate placement for your child they are obliged to find him a suitable program either privately or through an arrangment with another school district.

positively, I guess this means I get to learn about many different things that can go wrong with the brain and then get to play armchair doctor and make my own determination whether Jack has the diagnosis that the medical team made.

February 3rd
Taking Jack to Wooster Street for dinner on pass night is bittersweet for me. As a child, my family used to go to Wooster Street quite often for the meanest pizza in the city. Now, I am coming with a child who is out for an hour on a special pass from a psychiatric facility. It sure is good that you never know what the future holds—I probably would have spent a lot of my previous years dreading this revisit back to the stomping ground of my youth.

The first time that I took Jack to Wooster Street we went to Tony and Lucille's, an Italian restaurant. Tony and Lucille's has been around for years and years and my family, particularly my mother, is well known to the owners.

Coming here is like coming to your aunt's house. In one of our first visits, the waitresses and cooks (all brothers and sisters working for their parents) discovered who I was and that Jack was an in-patient at the hospital. They took him under their wing as if he were a long-lost cousin. Tonight, we were officially made part of the family as they suggested that we eat in the back room where the family relaxes and their children play. This, along with the fabulous mussels and calamari, is the reason Jack always chooses Tony and Lucille's for dinner during a pass night. Where else can you play with four children all your age and get terrific Italian fare?

I was impressed with Jack's abilities today. He negotiated questions, hugs and cheek pinching from six adults and shouts of "come join us" from three cousins. He remained pretty much on topic and appropriate with the kids. Only once we were back in the car and headed to the hospital did Jack revert to his baby talk and silliness. Now, was this loose thinking and behavior a result of the over-stimulating dinner environment? A change in biochemistry? Or, some learned behavior that he employs when he's with Mom?

February 10th
Dr. Burton is out of town for a few days and Dr. Drake is the covering doctor.

Dr. Drake is another Fellow, here at the hospital for one year before he begins his next psychiatric rotation. Dr. Drake has only met with me briefly during the past weeks; he answered a question or two when Dr. Burton has been off duty.

Today, Dr. Drake asked if I'd join him in his office for a few minutes. He reviewed a test that had come in. I asked Dr. Drake the same question that has been nagging me since we received the bipolar diagnosis in the second week of Jack's stay. "Why do you think Jack has bipolar disorder?" I keep asking the question because no one has given me a good answer. They point to behaviors that could easily be reactions to a scary environment or responses to incorrect drugs.

Dr. Drake looked at me and said the following, "Look at yourself. Did you ever think that you might be bipolar? I saw a letter that you wrote to Dr. Burton about Jack that you faxed to us at 4 a.m. You are very thin; in fact, you probably have an eating disorder. Did you ever think about going to a psychiatrist and getting yourself evaluated? I think you need to do that."

I was so stunned that I didn't ask a single question. I staggered out of the building, fuming that here I was, a mother who happened to be lucky enough to have a background that could help the doctors by providing organized information and data to help them with their diagnosis of Jack and instead, they slammed me into the Blame the Mother role.

February 11th
I called Dr. Hornsby, Jack's psychiatrist, today. I just can't move on until I tell someone about Dr. Drake's conversation with me. Why was the letter faxed to Dr. Burton at 4 a.m.? Well, I dare anyone to try to get a good night's sleep when his or her child is in a psychiatric ward. It is just not possible. John and I are up and down all night long, thinking and worrying. I am a fixer person. And, the hospital's diagnosis just doesn't feel right to John and me. We want to help the medical staff with any information that we can give so that they can get a balanced picture of Jack.

I told Dr. Hornsby, who didn't place any blame on me but asked if I would, in fact, just go talk to a psychiatrist or psychologist to satisfy the hospital. We agreed that

FROM THE HOSPITAL
WAITING ROOM

instead of this, Dr. Hornsby can call Sally, the psychotherapist that John and I have been seeing for the past five years. If they both decide that I need an evaluation I'll go. How did this get turned around on me?

February 14
Happy Valentines Day! After speaking to Sally, Dr. Hornsby is comfortable that an evaluation is not necessary. (How can all these hospital doctors make these accusations when they've never spent even one solid hour with me? Thank goodness that Sally, who has spent many hours with me, was in the picture.)

Time to deal with Dr. Drake. He actually approached me today, saying that he had heard through the grapevine that I wasn't very happy with him. I welcomed the opportunity to tell him that it was completely inappropriate to attack someone as he did when he'd never spent more than six minutes with me. I tried to explain how a psychiatric hospital might bring out tremendous stress in parents (you think they'd learn that in medical school). I suggested that he not take the Attack-The-Parent approach again.

The Bottom Line on the Hospital Experience

These diary excerpts may seem a little wishy-washy in terms of how I ultimately felt about the center. This is probably because I wanted to believe that this highly respected institution knew what it was doing. But, I'm not sure that's the case.

John, and my gut, said that the young Fellows had made diagnosis decisions too quickly and without listening to our thoughts or data or looking at recent history. The Fellows seemed to stay in a little box. They looked at an isolated behavior in an unnatural environment and then made a conclusion—without trying to understand anything behind the behavior.

All that said, the Child Center did have one great benefit, and that was the behavior management program followed by the nursing staff. The nurses and aides were the ones who tried to understand Jack and figure out why he might be behaving as he was. A nurse actually cornered me one night and said, "If you have doubts about the bipolar diagnosis, follow your gut. I think that you are on the right track. I think you are right—he's not having bipolar mood episodes."

If you can find someone within the staff who seems to understand and connect with your child, try to stay close to them and have them involved in the case as much as possible.

From An In-Patient to a Day Student at the Hospital's School

In mid February, nine weeks after Jack's admittance to the hospital, he was still not himself, but had figured out enough of the system to pretty much stay on the behavior management program's Leader level. In-patient hospital insurance was running out and John and I weren't convinced that the hospital team was headed in the right direction with the bipolar diagnosis. We didn't see that any gains were being made that would justify a further stay at the hospital.

However, the hospital team was still convinced that here was an incredibly ill child, and suggested that Jack attend their partial hospital program (PHP). PHP is a classroom of individualized instruction every weekday morning followed by afternoon therapies. Jack would make the hour-and-ten-minute trip—each way—in a school bus, courtesy of our town.

The partial hospital program had a very nice behavior management program. It used a goal sheet for the program that provided the same procedure for home on the reverse side. In this way, when Jack returned home from school, we could see what goals he was working on and how he was performing against these goals. I could then choose to either dovetail those goals or create ones that were more important for our home situation.

Jack started out the program having solid success each day, but as time wore on, we began to see the silliness increase and he began to have more and more trouble focusing—a dilemma when you must spend six hours in a single classroom. Week after week passed and Jack went back and forth to PHP. At the beginning of the program, Jack's three daily goals included things like displaying appropriate behavior (do not make animal noises), using chairs correctly, and looking at staff when they are talking to him. He could earn three levels of rewards in the PHP program, depending upon how many points he accumulated against his three goals.

Every student was evaluated twice each day, at noon and at 3:00 p.m. Two points meant you were doing Super, one point meant you were doing Good, and zero was equivalent to Keep On Trying. The first few weeks Jack landed on the bottom reward rung. Six weeks later, Jack's goals were "Be a good friend," "Follow directions," and "Limit silly behavior." More often than not, I was greeted at the door by a still somewhat silly, but very proud, little boy who had earned top reward for the day. Slowly, behavioral improvements were falling into place.

Each day when Jack arrived home, we agreed on his three goals for home. He got clever and tried to suggest shoe-ins like "Be nice to Mom" or "Play fairly with Mom." When I suggested that "Be nice to Mom" should include following directions and limiting silliness he insisted that you can't merge goals—and either refused to or couldn't understand how things like following directions and not being too silly were part of being a good friend to Mom. The home program was costly. Either I ran around all day finding tchockies to put into a top reward bag or Jack got three dollars a day for top reward. One week, in a weak moment, I agreed to purchase animals as top reward and we got two fish and an albino frog. Thank God I held my ground and nixed the nurse shark—even if it didn't bite.

We had targeted mid-March as the time to leave the hospital completely. Jack was at a standstill in terms of progress. Insurance for the partial hospital program was running out. We had found a school placement for him. The medications that Jack had tried at the hospital had not brought him back to the way he had been prior to second grade. He was on a better path than the fall, but it was a fragile one.

I realized just *how* fragile the path was when Jack developed a rash all over his body the week before we left PHP. Fearing that this was a drug reaction,

Dr. Hornsby took Jack off the last two drugs of his medication plan, Lithium and Thorazine.

Miracle of miracles. Jack began to look and act like himself again. Still a little silly and inappropriate, he was no longer foggy or lackluster. We began to see the old Jack returning. Ironically, after eighteen weeks of trying different medications, we left the hospital with no medication except for Benadryl (to try to bring his hyperactivity level down a bit) and with no clear diagnosis. We had learned that a highly structured behavior management program could change behavior. But we didn't seem to learn anything else.

The minute we got home, I took Jack to our pediatrician, who examined him and found that he wasn't having a drug reaction at all. He had scarlet fever. There is an illness called PANDAS (Pediatric Autoimmune Neuropsychiatric Disorders Associated with Streptococcal Infections), which is a strep-related infection that appears to affect behavior, often triggering obsessive-compulsive behaviors, among others. The doctor wondered if this could be what Jack was going through. Since he was already on medication we couldn't do the appropriate blood tests to tell, but it gave us something to think about.

When I now step back from this situation for a minute, I am amazed at what this small boy had been through and handled with aplomb. He had been at a psychiatric hospital for eighteen weeks and had seen all that one would expect in such a place. He traveled sometimes close to three hours a day to attend a school that keeps you on a behavioral tightrope, and he had willingly visited therapists and doctors after school three to four times a week.

On the last day, I picked Jack up and celebrated his hospital discharge with his favorite dinner of steamers at Tony and Lucille's, followed by a new movie which had just been released that night. For a seven year old, what better way to celebrate? Throw in a package of Skittles and it's truly a night in heaven.

The Hospital's Behavior Management Program Basics

The hospital showed a masterful display of behavior management. The consistency in philosophy exhibited in the staff's approach, language and style is remarkable. When Jack was discharged, I decided it was time to fine-tune my own management style with the children.

Sarah, one of the nurses at the hospital, was a pro at behavior management and gave me a crash course on the nuances that go into this methodology one evening during visiting hours. Here is how it goes as I understand it—courtesy of Sarah:

First of all, time-outs (the first line of defense when a request is not complied with) are not used as a punishment. Time-outs are used to break the behavior chain that a child is stuck in. Time-outs (or whatever consequence you use) should not be an "instead of," as in, "instead of a yell or a threat." They are used to give the child the space and time to regroup and reorient himself. You need to remain unemotional and calm while going through these steps. If you become emotionally upset or involved, no learning or behavior modifying will occur. All that will happen is more problem-creating that you will need to undo later. Below is the step-by-step behavior management system that the hospital so effectively uses when a child is exhibiting a behavior that needs to be changed:

> 1. Tell the child what behavior needs to be changed, such as, "Jack, stop bouncing the ball against the wall." You can add a very short explanation as to why bouncing the ball on the wall isn't good but don't get too wordy—children are already masters of the tune-out art. If the action continues, move to Step 2.
>
> 2. Let the child know that this is the last time you will be making a verbal request without his compliance, "Jack, *this is a prompt.* Stop bouncing the ball against the wall." Using the same language each time: *"This is a prompt,"* will set the system up. Using the word "prompt" instead of "warning" seems a little less threatening and less

controlling. The child will become accustomed to hearing the phrase, "this is a prompt" as a precursor to the next level, Step 3.

3. Time to break the cycle of behavior. "Jack, you need to take a time-out." As in all good time-out systems, have a designated chair that is in a quiet, non-stimulating environment for time-outs (obviously, in front of the television or a window is not a good idea). Ideally, the child will move quietly and compliantly to the chair. If this is the case, set the timer for an appropriate amount of time (maybe five minutes for a minor situation, ten or fifteen minutes for incidents where the child argued, lost control or defied the time-out for a brief period of time). If the child just can't settle into the time-out, you'll have to move to Step 4.

4. It is now necessary for the child to have a greater area of physical space where he can lose control in a safe manner. At the hospital, there are small (5'x5') quiet rooms that have a built-in bench, are sound proof and have soft surfaces. Since we don't (and shouldn't) have such rooms in our homes, try to designate the room that is safest and with the fewest distractions. Firmly and calmly, lead (or carry) the child to his room. "Jack, since you can't handle the time-out you are going to need some quiet time alone in your room."

It may be a good idea to keep toys to a minimum in a bedroom so that children know this is a place to sleep and not to play, and, when you need to use the room for a quiet room purpose it is not too inviting. Again, set the timer for an appropriate amount of time for the child, depending on age and level of upsetness (usually somewhere between ten and thirty minutes). The time begins once the child is quiet inside of the room.

5. Processing is a key step of this whole system. After the time-out or quiet room time has been completed, you need to then process (i.e., talk about what happened and what could be done differently next time). This is the last link in the learning chain. Again, the word "process" will become a key word for the child. "Jack, we need to process what happened now." Get the child to talk about why they

think what happened, happened and what could be done differently next time. Affirm the inherent goodness of the child; be sure to demonstrate your love for him.

Managing the behavior of a child is not akin to controlling the child. It is meant to be a growing process by which a child learns how to manage himself. It is not unlike a successful employer-employee relationship. I always considered myself a good manager when those under me grew to a point of such performance that they needed nothing more than a tweak here or a different perspective there.

HOSPITALIZATION

 *Strategies*

- BEFORE YOUR CHILD IS ADMITTED TO THE HOSPITAL, CONTACT YOUR INSURANCE COMPANY TO MAKE SURE YOU UNDERSTAND THE REQUIREMENTS AND COVERAGE FOR A PSYCHIATRIC HOSPITALIZATION.

Insurance coverage can be confusing these days. If you think there might be a need for hospitalization in the near future, contact your insurance company to understand what will and will not be covered. You may want to ask the insurance company if your policy offers a case manager to assist you. This is a service where an individual (usually contracted by the insurance company) with a medical background keeps in regular touch with the treatment team at the hospital, authorizing (or not) the stay, tests and medical procedures.

I contacted a case manager and reviewed the basics of Jack's case with her a couple of weeks before he was admitted to the hospital. Since insurance for psychiatric conditions is usually covered only in the event that an individual is a threat to himself or others, probably the situation needs to be very bad to be covered. I did not want to be taking a child that was out of control and in crisis to the hospital, and juggling insurance approvals at the same time. I wanted to have the insurance company be familiar with Jack's case in the event that a hospitalization was necessary.

- VISIT THE HOSPITAL FACILITY AND MEET WITH THE MEDICAL OR NURSING DIRECTOR BEFORE YOU BRING YOUR CHILD TO THE HOSPITAL.

There is a lot to stomach in a children's psychiatric facility. Visiting the ward before you take your child will reduce the initial shock. When you take your child in, he is going to be upset enough—someone is going to have to keep it together, and that someone should be you.

- **UNDERSTAND THE BEHAVIOR MANAGEMENT PROGRAM THAT THE HOSPITAL EMPLOYS AND BE SURE THAT YOU ARE COMFORTABLE WITH IT.**

The hospital has a very strict behavior management program that, at the highest degree of unsafe behavior and lack of cooperation, results in physical restraints. The nursing director who provided me with a tour was careful to familiarize me with each of the levels of behavioral control—showing me the time-out chair (Level 1), the quiet room (Level 2) and the use of physical restraining devices (Level 3). Although she assured me that Level 3 was rarely used and usually only for adolescent children, she needed me to be familiar with, and accepting of, the continuum of behavioral controls. This familiarity would later prove invaluable in saving my sanity.

- **GATHER EVALUATIONS AND SUMMARIES (RECENT AND HISTORICAL) THAT YOU THINK MIGHT GIVE DOCTORS A THOROUGH PICTURE OF YOUR CHILD.**

The hospital staff only knows a child in crisis—they have no concept of what he's like in his own environment and in a non-crisis state. Only you can provide them with that perspective. In addition to evaluations, I wrote a letter to the hospital staff in which I gave Jack's history, what he is generally like, and what we believed were the circumstances that led to his needing hospitalization.

- **KEEP A DIARY.**

The diary is useful for two reasons. First, it can be a great outlet for your emotions during this turbulent period. Second, medicines, treatments and plans change fast, and the diary can serve as a tracking system for you and your private doctor to refer to later. I recorded medicines that were being tried and reactions, as I saw them, in Jack.

- **DON'T BE AFRAID TO ASK QUESTIONS AND TO QUESTION TREATMENT PLANS AND DIAGNOSIS.**

John and I were so afraid of alienating the hospital staff that we did not challenge as strongly as we should have the nearly immediate bipolar disorder diagnosis. Although I wrote several letters outlining reasons and providing examples of why we thought the diagnosis was incorrect, we should have had more face-to-face meetings and asked for back-up proof, supporting the doctors' diagnosis and treatment plan.

- TALK TO THE NURSES AND NURSES' AIDES AND LISTEN TO WHAT THEY ARE SEEING IN YOUR CHILD.

One of the nurses pulled me aside halfway through Jack's hospital stay and indicated that she did not agree with the bipolar diagnosis. She carefully suggested that we follow our own instincts when Jack was discharged and supported our feeling that a second opinion would be useful.

- BRING GAMES THAT REQUIRE MORE THAN TWO PEOPLE TO PLAY.

Star Wars Monopoly was the biggest hit at the Child Center. Board games brought more children to our table than we could accommodate during visiting time. Each day, Jack and I would invite two children to stay. What a way to encourage friendships.

- HAVE FRIENDS AND FAMILY SEND UPBEAT CARDS.

We had a whole wall of Jack's room wallpapered with cards and photos.

V. Dealing With Doctors and Therapists

Don't Buff and Polish My Kid, Thanks

Second Opinions and Medications

Outside the Standard Approach

Don't Buff and Polish
My Kid, Thanks
Trust Your Instincts

One of my key operating methods is to find the top two or three persons in a field for what I need, listen to their opinions and then turn inward and add their input to my own thinking. My own intuition and the results from bouncing my thoughts off trusted friends and team members are the bottom line.

Two weeks after Jack had left the partial hospitalization program and was settling into CES, I had one of the strangest telephone calls of my life. It was from the young psychiatric Fellow who had been managing Jack's case at the hospital. Dr. Burton called to return a video that he had taken of Jack for use in one of his classes. As much as I like to be helpful to the teaching of doctors-to-be, I don't like having footage like that on the loose and had requested it back after Dr. Burton had used it.

I updated Dr. Burton on Jack, sharing the good news of his first two weeks at school. I told Dr. Burton that we had kept Jack off all the medications that we had discontinued at the end of his hospital stay, when we thought he was having a drug reaction. I concluded by telling him that essentially, we were returning to square one.

Less than five minutes after I hung up the phone, I received a second call from Dr. Burton. He had just met with the director of the pediatric psychiatric program and wanted to make me the following offer. Did John and I want to return Jack to the hospital's in-patient unit so that he could be "buffed and polished"? I didn't make this up. Those were his exact words. Dr. Burton added that the hospital team wanted us to know that we were not abandoned. End of second call.

Sometimes, I wonder if doctors' familiarity with their field breeds a certain detachment and loss of perspective. How could a doctor be so casual about a return to an in-hospital stay? And how does he think it makes a parent feel to hear their child described in such a flippant manner? I don't think for one minute that Dr. Burton meant to be smarmy. In fact, it was so innocently said that I didn't even take offense. I just think that there is a connection with reality that is lost.

And this may go for psychiatric medications. Here was a psychiatric facility which had refused to take Jack off all medications because they were afraid he would be too manic and psychotic. IT'S A PSYCHIATRIC UNIT! That's what they are supposed to be able to deal with. Now, here we were two weeks into a drug-free period and the child was hyper as all get out but he was alive, his eyes looked bright, he was connected with the world almost more than ever before, and, he was happy.

A short while later I received yet a third call from Dr. Burton. It seems that the director of the program was continuing to think, think, think and could offer me a special fifty percent off rate if we decided to return to the in-patient unit. An Easter special? Really? This was beginning to sound more like a car wash every minute.

Throughout the course of dealing with a child's illness there are times when you feel more or less knowledgeable about what is going on with your child. Six months earlier, we could not seem to break Jack's flight and fight at school. We had had no idea where to turn. The hospital stay seemed like the only choice.

In hindsight, I watched weeks of drug testing that only made Jack worse. I also saw weeks of behavior management that pulled Jack together. These observations reinforced my initial instincts that the second grade program had been too overwhelming for Jack and had brought him over an edge. My hunch was that Jack's decline had been due to environmental factors. And as I watched the doctors at the hospital go through their pro forma tests only to see normal results—MRI, EEG and a sleep study--I relaxed, knowing there was no underlying biological concern.

Drug after drug, anti-psychotic and mood stabilizer, had been tried to treat Jack's supposed bipolar and psychotic thinking. He had become hazy, fuzzy, sluggish, silly, and nonsensical. John and I had the perspective which a long history gives you. We had seen Jack at his best and worst. And we concluded that the drug trials were not, in Jack's case, going in the right direction.

The school's short drug free test could mean two things. It could mean that Jack was in a stable period of the bipolar illness. Or, it could mean that the drugs that Jack was taking at the hospital were making him psychotic.

This was all in my mind as I readily thanked Dr. Burton for the offer and declined. At this point, with an excellent school situation by our side, I knew that we were better off on our own.

We have been very lucky in that the majority of our experiences with professionals have been really good, built up from mutual respect and honesty. True partnerships. Sometimes you will run into a professional who is just in a different mindset and perhaps doesn't deal with you in a way that is effective for you. Try to remember that this is not your issue. Try to take the emotion out of the situation. Acknowledge the frustration and anger that you feel— and then *let it go.* It's not realistic to think that every doctor or therapist is going to be near-perfect. You may need to maintain a relationship that is imperfect and accept there will be fundamental differences that cannot be overcome. Or, you may need to end the relationship.

Try to remain even tempered and keep focused on doing what is best for your child—which occasionally will mean walking away. Because of Jack's behavior management gains, we will never regret the hospital experience. However, we knew, even while we were living through it, that the medication part of the experience was not right and we'd have to gut it out until we figured out where to go next.

DECISION-MAKING

 *Strategies*

• YOU ARE THE FINAL DECISION-MAKER.

If something doesn't ring true to you, question it and double-check it. It is perfectly acceptable to get a second and even third opinion. Take in the information that makes sense to you and along with it, listen to your own intuition. You know your child best.

• RECOGNIZE THAT DOCTORS AND OTHER PROFESSIONALS ARE HUMAN, TOO.

And since they are human, they can err in a number of ways—what they say, how they say it, what they do and what they don't do. Only you know what you can and should tolerate and if it is worth saving a relationship that is hiccupping along.

• BE BOLD ENOUGH TO ADMIT A MISTAKE, AND TAKE THE NECESSARY ACTION TO MAKE IT RIGHT.

Sometimes, decisions are not clear and you have to go with your best guess at the time. Often the choice will be right, but not always. Don't just pick a path and stick blindly to it. Keep assessing what choices you have made in the treatment plan, professional supports and program that are in place for your child. If something is not working, make a change.

The Twenty-Six Hour Doctor Visit

Second Opinions and Medication

The decision to medicate or not medicate is an important one. For every reason why a medication should be considered, there are side effect concerns and emotional aspects to be looked at. When Jack was hospitalized, a new disorder was proposed. And the new disorder had a whole host of very different medications prescribed for managing it. Because of Jack's poor response to the realm of drugs that were tried in the hospital setting, and based on John's and my own history with Jack, we began to question the diagnosis and medication choices.

Questioning your child's diagnosis or the choice to medicate or not to medicate, and if so, what medication should be used, raises difficult issues. This chapter shares our experience with these questions.

SECOND OPINIONS

Jack had been in the hospital for a very short period when Dr. Burton told us that they believed Jack had bipolar disorder. Curiously, bipolar is a highly genetic disorder and to the best of our knowledge there is no history of this in our family. Furthermore, by this time Jack had had two comprehensive psychological assessments and a three hour assessment by a noted psychologist who specialized in Pervasive Developmental Disorders. No one had ever thought bipolar was at hand.

But, just to double-check, I scheduled a visit to one of the top pediatric psychiatrists in the country who specialized in bipolar disorder. Dr. Mitchell was located at a university hospital in the Midwest. I was told that the standard procedure for an evaluation and diagnosis took place over three days. The first two days the child would work with her psychiatric Fellow. Dr. Mitchell would only be visiting with Jack and me during the last day. Because of the distance we would have to travel, Dr. Mitchell agreed to a shortened evaluation to be completed in one three-hour visit.

Whenever I go to see a doctor, and particularly a new doctor, I try to think of the sorts of information that could be helpful to her. In this case, I developed a tracking method which would chart Jack's symptoms of different disorders over a two-week period. An example of my daily log and the final graphing of data is provided in Appendix II, Logs and Tracking Tools. Every half hour I rated Jack's behavior, on a scale of 1-10, in symptoms that were ADHD-like and symptoms that were bipolar-like. Then I plugged the ratings and the dates into a worksheet in Microsoft Excel and looked at the resulting graph. There was no fluctuation in moods (i.e., bipolar symptoms), my charts said. The symptoms were exclusively clustered and elevated in the ADHD realm. I sent ahead these symptom charts, the hospital evaluation, and teacher observations, along with my own historical review of Jack.

We arrived at the clinic thirteen hours after we left home. Jack had gotten so dirty by the second leg of the flight that I began to tell fellow passengers we were on our way to an audition for The Clorox Kid commercial.

Tired, but eager, Jack played with children in the waiting room while we waited for our names to be called. Eventually, Dr. Mitchell's psychiatric Fellow came out and brought me in to his office. It was clear that the packet I had carefully sent in advance had not been read. I reviewed Jack's basic history and answered the questions off a routine worksheet as patiently as I could.

I knew within the first hour that the Fellow was not insightful or particularly familiar with bipolar disorder. He next invited Jack in but did not attempt to win him over. In a doctor-like voice, he asked Jack several mundane questions, which I knew Jack would not bother to answer. I had tried to explain that in Jack's life, anyone wanting to connect with him would need to take the bigger step, but I guess this had not registered. Jack gave the gentleman no answers.

Next we were asked to go back to the waiting room while Dr. Mitchell reviewed our file. Finally, we met the renowned doctor. She asked Jack a few questions, which he barely answered. When she asked, "What do you do when you get home from school?" Jack replied, "Open the door and walk in the house." He wasn't playing along, no matter how great I had told him this doctor was supposed to be. After I suggested that Jack return to the waiting room (so that Dr. Mitchell and I could really talk), Dr. Mitchell told me that based on my recent data collection and Jack's past history it did not look like he was bipolar *at this time*. There was no way that she was going to contradict another prestigious teaching hospital and so, she hedged my question as to why the first had given Jack such a label. Dr. Mitchell kept repeating that she could not comment on the boy's diagnosis during that time. Two hours, and it was all over. The entire trip took twenty-three hours. I don't doubt that this doctor had earned her reputation for being a guru in the realm of bipolar in children. But, in a brief visit, the doctor was not able to give any specific, relevant information about Jack. I wished that she had told me that before I invested all that time and money in the trip.

We sought a second opinion several months later on the advice of Dr. Hornsby, Jack's psychiatrist, and our pediatrician. Both doctors had wondered if Jack might have PANDAS—a strep-induced virus that changes people's behavior dramatically, often turning them into obsessive-compulsive individuals. The fact that Jack had had scarlet fever (a form of strep) at the end of his hospital stay opened the idea that perhaps he had had the strep for a period of time and we had not known it.

This time we traveled to Rhode Island, to another university-based hospital setting. At least the travel wasn't as taxing this time. After an hour and half review of records and a brief meeting with Jack the doctor informed us that the only way she could tell if he suffered from PANDAS was to do a blood test when he was actually going through one of his dips. Since, when we went to her, Jack was looking (and acting) pretty good, the visit was limited in its immediate usefulness.

The Twenty-Six Hour
Doctor Visit

MEDICATIONS

We had decided to include medication as part of Jack's treatment program when he was first diagnosed with ADHD at age 2½. He was getting into so much trouble, receiving constant reprimands everywhere he went, that we felt it was far better for him to have a reasonable chance of getting along in the world by using medication.

For John and me there was simply no choice. We could not control or connect with the child we had. With Ritalin, we immediately saw less impulsivity and a slight pause in Jack's otherwise high speed flight pattern. Yet, although we chose to medicate, I cannot say that I don't have questions whether medication (Ritalin, later joined by Risperdal) was at the root of the breakdown that Jack suffered in second grade. The results of adding the Risperdal may have pushed Jack over the edge. We will never know.

Each child is different and reacts differently to medication. On top of this, the brain changes constantly. What worked yesterday may not work tomorrow. It may not be needed tomorrow. We have learned that Jack is highly sensitive to medications. With him, less is definitely more. We keep a very close eye on Jack and take no medication program for granted.

We found that, as friends had promised, when Jack reached the age of eight or nine, he began to be able to use his reasoning skills to think through some of his behaviors. It was also around this time that Jack's own chemistry seemed to right itself a little—he was no longer the whirlwind of his early years. As he grew older the "H" of his ADHD subsided. He began to understand his disorder and we talked about the behavior areas that needed work.

Medication Decision  Strategies

- **Listen to the experiences of others.**

Read books on psychiatric medications for children. There are some easy to understand books, which give you the basics of medication, such as *Psychiatric Medications for Children* by Dr. Timothy Wilens or *Taking the Mystery Out of Medications in Autism / Asperger Syndromes* by Dr. Luke Tsai.

- **Talk to your doctor.**

Ask what the risks, side effects, and potential dangers are of the drug. Find out what the doctor's experience has been with children who are on this medication.

- **Get current information on the medication.**

Do a literature search in the library or on the internet to see what has been written recently about the medication that your doctor is thinking of using.

- **Keep a diary of your own observations when you begin a new medication.**

In order to help the doctor assess the efficacy of a drug, he needs information. Keep a log when you begin a new drug and ask your child's teacher to do the same. (See Appendix II, Logs and Tracking Tools.) Note any positive or negative behavioral changes and when they occur, in relation to when your child has taken the medication. Also, be on the lookout for changes in appetite, sleeping patterns, and any physical changes, such as the development of facial tics.

- **If you don't like what you see, call the doctor.**

Psychiatric medications are not to be fooled around with. If you don't like the reaction that you are seeing in your child, call your doctor.

OUTSIDE THE STANDARD APPROACH
A Review of Some Alternative Therapies

Along our journey, we have learned of many alternative therapies which claim success for managing ADHD and other disorders. We have tried four alternative therapies for Jack. The research and learning behind each one sounded reasonable to John and me. Until we showed the information to Jack's psychiatrist. He took a very conservative approach to alternative therapies and questioned their validity.

We have tried alternative routes in conjunction with the more tried and true methods and ALWAYS with the psychiatrist and psychologist's knowledge of what we were doing. In two of the four cases, we couldn't gain Jack's cooperation long enough to see if these approaches were helpful. I am sharing what we tried in case you have been thinking about one of these routes and want to hear one person's experience. Remember, we are only one family who tried a few different alternative approaches. That's hardly enough to base your decision on. It's just a first glance.

CRANIOSACRAL THERAPY

The craniosacral system is like the electrical generator behind the nerve impulse. It is made up of the brain and the spinal cord and includes all the attachments to the skull, spine and tailbone (sacrum). In order for the nervous system to function properly, spinal fluid must flow freely up and down the spinal cord to and from the brain. There is a reciprocal movement between the brain and the spinal cord that must be stress-free and fluid in order to have normal nerve functioning.

Craniosacral therapy uses light touch on the critical sensory areas in the body where energy may be getting stuck or distorted. It is a process of healing—not a one time event.

Jack's presentation to Dr. Trent during the first visit was revealing. He couldn't seem to stay in one place nor keep his hands from wandering to every thing that they shouldn't. With the wisdom and calm of an eastern thinker, Dr. Trent took one look at Jack and said to me, "We're going to go with this and not get upset. We will see where it leads." Where it led was a child who wiggled every which way on the table while Dr. Trent gently probed and evaluated Jack's functioning.

Dr. Trent did not get frazzled easily. Jack didn't like the feeling of the doctor manipulating his head and didn't understand why it was okay for this man to slightly pull his pants down in back to feel the base of the spine as he tried to balance the nervous system.

Dr. Trent talked to me about the tightness that he found in the left side of Jack's scalp, the tension in his brain and the lack of energy traveling through his spinal cord. Understanding little, I went on trust.

We continued with this program for a couple of months but it was getting exceedingly difficult. Jack told me again that he couldn't stand the doctor touching his head. Jack has had to overcome great tactile defensiveness. It didn't surprise me that he wouldn't like this sensation.

Whenever it makes sense, I try to experience what Jack experiences. Dr. Trent had inspected me, declared me highly stressed and off balance, and had treated me a couple of times. I must say, I did feel better but maybe I would have been with any relaxation method. We finally had to stop treatments because of Jack's non-cooperation.

ACUPUNCTURE

About the same time that I heard of craniosacrial therapy, I was introduced to acupuncture as a means of balancing the energies in the body. The doctor's hypothesis was that different energies within the body (electromagnetic fields) were misfiring, firing too much or not firing enough in Jack. Strangely enough, this sounded similar to what the homeopathic doctor had said was taking place in me both times I tried to become pregnant. It wasn't inconceivable that the same imbalance was passed along to Jack.

The acupuncturist had worked with ADD and ADHD children and claimed to have success in calming them down and improving their focus. We were willing to give it a go.

Dr. Zimmer did not use needles with his patients. He worked his hands about five inches above Jack's body, seeming to smooth and balance the energy field that surrounded the child. I must admit that, within a single session, we went from a child that was squirmy, unfocused and impulsive to a child who was calm and centered.

It was difficult for me to get Jack to Dr. Zimmer, though the obstacles were different than those presented at craniosacral therapy. There was an appealing swing set and tree house just outside the doctor's house. Each week presented a new challenge trying to make it past the swing and into the doctor's office.

I wanted to experience what Jack was going through with Dr. Zimmer. Also, I was looking for a way to manage my frequent migraines. So I had Dr. Zimmer treat me several times. Once, I went to him while suffering from one of my weekly migraines. As he moved the energy using hands raised a few inches above me, I could feel the headache lifting. No one was more amazed than me. I think that Dr. Zimmer probably could have helped Jack, based upon the effectiveness that I saw Dr. Zimmer work in me, but again, Jack's non-cooperation made me pull the plug.

Acupuncture, craniosacral therapy and alternative approaches require patience. Both doctors cautioned me against looking for any instantaneous results. After a few months, during which I think we spent more time pleading than actually getting any work done (at least in the case of the craniosacral therapy), I decided that although it might be helpful, emotionally it was too draining for me. Given our short experience, I really cannot recommend or dissuade anyone from trying these approaches. Although Dr. Jackson was quick to point out that there is absolutely no research that supports the work in any of these alternative therapies, I believe it is up to the individual to look at and assess her own experience to draw her own conclusions.

Diet and the Gluten-Free, Wheat-Free, Sugar-Free Approach

Many parents in one of my support groups were huge advocates of restricted diets and homeopathic supplements. Their children were all patients of a doctor who left the helm of a child institute at a respected university to take up this alternate route. Never knowing what might hold the key to an improvement for Jack, I felt that I had to at least try this course.

Dr. James' practice was closed but he had an associate, a nurse, in Philadelphia who had trained with him and was able to coordinate patient programs with him. After a very thorough history, the nurse ordered a battery of tests including extensive allergy tests, tests to identify fungi and other bacteria, and comprehensive blood, urine and stool analyses. Results showed that Jack had high levels of yeast, was allergic to twenty-six foods and had trouble digesting food, which was the cause of constant constipation. Jack was three years old at this point.

To get rid of the yeast, Jack was put on Diflucan, a powerful yeast killer. His liver function had to be monitored for as long as he was on this medication. Homeopathetic remedies were presented for vitamin and mineral deficiencies as well as to rectify the problems with Jack's digestive tract. Anything made with yeast was out (due to the high levels in his system), the twenty-six supposed allergic foods removed from the diet and a gluten-free, wheat-free, sugar-free diet encouraged. Luckily, Jack was young enough that he didn't think much about the changes in his food. Other parents following the diet went with me on a food shop to the large whole foods store in our town and shared their recipes.

I give total credit to the regime for regulating Jack's intestinal tract so that by four years old he was finally fully toilet trained. I just wouldn't say with certainty that the diet impacted his behavior. Yet, there were many parents in our parenting group who believed strongly that the diet changed their child's behavior.

Fish Oil (omega 3 fatty acids)

I became friends with the former chief of the psychopharmacology research program at the National Institute of Mental Health, via the bipolar parents web site, during the time that Jack was hospitalized and we were being told that he was bipolar. Dr. Cott was the first to introduce me to omega 3 fatty acids. Omega 3s are essential for healthy brains.

The brain needs omega 3s. Here's why. Two layers of fat protect every one of the billion brain cells that make up your brain. Through these fat layers messages are sent to other cells. Messages like: "Time to get ready for school," "Listen to the teacher," and so on. (Sounds curiously like message for attention, focus and action, right?)

For the communication to go smoothly the cell membranes need to be flexible—and here's where the fat part comes in. The omega 3s are what keep the membranes flexible, which improves the communication ability. When the cell membranes become stiff they can't easily pass the messages back and forth between cells because the chemicals (such as serotonin) are not easily traveling along their pathways. Attention, impulsivity, and mood equilibrium seem to be affected by such poor functioning chemical messengers. Since sixty percent of the brain is made up of fat, it is important that it is kept healthy and supple.

Since our diet today is much lower in fish and other excellent sources of omega 3s, proponents of omega 3s suggest that fish oil be taken as a supplement. Jack takes fish oil daily now, along with vitamins C and E to increase fish oil's absorption into the system. We have also adjusted our diet to include more salmon, tuna and walnuts—all great sources of omega 3s. John and I can clearly see a smoothing of personality and better emotional keel on the days that Jack has taken his fish oil. There are now books written on the benefits of the omega 3 fatty acids, and much information is available via the internet.

IF YOUR ARE THINKING ABOUT ANY NON-TRADITIONAL THERAPY

As parents, we are all so anxious to keep ourselves open to new ideas and approaches in our very diligent effort not to miss what could be the magic bullet for our child. Each time we tried an alternative approach, we had invariably heard about the idea from a parent or group of parents who were convinced that the program was making a true change in their child. And certainly, in this group of disorders, different things seem to be working for different children. Just be careful that you don't get so caught up in the momentum of the advocates of the program that you lose your rational sense.

It is a good feeling to be part of a group. And the stronger the group's support of the therapy, the more convinced you might become that it is working or going to work for your child. Try to maintain your objectivity and continue to look carefully at how the therapy or program is really affecting your child. Don't just go along because it feels good. Be equally tough evaluating the effectiveness of alternative therapies as you are with the traditional ones.

Think through what the goal of the therapy is and determine where it fits in the priority list of therapies. Specifically, find out how your child will change as a result of the therapy. There is a limit to how many therapies your child can take on so if the goal isn't in the top priority list, trying the therapy will have to wait. Remember, taking on a new discipline drains all sorts of energies—your time, your finances, and your child's sustenance. Being careful about what is in the program bag is practical and logical.

If you decide to proceed with an alternative therapy, discuss the treatment program in detail, before you begin. Find out what the program will consist of, including what each treatment session is like, how long it lasts, how often your child will need to go, and the costs. Insurance providers often do not reimburse for alternative health care choices. You may want to ask your insurance company what your policy covers before you undertake the program, to understand what your out-of-pocket commitment might be.

ALTERNATIVE THERAPY

★ Strategies

- **RESEARCH THE THERAPY AND THE DOCTOR OR THERAPIST CAREFULLY.**

There are so many alternative therapies being tossed around today and so many so-called experts on each of them. Ask the provider for information that validates the therapy. The more scientific studies or good hard data that you can review, the better. Look for published studies by reputable magazines and organizations. I never like an answer that starts out with, "Although there is no hard evidence…"

- **TRY ONE NEW THERAPY AT A TIME.**

We started craniosacral therapy and acupuncture at the same time and were never able to tell which might be making an impact.

- **TALK TO OTHER PEOPLE WHO USE THE DOCTOR OR THERAPIST THAT YOU ARE CONSIDERING USING.**

There is nothing like personal recommendations and real life experiences. Don't be afraid to ask the doctor for references but do recognize that he will probably give you his most supportive patients. Ask the parents questions like, "Do you see a change in your child?" "How do you know that this doctor is responsible for the change that you see in your child?" and, "What is one negative about the doctor?"

- **BE CONSISTENT.**

If you are going to try a special diet or fish oil, for example, don't just do it some of the time. You will not be able to get a good read on the therapy's effectiveness if you are only partly following the regime.

• KEEP A DIARY OF BEHAVIOR AND CHANGE IN YOUR CHILD, BEFORE AND DURING THE NEW THERAPY.

About two weeks before you begin a new regime, keep a daily log of behaviors that you see in your child. Continue your log after he begins the new regime. You might want to make particular note of the key behaviors that you are trying to change. There is nothing like the written word to help you decipher what is really going on day-to-day.

• UNDERSTAND WHAT YOUR ROLE WILL BE AND IF THERE ARE REQUIREMENTS FOR TEACHERS, OTHER THERAPISTS, OR OTHERS INVOLVED IN YOUR CHILD'S CARE.

VI. Circle of Support

With a Little Help From My Friends

Babysitters and Angels

Sleepover Central

WITH A LITTLE HELP
FROM MY FRIENDS
The Importance Of Friendships And Networks

I would have been nowhere without my friends. The first two years after Jack was diagnosed were the loneliest that I have ever experienced. I never went through a denial phase, probably because in our case it was so obvious from the beginning that something was wrong. But once I received the official diagnosis, I had a long period where I just needed to cocoon and absorb the information, and process what it would mean for the rest of my life.

I cocooned before I worked on getting an action plan together and I cocooned after the plan was in place. It took a while to digest what was to be my unchangeable experience of life. I had to adjust my expectations and my sense of who our family was, to accommodate this curveball. I could not do this with anyone, except my husband. Even then, a lot of my adjusting could only be with myself.

Many mothers of special needs children whom I know talk about feeling isolated and alone. I understand how this can happen. You don't want to take the child anywhere with you. You have to decline family invitations. You are frequently embarrassed in public. And you are raw and hurting.

Having a special needs child separates out those who are your true blue, tried and true, forever and ever friends. And in a way, it is worth having to go through this exercise because you end up with a meaty group of friends. That has been my experience. I have let the superficial friendships go a lot sooner than I might have.

It is hard enough figuring out how to get through each day with a child who thinks he can operate as he wants to. Even today, I use up a lot of emotional energy just trying to get through the ordinary parts of a day. Add to that trying to keep friendships and relationships in tact, and it's almost overwhelming.

My friends basically fell into three camps:

1) Friends who couldn't understand Jack's disorder (even after I explained it to them) and thought that we just needed to do a better job parenting---or mistook the disorder for a communicable disease.
2) Friends who acknowledged our situation and were sympathetic but couldn't relate to it.
3) Friends who were supportive.

When I was growing up my parents owned and operated a nursing home. I have been around the elderly since the time that I could walk. Nursing homes, the infirm and the dying do not scare me. In fact, I am quite comfortable around all three. But as a child and young adult, I didn't feel the same depth of compassion for those with physical disabilities. I tried to think about what their world was like, but I couldn't grasp it. So, I understood that for some of our friends, seeing a child who did not obey, did not cooperate, and did not even participate in what was going on around him was more than foreign. It was unimaginable to them.

They could not fathom that parenting would not correct how Jack behaved. Social behavior as related to a neurological disorder? This was beyond them. I could read it in their eyes, their interactions with Jack, and in their comments to me. What I was experiencing was as unreal to them as those with physical disabilities were to me years ago. This was not a fault of theirs. I wasn't mad at or disappointed in them. It just meant that our relationship could go only so far.

Those friendships ended up being the social and fun. I appreciated the laughter and lightness that John and I enjoyed for the night. A night of laughter was sure restful after a week of praising, coaching, coaxing, reminding and remedying the week's disasters with Jack. Since we knew that these same friends could not relate to, and probably were uncomfortable with, our situation, we never suggested family gatherings and we rarely discussed our trials with Jack with them. Although I appreciated these relationships, I drew on the sustenance and support of my very special friends to survive.

Most compelling were the friends who embraced our situation and Jack as well. These were the families who were always welcoming of Jack, called daily when we were in a dip with him, and took Sarah in when we had to respond to an emergency with Jack. While these friends were rare, we only needed a few. We were lucky enough to have some of them in our weekly lives, like the nurse and doctor couple who have three children, two dogs, a cat, a cockatiel and a dwarf hamster. Their house was always filled with furry animals willing to be hugged and played with. There was plenty of down-home cooking and genuine warmth and love to go around at least three times at that house. Going to their house was like cuddling up in a warm blanket.

I have another friend who lives just around the corner, who started many mornings with a cheery phone call of "Hi, Buddy!" That's enough to put a bounce in your step and a positive beat in your attitude.

There were the friends that I did not see as often, but who were just as wonderful. Like my grammar school friend who lives in the country. I hadn't seen her in several years but she could get into Jack's head and understand how he thought. She was my e-mail confidant and resident philosopher and psychologist. Then there was my thirty-plus year friendship with the gal who made sure I was stocked with silly jokes. Each of these friends, in their own way, kept me whole.

I also met some fabulous parents of special needs children who ended up being great sources of information. Soon after Jack was diagnosed, we learned about an integrated pre-school class offered by the public school system. I didn't know what IEP or anything other than SOS meant. I had heard of a support group for parents of special needs children called PICD, Parents Interested in Children's Development. It was through the monthly meetings at PICD that

WITH A LITTLE HELP
FROM MY FRIENDS

I learned how the school system for kids with special needs really worked. I became educated about the process but more importantly, I was given the inside scoop—which school system personnel truly considered your child's needs and which was committed to the system and the system alone. Who you could count on to get things done and who would drag their heels. I was given advice on how to get the proper special services, where to go for outside therapies, and what summer programs we were entitled to. I also heard about alternative therapies. PICD is where I cut my teeth on special education, then moved into the driver's seat.

As useful as the practical tips and being shown the ropes were, it was invaluable to listen to other parents' experiences, particularly if they had a slightly older child with a diagnosis similar to Jack's. This is how I heard which hair salons in town were best with children who couldn't stand to be touched, where to shop for foods with the least additives, what candy had the lowest sugar content, who was the most patient Little League coach in town, and which behavior modification programs seemed to be working.

For a year, I attended every PICD meeting, often getting together for coffee with other mothers for follow-up conversations. After about a year, I found that the bulk of information being discussed was not new news to me. It was time to look for another group that more closely targeted our son's disorder.

Jack's psychiatrist introduced us to the Asperger's Syndrome support group. This group was more riveting even than PICD. Here was a room full of parents who had children like Jack. The group had a similar format to PICD—one month was networking, the next was a guest speaker. My learning curve took another big tick upwards.

I have also found support groups and information via the internet. When Jack was mistakenly diagnosed with bipolar disorder, I went to the internet at once. There I found an incredible on-line support group of parents who had bipolar children. Membership was free and information plentiful. When you joined the group, you provided a thumbnail sketch of your child; anytime you gave a response to the group you were required to provide your child's diagnosis, age and current medications. Reading what twenty or more parents were going through on a daily basis proved to us that Jack was no bipolar child. In fact, more than four of the members warned me about the hospital's reputation for misdiagnosing—particularly in the bipolar category.

I used a search engine whenever I was looking for information on the internet. I found the most helpful sites by typing in the name of the disorder in the keyword section of the search module. Sites related to the keyword that you've typed in will pop up and you can choose from there. Appendix IV, Resources, provides some sites in the ADHD, PDD and Asperger's Syndrome areas.

Finally, I will never forget sitting on a plane and ending up in deep conversation with a woman who was a professor in psychology at Columbia University. At that time, we were just starting to ask questions about Jack's behavior. The professor was the one who first outlined a game plan for me. Right there on a napkin on a plane. She gave me the names of psychiatrists and neurologists in my geographic area and she walked me through the evaluation process. I keep her business card in my file of special letters. She was the first angel in Jack's life.

The bottom line is that you never know where you will find friends. Keep yourself open to the possibilities.

Networking

 *Strategies*

- Ask your child's psychiatrist and therapists for names of support groups in your area.

- Call local special education schools and ask about conferences they may know of, as well as local organizations that they recommend. I've attended some excellent conferences at the local private school for exceptional children and have been able to talk directly with some nationally recognized leaders in the field.

- Surf the internet using the keyword feature.

- Contact national organizations and get the name of their local branches.

You and Your Better Half
Trying to See Eye To Eye

All along the road with Jack, friends, family and professionals had lots of ideas as to what John and I should be doing as parents. John and I often had different opinions as to what we should be doing as parents, how Jack should be disciplined and how we should cope with the situation. Since I was the one doing eighty percent of the day-to-day, minute-to-minute interfacing with professionals and with Jack, I was higher up on the learning curve than John. We had to double back on the weekends, when John was more involved, as he tried the approaches that I had already tested during the week. He was frustrated and I was resentful. In general, life was exhausting. John and I were depressed and bewildered. Having fun? No, not yet. Maybe tomorrow.

The whole experience affected our relationship with each other and as a family. I can see how it would be easy to begin operating solo when you are in the midst of such pressure. We might have been part of the high statistics of divorce among special needs families had it not been for therapy and prayer. One of the best investments we made during this period was to find an excellent marriage and family counselor, Sally. Luckily, we recognized early on that we needed counseling.

I had heard Sally speak at a parenting class at Sarah's school. She was straightforward and full of common sense and insight. Instinctively, I liked her. I began working with her, both on my own and with John. My instincts were right on. Sally has been a lifeline for me and for our marriage.

During our roughest patch, one of my dear college friends, Jill, spent a few days with me in the mountains of Vermont, four children between us. She had come armed for action. She walked in the door with a book called *Divorce Busters* and the Bible. Jill spent five days reading, praying and talking, talking, talking with me. She helped me turn around my attitude and get God back into the loop.

When John and I were nearing marriage we talked a lot about the triangle nature of our relationship. For us, this meant that God was an equal part of our relationship. With Jack, although I constantly turned to God in frustration, thanksgiving, upset and alarm, I became absorbed with managing the situation, and forgot about others. Every conversation worked its way back to what was going on with Jack. What a bore this must have been. Getting re-centered—putting God at the center of my life and leaning on him for support pulled me, and our family, together.

Of course, not every marriage is salvageable. I cannot even pretend to imagine the burden upon people who receive no emotional or practical support from their spouses. Sometimes, it is probably easier to cope with the situation on your own, than to live with the additional stress of a destructive or emotionally absent spouse.

If there is some thread of connection or glimmer of hope, try first seeing a psychotherapist or marriage counselor. There are many out there and some are better than others. As you found health care professionals for your special needs child, use the same tenacity to find a top notch, highly recommended professional who can help you and your spouse.

Head and Heart

 *Strategies*

• **Bring in a marriage counselor and keep her on board.**

Even if you are not having a rough time right now, there will be challenges ahead. You will be glad that you have an objective person who knows your personalities and situation and can look at your crises with a practiced eye.

• **Work as a team.**

If parents of typical children need to do this, parents of special needs children need to do this twice as much. Teamwork starts with giving your spouse understanding and empathy. After all, who better than you knows what he or she is going through? But beyond the comforting shoulder and listening ear there needs to be someone who can share the workload—either with the child or running the household. Double the hands not only makes the work light, it offers companionship.

• **Act as a tag team.**

John and I know when one or the other of us is about to lose it with Jack. We have finally figured out the art of cutting in. Just before the big blow-up, the uninvolved parent will suggest that the one about to lose his or her cool step aside and let a fresh parent take over.

• **You have a long road ahead of you—that part won't change. But HOW you set your attitude and heart as you journey along is something that you have full control over.**

Someone once told me to be careful to set good habits in the early days of marriage, for those routines and ways of being with each other would become set patterns much more quickly than we would realize. The same is true of your mindset and heartset as special needs parents. Will you be martyrs? Will you be complainers? Will you take it in stride? Will you show courage? You are the one who will determine how you approach the world in this new place that you find yourself. Think carefully and be sure that how you are, is how you want others to see you.

• LOOK FOR YOUR LIFELINES.
You will need people who can support you and raise you up individually and as a couple. These are people who you can lean into during the tough periods and bad news days. Choose carefully.

BABYSITTERS AND ANGELS
Finding the Right Babysitter and Other Help

BABYSITTERS

I truly believe that angels walk beside Jack. I can remember times when Jack ran across a parking lot, got lost in a toy store, climbed to the tippy top of a tree at a friend's house (he was trying to be like Tarzan) or went somewhere or did something that was potentially disastrous. Each time, it is clear that someone had been there to catch Jack. This someone might be a stranger or friend, visible or not, but there is no doubt in my mind that Jack was being looked upon and cared for by others.

Besides those who protected Jack from physical dangers, were the angels that have saved him from emotional death. I've always known that Jack would need more than his immediate family to keep spirit and self-esteem pointed in the right direction.

Jack's feelings about himself soar when people cross his path who can develop friendships with him. Since kids like Jack really are not good at making friends on their own, I have been very deliberate about creating opportunities for relationships to develop. Even in Jack's most difficult periods, he has been able to hold on to friendships outside our family.

One of my rules in life is to be open to the possibilities that the Lord puts in my way. Margaret landed on our doorstep within the first six months of her coming to Connecticut. I had mentioned to our next door neighbor that we were in need of a babysitter for afternoons. Mrs. Tortora knew a young Polish man who had friends, a husband and wife, who had just moved to Connecticut from Brooklyn. Did I want to meet the wife?

Margaret was twenty-three when she first came to us, but had the insight and knowledge of someone much older. She had an intuitive feel for children and a remarkable acceptance of people. Margaret had a strong, inherent belief in the capability of others—this was evident in her relationship with Jack. Even during his toughest times, Margaret's message to Jack that she believed in him was loud and clear. She loved him unconditionally. Jack felt her acceptance strongly, and this resulted in a friendship that went deeper than words can express. Above all else, Jack and Margaret had tons of fun together. In my mind's eye, I see her swinging him high in the air, roughhousing to no end and racing him up and down a long driveway on a bicycle. Margaret's husband, Alex, was equally fun-loving and had a strong friendship with Jack as well.

Jack's most important friendship has been with Margaret. It was always a source of comfort to know that Jack was connecting with Margaret and enjoying his relationship with her, even when he couldn't connect with anyone else. I firmly believe that this relationship will be one of the cornerstones of Jack's lessons and experiences in friendship. In fact, seeing the power that this relationship has had in Jack's life, I now evaluate what we do and what activities he participates in based on my read of what I think the potential of the relationship might be.

We have a number of strategies to find babysitters. Depending upon your location, you may find one approach is more helpful than another. Although my goal is to use the same sitter as often as I can (so the children get into a groove with her), this is not always possible. People's circumstances change; they move or take on other responsibilities that prohibit babysitting.

Before I begin making telephone calls to find a sitter, I take the time to write a profile of what Jack and Sarah are like, a description of what the ideal babysitter would be like, requirements of the position, schedule, and pay scale. The goal of the profile is to give an accurate picture of our situation but not give so much information that we inundate candidates. It is a means to screen out people who have no interest or background in what the situation is about.

Babysitting a child like Jack involves a few adjustments. For one thing, I have found time and again that babysitters have difficulty juggling the demands of Jack with the needs of Sarah. What usually happens (on the theory that the squeaky wheel gets the oil) is that Jack demands and gets the full attention of the babysitter—using either negative or positive tactics. Sarah is left with the promise that "I'll spend time with you as soon as I get Jack settled," but that time never seems to arrive. Countless times John and I have arrived home after an evening out to find a babysitter who was all too conscious and even guilty that she had spent nearly all of her time managing Jack while a dejected Sarah finally took herself off to bed. Not surprisingly, the next time we mentioned that this particular babysitter was coming, Sarah was not enthused.

There are, however, some types of people who make great babysitters. Teachers and teachers' aides fall into this camp. I particularly like Jack's past teachers and teachers' aides because they have first-hand experience working with him. Knowing how Jack functions usually means they can get him on a program that leaves them time to spend with Sarah as well.

Jack's second grade special education teacher has been a marvel. She helped us implement the Point Sheet program at home and could carry it out even when we weren't there. Though strict in her expectations, she loves to have fun and is always game to do something or go somewhere.

Colleges are another source of babysitters. If you are fortunate enough to have local colleges with departments in any of the disciplines related to special education or children—social work, psychology, elementary education, or nursing—you have an additional piece of luck going your way. When I finally took the time to visit all the colleges in our area, I was richly rewarded. I wrote a specific advertisement for the college campuses that I thought might appeal to students. In addition to talking about the children and briefly describing Jack's needs, I mentioned that the experience might be great hands-on experience for students.

Jack hand-picked our first college sitter. We had just finished an appointment with the psychiatrist and were within ten minutes of a Catholic university. Besides being Jesuit-run (an instant plus in my book), the school had a number of programs that were well suited for what we needed. After we went to a few of the departments and were told that putting up posters was no longer allowed, we were redirected to the career placement office.

You need to leave ample time when you go onto a campus today, because typically, the career placement office is not in an obvious location. Such is the case at this school. As Jack and I were driving around the campus we stopped to ask a young man the directions to the placement office. He had obvious spunk and the sparkle in his eye that Jack and I both gravitate to. After we received directions and I began to pull away, Jack said, "Wait, let's give him a poster. He looks like a good sitter." Although a twinkle in the eye does not a good sitter make, I agreed that the lad had something about him. We turned around and Jack jumped out to hand Gary a poster.

Later that night I received the message, spoken in thick Scottish brogue, that introduced Gary to our family. Gary's message said that he had read our ad and although he had no babysitting experience, he was a psychology major and very interested in the challenge. Gary was co-captain of the varsity soccer team. This was a major asset for Sarah, an enthusiastic soccer player herself. We enjoyed Gary's company and sitting for several months until his lack of a car and a demanding soccer schedule made the arrangement too complicated.

This was the beginning of what has become one of my best babysitting strategies. I ultimately visited four different colleges and had my best luck at the school where I was able to personally meet with the director of career placement and lay out the very special requirements that we had. This woman was extraordinarily sympathetic, and helped me to look through the listing of students who had signed up seeking babysitting employment.

Going on her recommendations, I was able to meet and hire Blakely, who became one of our top babysitters. College students can be totally fun. They have lots of energy and have a perspective that is as refreshing for the children as it is for us. College students are usually more reasonably priced than teachers or older sitters. For us, this means that we can hire a pair of roommates to sit on a Saturday evening when we know that we will be out late, or during times when Jack is a bit more difficult to handle. The sitters have a great time and neither child gets short-changed. The whole arrangement only costs us slightly more than when we hire one older sitter.

What is most, most important—regardless of the where you find the sitter—is the personal interview. There have been a number of times that I have been impressed by someone's telephone interview, have had a favorable reference check, but have been disappointed when we meet in person.

One time, a candidate came to visit and paid absolutely no attention to the children past the initial hello. She could not have been less interested in them. Like any relationship, when babysitting begins at a point where both people are truly interested in developing a friendship, it is already on the road to success.

Once a strong relationship has been established between Jack and a sitter, we look for ways to maintain the connection, even when our schedules or needs change. Margaret became our full-time sitter for the year that we withdrew Jack from the Montessori school. I could never have kept the patience and energy required to care for Jack alone in those days, when his self-agenda was high and his cooperation was low. We operated as a tag team. Margaret would take Jack to therapies, to the aquarium, library and other fun places to fill the day, and I would be with him in the early morning and the late afternoon through to bedtime. However, the following year Jack started pre-kindergarten and I only needed Margaret after school.

There is a risk when you need to shift a sitter from full to part-time employment that you will lose the sitter. This could be devastating for someone like Jack who thrives on sameness and has difficulty establishing relationships. I looked for situations that needed part-time help that might complement Margaret's experience with us. There are a few things to think about if you and your babysitter agree on a part-time arrangement, where she will need to take on a second job if she wants to work full-time.

Suggestions for Helping Your Babysitter Find Additional Work

• *Do not have her look for another special needs situation.* I can't imagine a more draining experience than going from one special needs assignment to another. Not only is it physically demanding, but the emotional investment in one child requires quite a commitment—trying to balance the emotional wires of two special needs children and their families would likely be a formula for quick burn-out.

• *Help explore ways that she can turn her hobbies and interests into employment.* Having a part-time job in a field that is a hobby or interest might be relaxing and fun for the sitter. With the stability of your assignment, she may be able to sacrifice pay in favor of experience. Another approach might be for the sitter to explore a field that she is considering for the long-term.

• *Consider the logistics of your location and the other part-time employment.* Long travel distances between assignments can be wearing and create stress. We have used this strategy effectively with a housekeeper, who now splits her time between our house and a friend who lives within a quarter of a mile. It makes for easy last minute changes in schedule and emergency coverage, and is less taxing all the way around.

• *Don't be afraid to spread the word among friends as well as to local places of business where the sitter has expressed an interest.* We eventually helped Margaret secure part-time work with a children's dance school. At first, she worked half-time at the school, acting as receptionist and bookkeeper. Now that she is in graduate school, she continues to work ten hours a week, keeping the books for the school.

Remember, you are somebody who is between an employer and a friend to your sitter. You need to be available for moral support, to be a source of ideas, and to be willing to extend yourself to help in her job search. As the sitter invests in your family, invest in hers. I have been a ready reference for Margaret, have written letters of support for school applications and job wanted ads, and have helped her brainstorm long-term career choices and how to pursue them.

The hope is that your relationship has progressed to the point where you naturally want to help your sitter achieve her personal goals. But just in case this has not happened, remember that the sitter is a vital part of your survival network and a critical component of your core team. Take care of her.

If you find that your needs change and you truly don't require the employment of someone who has established a strong rapport with your child, try to find some way to continue regular contact. Margaret's return to school to pursue occupational therapy degree and Jack's full-time school schedule ended her regular position with us. But, knowing the importance of that relationship to Jack, we continued to have Margaret in our lives by having her sit each Saturday afternoon. Her five hour adventure with Jack gave us relief on the weekend and maintained the deep friendship.

I am not sure how many Margarets are out there. But there may be more than any of us think. Our search has resulted in a fabulous team composed of Margaret, roommates from a local college, and a seamstress who has grown children, who is patient and kind and who loves arts, crafts and the like.

GETTING THE (HOUSEHOLD) HELP YOU NEED

Decisions about the help you need—from financial and workload perspectives—must be made on an individual basis and requires some thought and discussion. We have found that as our children grow older, household help requirements change, too. How healthy Jack is at the time and who is able to manage him also influence our help decisions. We try to review the household help situation biannually—again, trying to be a step ahead of what we need.

We begin the review by determining how much money we have for household help. This includes weekday sitters, evening and weekend sitters, cleaning help, and any other person who supplies a service in the house. Once we agree on a weekly figure, we write down our needs. The primary caregiver for the children and the one generally responsible for the humming of the house should probably take the lead in this exercise.

When the children were pre-kindergarten age, babysitter help was consistently at the top of our list. Since I was working full-time during this period, there was really no choice. Between the hours of 7:30 a.m. and 5:30 p.m. someone needed to care for the children. Once they started school, it became more important to have someone to help with the cleaning and errands so that I could devote more time to the afternoon activities and therapies.

We never know what sort of Jack will step off the bus at the end of the day. Will it be a child needing my attention? Or, will it be the Jack who craves running outside, exploring his beloved brook and the frogs that lie unsuspecting beneath its surface? Since the only thing that I can count on is the inconsistency of each day, I try to be prepared for whatever child might step off the bus. If I am busy preparing dinner or doing laundry and he is desperate for me to be with him, something has to give. Either Jack will be frustrated or dinner will be short-changed. If I am unable to get things ready before 3:00 p.m., having the luxury of the housecleaner available to begin the meal, run to the store, or catch up on laundry is extremely helpful. For us, having a housecleaner come in a couple of hours each day to assist with the business of daily living is much more helpful than having someone spend one day a week in hard cleaning.

Obviously, whatever arrangement you settle on will depend first and foremost on what you can afford. I discovered that by cooking more meals at home and reducing the number of things that just seemed to find their way onto the must-have list, I saved enough money to hire the extra pair of hands that I needed. Try to be creative and you may be able to afford more help than you initially think.

Above all, as with any household help, keep the lines of communication flowing and keep everyone posted as to what emotional place your special needs child is in at any given time. A housecleaner who is aware that your child has less tolerance than most will be that much more aware of running the vacuum when he is in the room—a slight interruption for a typical child but, for a child who is sensitive to noise, one which can produce an unnecessary tantrum.

ANGELS — THE REAL McCOY'S

Call me nuts but I swear that I have seen a direct correlation between pumped up, S.O.S. prayer time and improvements in Jack. I've always been a big churchgoer during the week (well, especially when there were no children involved—these days my attendance record is pitiful). During some of my worst periods with Jack I'd go to 9 a.m. mass and just cry my eyes out. Help would come. I would have a good day or two with Jack. No miracle but enough to give me hope. Keep your eyes open and don't forget about the divine element.

Babysitting and Other Helping Hand *Strategies*

- **Contact employment agencies that have nurses and teachers in their network.**

Having someone already familiar with people who have special needs can be a great bonus.

- **Visit the local college career placement offices and its departments of education, psychology and nursing.**

Many times I had sent job ads to be posted but it wasn't until I visited the schools in person that the directors gave my need enough attention to get results.

- **Recruit special education aides within your school district and at local special education schools.**

While you probably cannot use the aides who are in your child's classroom, there may be other aides within the school building who would be happy to have a way to earn extra money. If none of these people are available, you might try asking someone at the department of special education if there is a listing of teachers in the district who have indicated interest in extra work. Finally, after the school year ends, the aides who have been with your child may be free agents, available for sitting.

- **Contact local hospitals and nursing homes for nurses and nurses' aides.**

Visiting pediatric wards and the employment center at your local hospital (and even pediatrician offices) may provide you with a nurse or nurse's aide who has an affinity for children with special needs.

• LOCAL AGENCIES MAY EXIST FOR FAMILIES WITH SPECIAL NEEDS CHILDREN.
I have a friend who has a wonderfully trained aide who provides regular respite care. Not only is the quality of the care wonderful, but my friend also qualifies for a financial subsidy so the help is very affordable.

• TELL MEMBERS OF YOUR CHILD'S TEAM OF PROFESSIONALS—SPEECH THERAPIST, OCCUPATIONAL THERAPIST, PHYSICAL THERAPIST, PSYCHOLOGIST, AND PSYCHIATRIST—ABOUT YOUR NEEDS.
These professionals see babysitters every day and may know which ones are looking for outside work. What's more, they will have had a good chance to eyeball the babysitter's interactions with children. You'll want to be very careful of protocol when finding babysitters who already have full-time assignments. If the employer allows outside employment, it would be courteous to first call the employer before contacting the sitter, to introduce yourself and share your timing needs and general assignment. You may want to take the opportunity to describe your children and the type of skills that you are seeking in a sitter; the employer may be able to give you a perspective on whether or not this person would be appropriate or not for your family.

• ONLY YOU KNOW WHICH PEOPLE WORKING FOR YOU ARE EQUIPPED TO BABY-SIT YOUR CHILD.
Asking the cleaning lady to baby-sit Jack while I run a quick errand is usually fine. However, it is not fair to her or Jack to put them in a situation that she can't manage.

SLEEPOVER CENTRAL
The Care and Keeping of Friends

I remember Jack's first playgroup. He was four months old. Of course there were older children there, the siblings, who were completely busy parallel playing, real playing, wandering, jumping, scooting, and plain old being busy toddlers. The first six months I would visit with the other moms while our babies progressed from gurgling to wiggling to crawling and finally joining their older sibs in some real moving and grooving.

Jack was extremely quiet and kept to himself from the get-go. In the early months he would lie complacently on his blanket. I thought this was because he was tired from having no sleep the night before (which was basically every night). But as the months rolled on and Jack had absolutely no interest in either exploring other children or playing with any toys that were placed in front of him, that nagging feeling from the first few days of his life came back to me.

Jack's disinterest in people, either of his age or otherwise, continued throughout his toddler years. Jack showed only slight interest even when his sister tried to play with him. In fact, the only people who got a reaction were me, John (and even so, much of the time it was only a slight reaction) and Margaret, the sitter that Jack adored. In fact, it wasn't until Jack's stay at the hospital, where he was absolutely forced to attend group meetings and participate in group activities, that he actually began to be interested in other people.

Jack had a roommate at the hospital. I had told the staff how poor Jack's sleeping habits were (i.e., that he basically only slept four hours each night and often wet the bed) and this staved off a roommate for the first six weeks. When Jack finally did get a roommate, he was a quiet boy of twelve who was very sweet to Jack, loaning him games and picture books. I really believe that having someone to share a cold room in a scary place where your parents couldn't be found, broke through to something in Jack. In fact, when the boy was discharged, Jack started asking when he could have his next sleepover guest. The idea of friendship had taken hold.

Jack made his first best friend soon after he left the hospital and began a therapeutic day school. Strangely enough, the boy, Brian, had been with Jack at the hospital. Only there, as Jack puts it, they had been rivals. He reminds me even today that he can't get over the fact that the boy who was his rival later became his best friend. I have responded to that by suggesting that with a changed perspective and flexible attitude perhaps more people who have supposed enemies could rediscover them as friends.

Like Jack, Brian had some very rough patches in his life and, like Jack, he showed those rougher edges from time to time. Yet, he and Jack accepted each other every which way, any day. The two were true friends. It also helped enormously that Brian's parents shared our parenting style and were as comfortable handling both boys as we were. In fact, the summer of third grade we began trying sleepovers. Once Jack and Brian got the first one under their belt, learning that staying up until 2 a.m. had consequences for how quickly they could have the next sleepover, they did a great job of being at each other's homes for a weekend.

About the time that this friendship began, we noticed that Jack had more confidence in himself and was more interested in what was going on around him. All of a sudden, the telephone's ring, which once had been an intrusion at best, held the possibility that Jack's friend could be at the other end. A Saturday and Sunday weren't just stretches of time to be filled; they held the opportunity of a play date. The nicest surprise was watching the boys move from a competition of who held the best Pokemon cards to the joy of helping the other person find cards that he didn't yet have. Not to say that Brian and Jack didn't have their share of disagreements. A play date wasn't complete unless one of them had a little meltdown—but they were getting easier. Both boys began to bloom.

With only a few children in his class and in a school that was forty-five minutes away from our home, Jack did not have much opportunity for school friendships. A friend of mine calls this predicament The Island Syndrome. This was a tough situation. Here was a child who needed social skills practice. But we didn't know many people to practice with. Jack was not interested in sports (or he was not confident playing team sports since his school didn't offer sports), so that was another avenue closed off for meeting and making friends. Our neighborhood didn't have sidewalks and the roads were windy—too dangerous for meeting kids in the neighborhood casually. For a number of years, John and I fretted about this situation, but we really didn't have any good solutions. Until I had a brainstorm when Jack entered third grade.

When Jack was in third grade, I began to look around for an older boy who could be a special friend to Jack. One of my friends had a twelve-year-old son, Julien. Julien was easy going, adventuresome, and socially astute. His mother and I knew a friendship between him and Jack would click or it wouldn't. I explained a little about Jack's condition to Julien but the bottom line was, they'd either have fun together or not. Luckily, they did. Julien now comes to hang out with Jack about once a week. The two can usually be found fishing, working on a science project, building a robot, adventuring or playing chess.

I knew that the boys had a true relationship the first week that Jack went to fourth grade. That summer, Jack had made the big move from tightie whities to boxer shorts. One day, I asked Sarah to run into the local clothing store to buy Jack an assortment of boxers while he and I ran to get a prescription filled at the drugstore. Sarah had assured Jack that since she was considering a career in fashion design, her selection of boxers would be a good demonstration of her innate talents. That night, as I laid out a suggested outfit for the next day, I added one of the new boxers—red boxers with orange polka dots. Jack was horrified. "What if my pants come down and everyone sees my shorts?" he cried, "I'll be humiliated."

I was pretty impressed that this child, who was not supposed to be so great at having feelings and knowing what is appropriate, could think through such a possibility. I managed to avoid a lengthy debate between the two children by suggesting that we call Julien, who was sure to know what's in and out in boxers.

Julien got quite a kick out of the call and (for those of you who are wondering) told Jack that the wilder the boxers, the cooler. Maybe Sarah does have a good instinct for fashion! We got quite a bit of mileage out of the phone call and you can guess what we got Julien for Christmas.

Some days Jack is connected and all works well with Julien. However, there are some days when Jack is too physical or too caught up in his Pokemon cards to offer much to Julien. Julien and I have a very good relationship. I try to keep an eye out for how taxing the day is for Julien. If I see Jack being particularly difficult, I suggest that Julien go home earlier than usual and we discuss what happened on the way home. One day that was going particularly well, Julien and Jack ended up pitching a tent and having a sleepover. The key with this kind of mentor relationship is finding the right child and staying tuned in during his visit in case your child is having a rough day.

Little by little Jack is picking up one friend here and one friend there. Our next door neighbors have a boy, Jason, who is just two years older than Jack. I knew that we had the potential for an unbelievable friendship when Jason told Jack, the avid fisherman, that ESPN has a great fishing show on television. This friendship provides me with frequent laughs, like the night the boys caught a fifteen inch bass in the neighbor's lake. There they were, dripping wet and tracking mud into our newly renovated house. The fish flopped around as the boys filled the kitchen sink so they could watch his last swim.

I suggested that Jason bring the fish back to his house so that his mom could filet it, but she had beaten me to the punch. Jason looked at me with his famous twinkle and said, "But that's why we're here. She said the same about you."

I proposed (since both dads were still working) that the boys try to find a neighbor who could do the honors. They agreed that Jack would bike around looking for a good-hearted soul and Jason would guard the fish. Thirty minutes later Jack wheeled back in, excited that the new neighbor who owned the lake where the fish was caught would do the honors. We arrived at the house of a willing soul who was only aghast for a minute when she learned that the fish was still flipping around. As the boys helped, she taught them how to skin a fish.

Near 9:30 p.m. Jason and Jack wore me down and I agreed to a late night fish fry. Actually, they were calling it a midnight snack. I don't know what made us laugh more—seeing the surprise of the neighbor when we displayed the very fresh fish, or watching Sarah scream at the top of her lungs as the boys presented her with a fish head (and tail) when she arrived in the kitchen. You can bet that we delivered some freshly baked chocolate chip cookies soon after to that kind neighbor—it's never too early to take advantage of an opportunity to teach Jack ways to be kind to others and to say thank you.

Social skills are one of the toughest things for Jack to master. His heart is in the right place but he has no clue how to go about the social process. Recently, our ninety-four year-old neighbor passed away. Sarah had the wonderful idea of inviting her daughter, Maria, over to our home for chocolate chip cookies on one of the first nights after Maria arrived from Chicago. I briefed the children and Jack's friend, Jason, on what to say when they saw Maria. They were to tell her that they were sorry that her mother had died.

The doorbell rang. Although a little loud, Jack yelled down the stairs the minute I opened the door, "Sorry that your mother died!" A few seconds later Jason appeared from upstairs and sweetly offered his condolences. As an exclamation point to Jason's offering, Jack brought up the rear, sliding down the banister. Dumped at the feet of Maria, he offered the same and proceeded to put on a pillow juggling show. Later that evening I asked Jack why he was so pepped up when we wanted to provide Maria with a little peace. He replied, "Gee, Mom, I was just trying to cheer her up." Perhaps his first step is to be interested and make an effort in relating. The next step will be the how. It's all a process.

PETS AS FRIENDS

One of my degrees is in nursing home administration. We have known for a long time that pets can influence the mood and well-being of the elderly. I think that the same is true for developmentally challenged children. Where else can you find someone that will tolerate crowding of their personal space and a few too many well-intentioned hugs, and put up with more than their fair share of silly games? That unconditional love of a dog, cat or other furry critter just can't be beat. I always thought that a pet would give Jack an opportunity to have a good friend. Maybe an uncomplicated, unemotional, pretty predictable pet would be able to meet Jack on his very basic emotional level. So, when Jack was four we got a rabbit. Not such a good choice of pet at this stage. Jack's hugs were a little too enthusiastic and too frequent. That poor rabbit got little rest. For the sake of Rosebud the Rabbit, we gave her away and waited until Jack had a little more self-control.

When Jack was eight, I looked around for an easy-going, full-grown dog to join our family. I knew that I could not manage the demands of a puppy, with all that I was dealing with. I began to ask people if they knew of anyone who had a young Labrador retriever for sale. This was the type of dog that we had decided we wanted.

One day, I was meeting with a homeopath. There at her feet was a calm, sweet yellow Lab. I mentioned that we were looking for a dog like hers. Bonnie said that as a matter-of-fact she was moving and could not bring her three year old dog, Gildy. Maybe this was meant to be.

For the next few months, we babysat Gildy on weekends. We wanted to see if she would fit in with the family. For us, she was the right kind of dog. Active outside, she chased tennis balls. For hours, Jack would throw the tennis ball and Gildy would hunt it down and bring it back. Inside, she could hang with the best of the couch potatoes.

Gildy became part of our family. Jack had a buddy to join him at the stream. The problem for me, and I must admit it was me alone, was that Gildy would go from the muddy stream to the house, only to be cleaned up and then bound back to test out the pool—and back in the house again. Between my animal allergies (which were in high gear) and the mess that water dog was creating all day long, I eventually knew that it was me or Gildy. One of us had to go.

We found Gildy a wonderful home on twelve country acres with two other dogs, and got the children pets that were more manageable for me—a gecko and a kitten.

Children can learn great lessons through pets. Jack and Sarah have had to take on the responsibility for the care of their pets, they are learning what commitment means, and best of all, they have someone who loves them unconditionally. These are lessons that no kind of behavior management could teach Jack.

The trick here is to figure out what kind of a pet is right for your family, before you go to the pet store or say "yes" to a pet. Try to think about things like: 1) What level of maintenance are you willing to put in to caring for the pet? 2) Are allergies an issue? 3) What kinds of pets can your children safely handle? And remember, the bottom line is that no matter what the children say, you will probably end up being the one who walks the dog.

FRIENDSHIP

 *Strategies*

- FIGURE OUT WHAT TYPE OF CHILD HAS THE BEST PERSONALITY FIT WITH YOUR CHILD.
For years we thought that an active child would be the best match for Jack.
Nope. The two would get each other hyped up and start spinning out of
control. Best is the child who is calm and on the mature side. Jack seems to
rise to that level.

- SET PLAY DATES UP FOR SUCCESS.
Keep the play date structured and supervised. Create a home that children will
want to visit by having fun things to do and yummy (but healthy) snacks. I
keep a few science and art projects on hand just for the play dates that need a
little extra zip.

- CONSIDER FINDING AN OLDER CHILD TO MENTOR YOUR CHILD.
Older children (in the big brother or sister vein) can be wonderful role models.
Ask your friends if they have a child who might want to make some extra
money and play this role, call the high school student employment office or
organizations like The Boys and Girls Club or YMCA.

- BE CREATIVE IN YOUR SEARCH FOR FRIENDS.
Look around your town and neighborhood to find places where kids hang out,
such as indoor roller rinks or parks. We used to go to the local playground
every weekend—it was an instant play date.

- HELP YOUR CHILD CONNECT WITH A CHILD THAT HE LIKES.
Initiate a phone call or offer to take your child and a friend on an outing, like a movie.

- DON'T BE A THIRD WHEEL.
Do keep an ear tuned for potential problems, but don't be the over-the-

shoulder third wheel. No child is going to feel comfortable or free to have a typical play date with a parent lurking in the background.

• BE PATIENT.
There are bound to be a few disasters. A bad play date doesn't necessarily mean that the relationship isn't a good one to work at.

• ERR ON THE SIDE OF A PLAY DATE BEING TOO SHORT.
I live by the adage, "Go while they're still asking for more." Better to leave when they are still clamoring for more time than when one or both is melting down.

• TRY TO DO A FEW THINGS IN THE COMMUNITY WITH YOUR CHILD.
Your child will begin to feel comfortable in the community by being a part of it.

• SEE WHAT YOUR CHURCH OFFERS FOR YOUTH GROUP ACTIVITIES.
Your church may have a youth choir or young people's group that your child can join. You should talk to whoever is in charge about the needs of your child and check back after the first week or two to see if it is working out. You don't ever want to put an unfair burden on a group or have your child not add to the group in a positive way.

VII. STAYING IN BALANCE

SCRAMBLED EGGS

THE STICKER SHIRT TURN-AROUND

SCRAMBLED EGGS
Attitude Precedes Action

There is absolutely no way around it. Having a special needs child in the family requires an enormous amount of energy, resilience, patience and flexibility from every other family member. From the first diagnosis to every day thereafter, your lives will be more complicated in numerous ways, from a demanding therapy schedule to added confusion at home. With a child who has social issues there will be an above average number of sibling squabbles and parent-child confrontations. The list of complications will change depending upon the age and stage but there will always be a list. It is critical to have a game plan in terms of how to manage the therapies and programs that your exceptional child will need. And having a plan for helping the family adjust to the added work and stress of the situation is a must.

The most important thing that John and I did was to get into Jack's world. We couldn't possibly help him negotiate our world if we didn't first understand where he was coming from and what his world looked like. I had to learn to put aside not just my own needs at the moment but also my preconceived ideas of what should be. Flexibility and creative solutions were the order of the day, as my lesson with scrambled eggs at 2 a.m. taught me.

When Jack was three years old, his speech pathologist told me he had mentioned that his favorite time of the day was when he ate scrambled eggs with Mom in the middle of the night. We were often up in the middle of the night because he had a sleep disorder. He fell asleep close to 11:00 p.m. or so each night, only to wake at 2:00 a.m. to start the next day. When he woke up he was famished. For months we had the same routine: Wake up at 2:00 a.m.

and make four scrambled eggs and four sausages. If I wanted to connect with Jack, that was the time of day to do it.

So, I trained myself to change my 2 a.m. attitude. At that time of his life the windows to Jack's social self were usually open just enough for him to get what he wanted, rather than to let the breath of friendship blow in and touch him. If 2 a.m. was where the wind was blowing me, I leaned on the Lord to give me the energy-- and matched my bedtime to the children's-- and did the best breakfasting that I could with Jack in the wee hours of the morning.

This story might suggest that you should work your schedule and family format around the needs and abilities of your child. I don't think it's that cut and dry. If you adapt to the child, and make everyone in the family do the same, you are actually reinforcing the child's limitations and not helping him learn how to adapt to the world. We are always very clear as to what the goal, the ideal situation, is. But we also try to figure out what Jack is seeing, feeling and interpreting. Then, we develop a plan of baby steps to help him build a bridge from his world to ours.

Before doing anything, however, I try to understand Jack's limitations. I now know what pushes Jack beyond what he can manage or even stretch to. Then I develop a plan to work gradually towards where I want him to be. In my scrambled eggs issue, I acknowledged that Jack had a real sleep disorder that he couldn't control. Years of battling him to bed where we would both end up exhausted and crying proved that trying to force him to sleep was ineffective. With so many other issues going on, the doctors and I weren't ready to tackle the sleep dilemma yet.

So, knowing that the sleep problem was not going to be one that could be solved through behavior management, I focused on the part of the 2:00 a.m. experience that I could work on: Jack's non-relating to others. Preparing a moonlight breakfast together would be our way to connect. From Jack's comment to his speech pathologist, the plan worked.

Try to be flexible, but keep your priorities in sight. Think of ways that you can adjust your life in a way that meets the unchangeable demands of your special child but *always, always* work toward what your ideal situation would be. In the short run I went to bed when the children did so that I would be able to deal with the early morning breakfast that gave me a chance to connect with my child.

Strategies FOR SETTING PRIORITIES

• TRY TO SEE YOUR CHILD'S WORLD THROUGH HIS EYES.

If you don't know what he can handle, what sets him off, what is safe for him and what opens a window to connect, you won't be able to develop an effective plan for your child.

• THINK OUTSIDE THE BOX.

Don't worry about what should be. You have a unique situation which calls for unique solutions.

• BE AVAILABLE TO YOUR CHILD.

You never know when your child is ready to take a step forward; be willing and able to be by his side—even if it's 2 a.m.

• HAVE A GOAL IN MIND.

Even if you can't get to it for awhile, knowing where you want your child to be will allow you to make a plan to get there. There is an old proverb that says, "If the mountain will not turn, I must be the road and do the turning myself."

THE STICKER SHIRT
TURN-AROUND
Using Behavior Management to Change Behavior

John and I never really thought that Jack had much of a sense of self-esteem. It seemed to us that in order to have self-esteem, you first needed to have a sense of yourself. Much of the time, particularly when he was under seven, Jack just seemed to be. He was not really conscious of anything or anyone around him and certainly not tuned into himself. Since we thought that Jack was pretty unaware of himself, we never really *worried* about his self-esteem, despite the enormous number of "no's" that Jack chalked up everyday at home, and almost anywhere else that he went.

That is, until the day when Jack began to say that he didn't like himself and, come to think of it, he wished he were dead. He was four years old. What a way to find out that the child did, in fact, have some sort of sense of his self. Unfortunately, the sense he had was one of worthlessness. This message came on so strong and so vocal that I knew we needed to do something to change our whole tenor towards Jack.

I made a plan. For one solid day, I worked hard to catch Jack doing things right. I went for the big things and I went for the very, very small things. Everytime that I gave Jack praise, "That was a nice job sitting down at the table, Jack," I would accompany the verbal praise with a sticker, slapped right on the front of his shirt.

I stuck by his side and looked for any little excuse to pop a sticker on his shirt. By the end of the day, there were more stickers showing than shirt. Funny as it seems, that day, the day of the sticker shirt, was a turn-around day for Jack.

Not a big turn around, but a little curve in his journey. Jack had done a few things well, and it showed. He was proud of his accomplishment—so proud that the shirt stayed on for a solid twenty-four hours.

Even today, my philosophy is to try to catch Jack in the act of doing something good. I figure that in a world where competition is a part of everything, home should be the place not only where you are loved unconditionally, but where you are valued. And that value needs to be felt in as many ways as possible.

At the time of the sticker shirt strategy, Jack's whole world consisted of John, Sarah, our babysitter, and me. This was the time when Jack had left the Montessori school and we were in the midst of a full evaluation. Jack's good feelings about himself had to come from this very tiny world in which he was newly operating—the immediate family plus a babysitter. Thank goodness Margaret was a natural cheerleader and could keep the cheers going throughout the day. Having people around him who loved him, obviously and unconditionally, and who validated who he was, played a critical part in helping Jack to build and sustain a foundation of self-worth. While we knew how important this process was, it was absolutely exhausting and emotionally draining for us, as the parents, to be as patient and understanding as was necessary.

During the sticker shirt period and first turn-around for Jack, there was a turn-around in John's and my attitude towards him. It is very easy to get into a nagging or a yelling streak. For me, it starts gradually and then builds, until even John notices that I am not the most pleasant to be around. As easy as it is to start, I find I can break the streak with the same focus and concentration that any behavior chart requires.

In fact, during one of my streaks Jack and Sarah put me on a behavior chart. We had it taped to the refrigerator alongside their charts. Jack was seven at the time and had finally gotten comfortable with the Point Sheet system at school. I was under the same plan. I started out every period of the day with 100 points and lost points for raising my voice and/or yelling. I also lost points if I didn't take the time to discuss whatever problem was at hand.

It took just a couple of days for me to change my tune and maintain most of my points each day. I must say, competing against a bunch of numbers is motivating for some strange reason. It really was the numbers, not the quarters that I would have to shell out if I blew my goal for the day, which got me motivated and taught me how to handle impatience without yelling.

Jack was equally tiring for John during these years. John has a great deal of fun in him and will happily rough house with Jack and spend hours in water gun wars. However, every grown-up has his or her limit. And unfortunately, with his inability to read social cues, Jack can't tell when John has had enough play for the day, and he can't recalibrate his system to tone back down. It is not unusual for John, like me, to start off with a good ten minutes of patient "Game's over, time to calm down," only to disintegrate into, "That's ENOUGH now, Jack!" Once we lose control, Jack loses control and all the investment we have put into building his foundation of self-esteem is instantly blown apart. It has taken both John and me a few years to learn how to control ourselves and manage the situation so that our hard work remains intact.

When he was five, six and seven, Jack could easily crumble and resort to running to his bedroom and taking everything out of the drawers, or locking himself in the bathroom. It was worth every bit of energy that we had not to let Jack get to the point where he couldn't control himself. We knew that he felt badly about how he'd behaved and what he'd done. These incidents added to his not-so-good feeling about himself. They became part of the videotape that he looked at when he defined himself.

The bottom line in telling you so many horror stories in a chapter on self-esteem is to say that when your child is having a really, really bad period it may be that the medication is off, the neurology is changing, or something else is going on. But it may be that there is some situational difficulty that is creating so much anxiety, angst or anger that your child's self-esteem is tanking. If it is important to heap compliments and focus on building self-esteem in the quiet periods, it is one hundred times more important to do the same during the hairy periods. Don't let it all just spiral down.

Even with all that we were trying to do at home, the next significant boost that we saw in Jack's opinion of himself didn't come from within our four walls. It came when he began to develop friends. I read somewhere that if you have seven good friends, not including those people that you are related to, you have a good chance of having a fulfilled life. The concept seems to make some sense.

School is a place where Jack's self-esteem can go way up or way down. I've noticed a pattern: when school is going well for Jack, he feels good about himself. He shows this not only in his relaxed manner and mood, but also in what he does. He is more willing to try new things and make new friends. I will never forget a phone call at 1 p.m. one Wednesday from Mr. Grasso, the vice principal of the elementary school where Jack was attending first grade. Mr. Grasso wanted to share with me that he had just seen Jack playing basketball with a group of other boys. What an improvement, he reminded me, over the days when Jack spent the entire thirty-five minutes of recess catching bugs and butterflies alone.

We try to take advantage of good periods, periods where school is really going well, to take some safe risks. We try to expand Jack's world with experiences that might help him continue to grow. The first sign that things are not going so well in school is Jack's retreat into anything electronic (television or Gameboy) and his frequent growling "Leave me alone!" to any of us who try to talk to him. In our worst years, he had no sense of safety and would often run out of the house and wander into a nearby forest to vent his frustration. In retrospect, during the times in school when things were going poorly—shown through a nosedive in behavior and using self-disparaging talk—we should have seen the red flag. John and I should not have been so patient, willing to try just a pinch of this or a little of that, as the school suggested. We should have tried to counterbalance what was going on at school with a full-court press of support and an overarching effort at home to pump up Jack's self-worth. At the same time, we should have pushed the school to help us sort out what we needed to change.

All in all, self-esteem is a slippery thing for Jack and probably always will be. The other night, I asked Jack to excuse himself from the table after dinner and to put his plate in the dishwasher.   Now, Jack has seen many, many old-fashioned cartoons and while they are much less harmful than a lot of what is available on television today, there are some dangers for a kid like Jack. One of his difficulties is distinguishing what is cartoon and should remain so, and what is okay in real life. This particular night I could almost see the scene from a cartoon where the man slides his glass down the long bar run for a refill. That's exactly what Jack imitated. The plate came towards me across the slick countertop of the island, only it didn't neatly stop just at the edge, as I'm sure it did in the cartoon. Swoosh, drop, plop, crash! The plate slid right into home base and shattered in a million (or maybe half a million) pieces.

Jack looked at me quickly and said, "Are you mad at me? Are you going to ground me?" I don't think I've ever grounded him (in part because, what would I ground him from?) but he always asks that same question when he breaks something. I was careful to take my time and explain that unless there is a raised edge at the end of a counter, things that slide across the smooth surface are, most likely, going to fall off the other side.

I asked Jack to help me clean up the mess and as we were doing so he said, "I bet you think I'm stupid now, don't you?" This was surprising as I had been very matter-of-fact in the clean up and the discussion about why the plate slide was not a good idea. The exchange did remind me that the slightest thing, if not handled right, could hit him right at his core. It comes as easily as it goes.

One summer day, John and Jack spent a day hunting tuna on Long Island Sound.   The day had been enormously successful from a father-son perspective. It didn't hurt that they had landed a few juicy fish.

As they were packing up on the marina, Jack spotted a particular fishing net for sale that he'd been looking all over for. We were leaving for Georgia in just a couple of weeks and he knew this net would be perfect for crabbing. Unfortunately, Jack didn't explain to John how long he had searched for this particular net and how important it was to him.   All John saw was an impractical, large item and what seemed to be a silly whim. So he didn't buy it.

To Jack's credit, he didn't absolutely fall apart (as he would have in the old days). He just repeated again and again, "I want the net."

I arrived home after the boys did, only to find Jack sitting cross-legged on the ground in the driveway, blocking a delivery truck that was trying to leave.

"Why are you doing this?" I asked.

Jack said, "This is how the kids at camp would handle the situation."

"Well Jack, these are kids with special needs. Don't follow their example."

To which he replied, "Well, why am I at the camp?"

I always wondered when and how I would explain Jack's disorder to him. Here was my opening. I wanted him to understand the basics in a way that made him feel highly valued, yet I didn't want to sugar-coat the fact that he had a little bit of work ahead.

Jack and I talked about how the world successfully functions—working alone and working in groups. I praised Jack for how well he worked alone and focused him on the need to be able to work well with others in a group. He was open and available on this particular day for such a discussion. So I seized the opportunity to have it.

Dr. Tony Attwood, author of the book, *Asperger's Syndrome,* adds a sixth sense, which he calls the social sense, to the other five. He suggests an exercise for children to explain what Asperger's Syndrome is. I've used this with Jack. It can be used for any disorder where a child has difficulty with social skills.

I blindfolded Jack and asked him to feel what it would be like if he couldn't see. Then I had him block his ears to experience what it felt like not to be able to hear. After we went through each of the senses I explained to Jack that if someone doesn't know how to act with others, that's not having a social sense. We then talked about how Jack can *learn* to develop this missing sense. I use many of the strategies in Dr. Attwood's book, either directly or indirectly, to help Jack develop this sense.

I see a direct relationship between strong social skills and good self-esteem in youngsters (and probably at any age). When the children have friends who treat them nicely and are good friends to them, they feel good about themselves. I can see it in little actions and big actions.

Self-Esteem Building

 *Strategies*

• **Make sure that your child has more positive experiences than negative experiences, so he feels that he is doing a good job managing himself.**
If you can help orchestrate a few good experiences to counteract a few not so good ones, you can tip the scales on the kind of day your child will have and perhaps remember. With Jack, it seems that meltdown begets meltdown and then we have a complete unraveling. Similarly, one little success builds upon another and soon we are going from half an hour of pleasantry to a little longer. Remember, it's the baby steps that lead to a long journey.

• **School can have a tremendous impact on self-esteem.**
Don't underestimate the impact that school and school friendships can have on your child. Stay involved and keep communicating with the teacher.

• **Try to find a hobby or area of interest where your child can develop an expertise.**
For years I tortured myself trying to get Jack interested in what I wanted him to be interested in—you know, the things in which every kid is supposed to participate in your town. Once we got over that mindset and encouraged the things he naturally gravitated to, we had more opportunities for positive experiences.

• **Be generous with your compliments and praises.**
We are really obvious and specific in our praise of Jack. We also have some well-worn phrases. In fact, when John asks Jack one of his favorite questions, "Jack, do you know how much I love you?" Jack says, almost in a monotone, "Yes, Dad. You tell me all the time. A whole bunch." He might act like he's hearing a broken record but we know he's humming the tune.

• PUT BOOKS OF HEROES—GREAT AND SMALL—INTO YOUR CHILD'S HANDS.

Or better yet, read him the stories. Stories of men and women who have done marvelous things inspire all of us. These stories can plant seeds of inspiration in children who have no strong internal moral or social compass. When Jack was five, he read the Children's Bible over and over again at bedtime, for nearly six months straight. During that time, whenever incidents occurred, Jack would refer back to one of the biblical stories, looking there for ways to handle the problem.

• PUT PEOPLE IN YOUR CHILD'S PATH WHO HE ENJOYS AND WHO MAKE HIM FEEL GOOD ABOUT HIMSELF.

We watched Jack participate in the same activity with two different teachers—one patient, one not. The difference in Jack 's attitude was remarkable. It is important to surround your child with people who make him feel good about himself.

VIII. It's What's Inside That Counts

A Road Map of Life

Seize the Moment

Black, White or Shades of Grey?

Keeping the Faith

A Road Map of Life
Thirteen Ways To Bring Out The Best
In Your Child

One of the scariest things that I do to myself is to try to imagine where Jack will be when he is twenty-three, thirty-three, and forty-three years old. If you let your mind go full throttle, you can drive yourself nuts. As easily as I can picture Jack in some university setting, holed up in a science laboratory studying a molecular structure, I can also let my mind create an image of some awful hole-in-the-wall town, influenced by shady characters, making prey of people like Jack.

I worry for both of our children in a number of ways. Of course, it is easy to imagine what kind of seriously dangerous things they might run across—violence, date rape, sexual promiscuity, addictions, and AIDS are all there. The world is a much scarier place today than when we were kids. The statistics show it, the media flashes it, and you can sense it. But then there are the less obvious threats—an inability to hold a responsible job, a sense of purposelessness, loneliness, selfishness, isolation, and self-centeredness come to mind immediately. While it sounds like a cliché, the more I listen and watch today's youth it seems to fit—the "me" generation seems to have returned. I hear it in Sarah's conversations with her friends as they discuss their next trip to the mall and I see it in how they choose to spend their free time. Whether it's the media, the latchkey kid syndrome, too much disposable income, not enough disposable income, or something else is irrelevant to our own immediate family. My concern is how to counterbalance the forces of society that influence our two children.

I must admit that in the last year I have become obsessed with this concern. I'm scared that we've made life too automatic for Jack and Sarah. John and I have unwittingly—in an effort to be better and more efficient parents—made family life hum along in a way that seems effortless. With computers, cell phones, palm pilots, voice mail, automatic dishwashers, garbage disposals, car washes, microwave meals, frozen meals, and wash and wear, we've managed to reduce everyone's workload so that things run faster and more smoothly. After all, isn't that what life is about? We've also reduced interaction with each other. Why meet someone for coffee when you can talk on the phone? Why talk on the phone when you can leave a message on the answering machine? Why leave a message when you can shoot a quick e-mail? If I'm not careful, I can spend my whole day not talking to any real person but spending a lot of time in front of a computer and clicking the button of lots of different things. What I've noticed over the past few years is that it's easy to lose the art of connecting to people.

I recently had lunch with a college friend whom I haven't seen in many years. She asked me if I spoiled my husband and children. Not spoiled in the sense of giving them many things, but by giving them my emotional time. This is what she remembered as one of my greatest gifts. She recalled that I was always willing to give my time and emotional energy to others. I can't tell you how awful that sinking feeling in the pit of my stomach felt. No. I don't think I spoil them with my emotional attention. And I don't think that I give the way I did in college—baking cookies or dropping off a little package of Hershey kisses for friends who were having a bad day or needed a lift. Nope. I sure am busy though. Can I tell you how many things I checked off my To Do list today?

Funny enough, just in the past year, as things have settled down a little with Jack, I've begun thinking about how I interact with others during the day. I must admit, being a list person, I still carry a daily list with me. But I am trying to put the list aside when I'm involved in each task. I'm trying to spend a minute or two, asking the counter person at the dry cleaner, "How are you today?" and really listening to the answer. I'm trying to put human touch back into my day. And the same with my family. Rather than let Jack and Sarah watch their hour of daily television (something I still kick myself for allowing back in the schedule), I am trying to pull them away and devote thirty minutes to each of them when I sit on their beds and get to know them. A friend of mine says her youth pastor calls it dating your child. I like that. I've been a big believer, the entirety of our fifteen years of marriage, in a weekly date night, but I've never thought about that in terms of children.

So back to my big worries. What can I do as Jack's and Sarah's mom, the person with the most everyday contact and probably the most influence on these two children, to ensure that they will be responsible, capable people and that they will be loving, giving individuals? I've come up with *Thirteen Habits That I Hope My Kids Leave Home With.* See if you agree with them.

1. ENCOURAGE THE SPIRITUAL LIFE IN YOUR CHILD.
Thirty or forty five minutes a week at a church school or service is not going to set spiritual habits in place. Spiritual habits begin at home.

2. GIVE CHILDREN LOTS OF OPPORTUNITY TO PRACTICE HOME SKILLS.
It has taken years for Jack to get into a regular routine of getting up in the morning and making his bed—and if I'm not in the hallway hanging out, the likelihood of the bed being made is still pretty low. (His latest rationalization was, "Why should I make the bed when I'm just going to get into it again tonight?") The old saying that it's easier to just do the chore yourself than have your child do it is sure true and a natural instinct in a world where you are rewarded more and more for speed. But it doesn't do anything to help children learn responsibility around the house.

I remember as a child that an unquestioned part of my Saturday routine was cleaning the bathrooms in our house—not an envied job with two boys in the family. Having the kids set the table, help with the dishes and assist me cook not only teaches them how dinner gets done in a family but gives us a time to chit-chat.

We recently bought a small boat so that John and Jack could take their fishing passion to a new level. The day that we bought the boat we brought the children and one of Sarah's friends down to the dock. It's an older boat and needed a day of cleaning and scrubbing. I pointed out a chore to Sarah and her friend and asked them to pitch in. The little girl said, "But in our house we have other people do work like this." I told her, "We don't have that help and besides, this is what a family does."

Maybe I'm just stupid but if you have someone else doing all of this work, what do you do with each other? Just play and have good times? Seems a little superficial to me. At ages ten and nine the children were responsible for making their beds and setting the dinner table and helping with clean up. Not only are these good life skills, practicing them means spending time together.

3. LEARN HOW TO HANDLE MONEY RESPONSIBLY.

With Jack's need for the here and how and impulsive tendencies, managing money responsibly could be a big issue. Part of our philosophy in giving Jack an allowance is to let him experience the impact of some poor financial decisions in a safe environment. We talk about money in our home. We talk about what is smart spending and what is not. What is unnecessary spending and what is not? I've developed a personal rule the last few years that really helps me think about things. "If something comes in, then something has to go out." If I bring home a new piece of clothing then I need to take one out of my closet and give it away. The same with toys. The kids don't even play with what they have, so why do they need more? This general guideline has been helpful to me. We also have the children give a portion of their allowance to the church and the less fortunate. At our church, the children have become part of the tithing process, and are asked to give a portion of their allowance to support a child in a less fortunate country.

4. USE FREE TIME IN A HEALTHY WAY.

There was a time when Jack would have played Gameboy in every free moment if I had allowed it. Enjoying a bike ride or nature walk or being able to pick up a book at a moment's notice are all things that I try to encourage. Anything outside gets a huge thumbs up. I try to encourage interests that can be done anywhere and anytime, such as reading and hiking.

5. Cultivate hobbies and interests.

Having a passion (or two or three) is a gift. I get hours of pleasure out of playing the piano, hitting a tennis ball, and reading. I try to tune into sparks of interest that I see in Jack and then put people and resources in his way to support their growth. I also try to expose the children to a range of arts, sports and other interests. I try to pair something cultural with something fun.

John and I took the children into the city recently to see a revival of the classical musical, *The Music Man.* I promised them a pre-show dinner at an old-fashioned ice cream parlor that has stacks of unusual toys out front. Jack literally got down on one knee begging me for a lollipop toy that claimed to play music in your head (how safe does that sound?). In front of a line of people that stretched out to the street I had to repeat "no" again and again. When we got out the door, Jack made one last pitch, "I'll give up my Gameboy for a month," he promised.

"Mommy that's worth it!" said Sarah, as weary of seeing Jack's head bent over the electronic game as I was. I marched back into the restaurant, plunked my fifteen dollars down, and, embarrassed that the queue of people would think here was another weak parent giving in, I explained Jack's offer. Without the Gameboy around, Jack has been reading more, riding his bike and searching out friends—a good investment of fifteen dollars.

6. Make good manners a natural part of who the children are.

I love to tell the children the story about how my mother would line up four little mirrors in front of our dinner plates once a week so that we could watch ourselves eat. Seeing yourself during dinner sure was a fast way to clean up sloppy manners. For a child like Jack, this is no easy feat. It's taken me two years just to have him follow my direction to put your napkin on your lap and say grace before eating.

From manners and etiquette to basic social skills, things have to be explained more often and more simply, and practiced forty times as much. I try to concoct ways of practicing these things at home, where the embarrassment factor is lowest and it's a safe place to fail. I also try to keep the lesson fun but make sure the message is heard. Manners and social skills are among the hardest things to teach exceptional children because they don't pick any of them up on their own. Being specific about what manners you are looking for, along with consistent repetition, will make a dent.

7. TEACH CHILDREN BASIC TIME MANAGEMENT AND A RESPECT FOR TIME.

The only unlimited resource that we have is our time. When you are young that's what time feels like. It is only in the last few years that I have begun to see the finality of time and to regard each day as a gift. I have been really looking at my time to see what I do with it and then challenging myself, was it time well spent? I am extremely conscious of using time wisely and efficiently. We are big schedulers in our family—we have to be with the lengthy transitions Jack requires. On the refrigerator I have posted the after school schedule:

> 4:30 Homework
> 5:30 Dinner
> 6:00 Bath
> 6:30 Free Time
> 8:30 Bed

We are not always able to follow this schedule but it's a goal. The first week of school everyone complained but complied about fifty percent. We got a rhythm down, after school activities kicked in, and there John and I were again, trying to hold the line while the hours slipped away. When this happens, I all too easily fall back into my nagging-yelling mode: "Get to bed, *Get to bed, **Get to bed,** **GET TO BED!**"* And still the children dabble and procrastinate. Unless the two are detained because they are involved in some project together (when we let bedtime slide a bit for the gain in growing together as a family), we try to stick to the schedule.

8. ENCOURAGE HEALTHY LIVING HABITS AND PERSONAL CARE.

A healthy diet, exercise and the proper amount of sleep not only make good sense, they keep kids healthy. I'm not a fanatic about eliminating sweets but I am big on a well-balanced diet. When the children were six and seven years old we talked about the food pyramid and looked at how we eat at home. I am a big believer in a varied diet, and also follow the thinking of the omega 3 fatty acids concept. We eat lots of fish, fruit, vegetables and chicken and limit breads and sweets.

9. TEACH YOUR CHILDREN TO FIND THE JOY IN BIG AND SMALL THINGS.

Did you ever notice how some people are consistently upbeat and positive in their approach to life while others seem worn down or numb? I am always amazed at how much the rest of the family takes their cue from my tone and attitude. When the children were quite young we took a vacation to a quiet, remote island. The pace of the island was completely different from our East Coast life. Everything from conversation to buses moved slowly, rhythmically. Errands weren't just things to be checked off of a list, they were opportunities for interaction. I try to remember this attitude towards life. Because of my background in nursing homes, I am always aware of the finality of life. I try to teach the children to appreciate all things in every day, and to share what they have and their joy of life with others.

10. YOUR CHILDREN LEARN THE DEFINITION OF FAMILY THROUGH THE FAMILY THAT YOU CREATE.

Did you ever notice how we sometimes are the grumpiest with the people that we love the most? Or that these are the people we have the least patience with at times? Jack doesn't develop attachments to people like most kids do. Everything needs to be magnified and more obvious than what is typically required. When we make corrections or give Jack a negative consequence, we have to tell him again and again that we still love and value him, it's just the behavior that we don't approve of. Our actions and our words are what Jack experiences as a family. We have gone through a lot of counseling and changes in our style so that we can do things and go places as a family.

11. HELP YOUR CHILD TO BUILD A CORE GROUP OF FRIENDS.

Friends are a mirror of yourself. They bring happiness and laughter, and challenge you to stretch. Once Jack had one true friend, it seemed that he found a whole new joy in life and enjoyment of his own life.

12. Teach moderation in all things.

There was a time when Jack would wolf down six desserts before I could intervene. If a little was good, a lot must be better. That was his motto. This could be dangerous later, with all the temptations that strike in the teenage years. Frequent discussions and limit-setting have helped Jack begin to learn that sometimes less is more.

13. Be aware of the less fortunate.

In our house, many decisions and discussions already center upon Jack. It is very easy for special needs children, already self-absorbed, to become more so. Although he is sometimes reluctant, I try to involve Jack in small acts of kindness to those who are less fortunate. These are tangible acts, like bringing flowers to our ninety four year old neighbor, or selecting a toy for an underprivileged child at Christmas. Even if it doesn't go over well, continue to make an effort—the message will get through.

Seize the Moment
Recognize Opportunities To Teach And Train

This morning I was preparing the bathtub water for Jack to take a quick dunk before camp. When he stepped into what (I trust you) was lukewarm water, he pulled his toes right back out of the water proclaiming, "That water is too hot!"

Without a second's hesitation I corrected him, "No, it's not."

Jack looked me squarely in the eye and said, "It might be cold to you but it's hot to me."

Perspective. When I remember to understand Jack's (and Sarah's and John's) perspective, the whole world looks different. If I stick with my own perspective, I move into a hyper-control mode, with a whole list of expectations and should be's. These are not only completely unrealistic in this family of strong wills and distinct opinions, they also do nothing to help the children learn how to make good decisions and develop as capable, independent people.

For us, getting rid of the specific mold that we want the children to fit into doesn't mean that we have no expectations. We definitely do have expectations and are not willing to compromise them because of Jack's disability. But what I try very hard to do is to seize the teachable moment.

Here's what I mean.

John had wanted a boat for as long as I can remember. He adores the water and is passionate about fishing. We have always seen John and Jack's common fishing interest as a jumping off point for deepening their relationship.

When Jack was younger and not as rational, his behavior was way too dangerous and unpredictable for us to even consider navigating the water. Finally, this summer, we decided he was ready. John and I spent a lot of the summer talking about and looking at boats. We traveled to several states to look at them and see how they handled. To his credit, John got himself on a very steep learning curve and finally found the perfect boat for our family. It had a great fishing format and not too uncomfortable for the girls in the family (who have little interest in catching a big one). It was called *Knot A Problem*.

John spent his first several weeks as a boat owner working on the boat; not even going out on the boat but just working on it. He had men teach him how it operated and how to drive it. He got his boat safety license. And he spent a lot of time talking to the people who ran the marina.

The big day finally arrived. John and Jack were set to go for their first trip. It would be just a short one in Long Island Sound because we had a party to go to at 5 p.m.

Sarah and I left for the party promptly at 5 p.m., knowing that the boys of our family might not have a good sense of time on their first trip. 5:30 came and went, 6:00, 6:30, 7:00 and finally at 7:30, the telephone rang. It was John. The boys had had a tremendous time. They weren't, in fact, stranded on some island as I had begun to imagine. They had gone to Martha's Vineyard and back! What a hit the day had been!

Charged up and ready for more, we made a plan for the following day. I would take the children and their friends apple picking in the morning while John did some work on the boat. We would meet at 5:00 p.m. and go out, the whole family, for a short cruise just one town over, where we would dock and have dinner. This was really exciting. For a family that can rarely travel together and has to have all kinds of contingency plans, this was a big step indeed. I felt like we were ready to take it.

I arrived with the children at 5:15 p.m. John was anxious to get going since our dinner reservation was at 6:00 p.m. and it took thirty minutes to get there. Jack started to work on the first mate jobs that had been assigned to him the day before. Sarah, who has some boating experience from being on a friend's boat, also wanted some jobs. (Why can't I get this kind of volunteer effort at home?) The competition for chores began. The bow line was the hot item of the day. Everyone wanted to hang off the front of the boat and toss the line. The aft lines and the buoys were chopped liver compared to the bow line. There was a fair amount of commotion as we prepared to leave. John called for everyone to be seated, but the kids were still arguing about who would do what. Somehow we all made it on and the boat pushed off.

John was frazzled and the kids were out of sync. I made sure all life jackets were on and zipped up. Sarah and I headed down to the cabin to play a game of cards. We had just begun to play a new game when we felt a jolt and heard a rumble. My first thought was, "Why is my life jacket upstairs?"

When I ran up to where John was, there was bridge everywhere-- in front of us, above us and on each side of us. Somehow, John had missed the lane line and we had gone into a shallow area, hitting the bottom of the boat. I don't need to tell you the rest of the story. The kids and I could barely breathe, we felt so, so sad for John. He said little. He did tell the children that he couldn't concentrate when people were hopping around and arguing about jobs.

We made it back to the dock, unfortunately amidst a crowd of spectators. The kids and I headed for the car so that John could have some peace in which to deal with finding out how much damage had been done. Sarah glanced back and said, "I guess we should change the name of the boat to *Knot A Problem Until Today.*"

I gave a lot of thought to what had gone wrong and how this experience could be a teachable moment. John and I quickly realized that the biggest problem had been our lack of preparation for family boating. We had never had a family meeting where we reviewed the rules of the boat, conducts of behavior, and who had what job. That night, we discussed all of these things. We divided up the jobs. Jack vented his feelings: he felt like John didn't want him as first mate anymore because he had given some of the jobs to Sarah. We laid out jobs for when just John and Jack were on the boat and for when there were the four of us. And we made a plan to try the same thing one week later.

As awful as the experience had been, I think it was a major lesson to both children that sometimes in life you just follow the directions of the guy in charge. While this was a big teachable moment, there are smaller ones at your finger tips every day. If you keep an ear open for a teachable moment, you can cover a lot of life's lessons.

Turning Disasters Into
Something Good *Strategies*

- **Be around and be listening.**
You can't make it a teachable moment if you are not around to hear what's going on.

- **Keep your temper in check.**
This is a tough one. When your child has just spilled eggs all over the counter because he was trying to make eggnog without waiting as you requested, the last thing you want to do is be patient. But if you start out by yelling at him (and we all do it so don't feel bad—just be aware of it), the child will probably shut down and not be available for the lesson that follows.

- **Use humor.**
Sarah reminds me that lectures are boring and now heads me off at the path. I've had to change my approach as the children have gotten older so that they don't guess what I am going to say and tune me out before I even begin.

- **Don't wait for later.**
Unless you are in a place where you really can't deal with the situation, try to seize the moment for teaching. Take your child aside and have a private discussion.

- **Compliment your child for his good listening skills and for learning an important lesson.**
Learning to take constructive criticism and to grow from your mistakes is a gift.

BLACK, WHITE, OR SHADES OF GREY?

Seeing The World Through Your Child's Eyes

One of our goals as parents is to help Jack move past the fact that though some things may be black or white in life, a lot of life is not so clear cut. It is all shades of grey. While a math problem has one right answer, and there is probably only one way to boil an egg, most aspects of life are filled with choices and decisions. Getting children like Jack to learn how to be flexible and not so literal is a challenge.

Jack was working on a research project for science one day recently. As part of the project, he needed to build a model of a planet that he had selected to study. It was the third time that Jack had studied the planets. For some strange reason, every time he changes schools, one of the first projects is the planet project. So he's a real pro at the solar system by now. He's also no slouch when it comes to efficiency.

When we arrived at the art store, prepared to buy the plaster of Paris to make Jupiter, we saw a styrofoam and wire art kit to construct the entire solar system. Jack looked the package over carefully and said, "This will be perfect. Then, when I change schools the next time and I'm asked to do the solar system project, I'll have it covered!" (I wrote a mental note to myself: Ask any new schools not to select the planets as a topic for a project)

Jack opened the package up to find out what sorts of supplies we might need. He read the colors that were required: Yellow, red, blue and green. We went to the acrylic paint aisle and found numerous brands and choices. I directed him to the group that looked the easiest to use. Jack began searching for the colors while

Sarah and I walked the nearby aisles, searching for projects that might strike her fancy. It wasn't long before I heard Jack cry, "Mmmmoooommmmmmeeeeeeee!" I ran back to where the voice was coming from. There was a look of exasperation on his face. "There is no yellow, red, blue or green!" Jack announced.

"Sure there is," I said to him, going over to the fourteen reds that were lined up. "You have Tomato Red, Ruby Red, Crimson Red, Dark Red, Cranberry, Apple Red, Fire Engine Red and Orange Red—which one do you want?"

"No, Mommy," Jack insisted, "The directions say "Red, just plain red." We spent no less than forty-five minutes discussing why any of the reds in the selection would *really* be okay for the project.

There is the literalism of Asperger's. I finally walked over to the manager and asked if he could recommend which red might be the closest to just plain red. That seemed to be the ticket to moving Jack beyond his need to match the paint to what the directions said exactly.

Nothing could be less black and white or have more shades of gray than how to raise a child with ADD, ADHD, PDD or Asperger's Syndrome. Jack is changing every day, affected by the chemical and neurological functioning of his brain, things in the environment, and experiences that he has. To meet Jack wherever he is on any given day means that we need all the cannons firing in the multidisciplinary plan. And those are:

- The right kind and dosage of medication.
- An effective behavior management plan is in place at school, home and anywhere else where Jack is spending considerable time.
- A school program that works.
- Therapies that move Jack forward.
- The family is humming along.
- That Jack has (for what he can manage) a good social life and fulfilling extra curricular activities.

Getting these canons lined up and lined up at the same time is no small achievement. We've had lots and lots of trial and error to finally reach a good functioning level, only to have something change either in Jack or the environment. And then we need to start rebuilding.

Medication alone is not the answer. In fact, in some cases it is no answer. I've listened to parents of children who could greatly benefit from medication, but absolutely refuse to consider it. I have also seen parents pushing a prescription when one might not even be needed. For us, without medication there is no focus in Jack. And with no focus, we have no opportunity to get his attention and get cooperation.

Behavior management alone is not the answer but it's a part of the answer. Selecting the right behavior management program is extremely important. The wrong one can send a child into orbit or leave the child unaffected but send the family spinning. We found the right program through careful thinking and discussions with our professional team, and through trial and error. Despite the difficulty of implementing and sticking to a behavior plan, the rewards can be monumental.

Each of the other components listed above is an ingredient. It's not unlike baking a loaf of bread. You absolutely have to have a few essential foodstuffs like flour and water. Without these, no bread making is possible. And then there are the additional ingredients that give the bread its character and flavor, like raisins and nuts. You can bake a basic loaf but it won't be as fine a loaf as it could be if you used all the ingredients in the recipe.

You have the opportunity to help craft someone really fine in this world. He or she won't fit a certain mold or image that you might have. If you can adopt the perspective that different is special and special is of value, than you can influence the blooming of an individual as wonderful and unique as each loaf of bread.

KEEPING FAITH
Recognize Opportunities to Teach and Train

At the end of it all, when I have put into place all of the routines, set all the schedules, reduced the uncertainties, adopted the most useful tips, committed to the most appropriate therapies, activities and schools, my challenging child's future is still out of my hands. And that, quite simply, is where I step out and let God step in. It is what sustains me in my daily struggles and keeps my sight straight for the long haul. A couple of thoughts on the short and the long journey, from a spiritual perspective.

One evening during Jack's hospitalization we were out to dinner with friends. One of the wives started to cry at the table. Her child had gotten a rejection notice from their first choice of private schools. He had been accepted to the other equally wonderful private school in town, but this wasn't the parents' first choice. Through her tears my friend looked at me and said, "You must think I'm pretty silly. Here I am crying over a rejection letter when you're dealing with what you're dealing with."

Actually, I hadn't traveled down that thought path. I hadn't thought like that because somewhere along our struggle to accept our path with Jack, John and I had simply thrown away the comparative, competitive mindset that usually starts with the school admissions process.

When I was an undergraduate at Georgetown I used to meet with a spiritual director. I remember saying to her, "My life is so easy right now. My faith is strong and everything is going my way. I feel very guilty."

Sister Mary replied, "Just store up this time that you are logging with God. Someday, you will need to draw on what you've built." She likened it to a bank account. "You are investing in your spiritual account right now. There will come a day when you will need to draw on the reserve. Being given much, much might be required at a later time."

It wasn't until we had Jack that I remembered the bank account.

For a very long time I believed that what I accomplished and what I did determined how successful my life was. And I held the same standard for my husband and my children. We had a plan that included demanding schools, Ivy League colleges, good careers, and so on. But when we had Jack, we began rethinking everything. We went back to square one, asking those age old questions like, "What does it mean to have a full life? What do we want our children to be like, as people, when they grow up?" Somewhere, very early on, our perspectives changed.

A Dartmouth alumna and Rhodes scholar, Mary Cleary Kiely, tells of the change in her perspective that her Down's syndrome child, Christina, brought about in her. One day, her young daughter Bridget approached her with this concern, "Mommy, it's okay to have Down's syndrome, right?" Mary assured her that it was and asked her child what she was thinking about. Her daughter replied, "Well, you said a few days ago that Christina had Down's syndrome because of a mistake that happened when she was in your tummy. Does that mean Christina is a mistake?"

Mary goes on to say, "Now I have a greater sense for how much life resists the little formulas that we would squeeze it into. While the pleasures and the powers of intelligence can be considerable, intelligence possessed is not necessarily intelligence used. And intelligence without heart can be a very dangerous thing—a lesson that we need to be reminded of over and over again. I watch my daughter, who cannot stand to see someone else in distress. She invariably rushes over, lips trembling or eyes filling, to comfort the other with a pat or a hug. Then I read about kids shooting other kids and I wonder:

Whose deficiencies are the more serious? Those of children like my daughter, or those of children like the shooters, who presumably came into this world labeled normal?" Mary concludes, "I am not suggesting that this is our choice—developmentally disabled children or emotionally disturbed children, but I am suggesting that a good heart is one of the greatest gifts of all time."

You see, there it is again, perspective. It is in your hands: Will you see the special gifts of your child and see him as one who is special, or will you only see the special needs?

The other day Jack woke up not feeling well, so I ran him to the doctor during the early morning sick child hour. In the waiting room we saw a father with a small child. Jack never hesitates to tell me that he really doesn't like babies. I guess he just can't figure out what to do with them. So I was surprised when he looked up at the child, who was whimpering, and began to talk to her in a soft voice, trying to cheer her up. This was a significant leap—big time stuff. It was nothing measurable, nothing you could put on a resume or use to get into a better school. However, for Jack, it was the kind of growth that I would trade over anything. My point is this: if you can change the way you view the world and your own experience, framing it in the bigger context, the context of life with a capital L, you may not only be more content, you might have a deeper, fuller life.

Friends who have known our family and know a little about Jack ask periodically, "So what will happen to Jack? Where will he end up? Will he ever be normal? Will he go to a regular college?" And again and again John and I have to answer them, and ourselves, with the honest answer. We Don't Know. We don't have a clue. He might go to a well-known university or he might go to a community college. Then again, he might not go to college at all.

Where he goes doesn't matter one bit. But who he becomes...now, that's everything.

At the end of it all, there is that saying of St. Paul's[4] "so faith, hope, love, remain these three; but the greatest of these is love." And my faith is in a God

4. I Corinthians 13:13

who always has the first and the last word. I have faith that God will bring Jack's journey, and our journey as a family, to a good conclusion.

When I first learned that the probability of having children was miniscule, I prayed the same prayer each day: "God, if it is Your Will for me to have children, than let me have them. Give to us children who will glorify your name, and do Your work on Earth." God, in turn, gave us Jack as part of the package. I don't think it was just an accident that we were given him. By fixing my eyes on God, I keep up hope for the long-term, and have the determination to try my best each day.

The day-to-day isn't easy. I can spend all day in relative peace and have Jack come home from school and unravel me in no time at all. Maintaining an inner calm and upbeat attitude doesn't just happen. I consciously work at it. And again, I lean on my faith and make sure that each day includes time with God.

Somewhere along the way, I have come to see Jack, in a way, as my destiny. I can reach back and pull forward experiences, friendships, events, activities— even my odd combination of studying philosophy and business—and see that it all prepared me for this moment. You can do the same. I bet if you dig inside, you will find things that can help you raise, magnificently, your special child. Don't think that this is the end of it. The ball keeps rolling forward. My experience with Jack is probably preparing me for something else down the road. And I'll get there with faith, the right attitude, and the right perspective.

This summer our family was again vacationing in Georgia. It had been a few years since I had last seen Connie, and Helen, her daughter with cerebral palsy. There they were, looking more radiant than ever. One day, my conversation with Connie turned to coping mechanisms, and we found that we shared a strong spiritual foundation. Connie said to me, "You know, many people who first meet me say they don't know how I cope with my situation. Then, when they get to know me, they say, 'I see why God gave Helen to you. Because you can handle it.'" Connie then said, "But you know Anne, they have it backwards. I am so honored that I was chosen for Helen."

I know what she means. My spiritual life these past nine years has grown by leaps because of Jack. I have memories so precious that I still cry when I recall them. The first time Jack actually held my hand when we crossed the street (it took him until age six to master this), when he first took an interest in a friend (age seven), the time he joined me to make egg nog, rather than work on his passion of the moment (age eight), and when he responded to a hug in a way that meant he felt it inside (age nine). I would never trade my experience with Jack, not even the painful days (well, maybe the most painful days).

I couldn't write this book in good conscience without sharing with you the number one tip, bar none, that has helped me cope with the daily stress as well as kept me on the right road, and given me the things I need to help Jack. Your faith walk is a completely personal thing. Inside of you are the tips that can increase your own spirituality and can get you through the day with strength and even joy.

God bless you, your special child and your family.

Appendix I
Sample Letters

Planning Meeting for Next Academic Year— Follow-Up Letter

TO: The names of the school based team

FROM: Anne Addison

RE: Placement and Planning Meeting Recap

DATE: Going into second grade

Cc: Private therapists and doctors

This memo follows up our meeting today, where we reviewed Jack's progress against his current academic year goals. This recaps the next steps that we agreed to, so that the success of first grade will be repeated in second grade.

AREAS OF FOCUS FOR THE ACADEMIC YEAR

Jack has progressed extremely well in terms of academic performance. He has been more willing to set aside his own agenda and follow the directions of the teacher and classroom. In addition to following teacher directions, he has made major gains in the areas of:

- Transitioning between activities.
- Reactions to schedule changes.
- Pragmatic language.
- Following routines and classroom agendas.
- Remaining on task and sustaining attention.
- Self-care responsibilities.

THE MAJOR AREAS OF CONCERN CONTINUE TO BE:

1. *Safety*—Jack continues to have a lack of self-awareness regarding unsafe actions affecting him and others. This is probably a combination of sensory impairments and the self-orientation of Asperger's Syndrome (AS) individuals.
2. *Regulating or Managing His Upsetness when Overstimulated or Upset*— Jack still responds physically and/or verbally when he is upset, his system is overloaded or something is off in him. Jack's first grade teacher has found that there is a window of opportunity before Jack loses it; if you can distract him

he can have the space and time to bring himself back in line.

3. *Social Abilities*—Learning how to make and have friends, be an active participant in a group, and successfully work with peers are what comes hardest to AS individuals. These will need to be nurtured in Jack and are of the highest priority in the next academic year.

WAYS TO DELIVER AGAINST THE PRIORITIES STATED ABOVE

1. *Safety*—Jack understands and responds to safety warnings when they are presented rationally with clear explanations about consequences. The Junior League offers a safety program for children that the school will investigate. The curriculum may be available to borrow for implementation in the classroom; the program may be an after school option that the PTA might consider or perhaps the League would consider running the safety program for the resource class that will be in place next year.

2. *Regulating or Managing Upsetness*—In addition to continuing the behavior intervention strategies that have been so successful in the first grade class, it is highly recommended that occupational therapy (OT) be delivered first thing in the morning (perhaps even twenty minutes before school opens) or at the end of the day. There is a belief in OT circles that a sensory diet, implemented twenty minutes each morning, can provide the necessary input for the sensory system to be ready for learning. I would be willing to come in with Jack early each morning and provide the diet myself if the OT feels that this would be beneficial—if no one is available to provide this function. John and I strongly believe that OT should not be done with Jack in the middle of the day, looking at the difficulties in transition and in his system that we observed this year.

In addition, the sensory integration program, How Does Your Engine Run? may now be appropriate for Jack. Our own OTs have discussed this program with us in the past and have identified it as a good choice for Jack. The special education coordinator will investigate who in the district is trained to deliver this curriculum and will work out a strategy for incorporating it into Jack's program for next year.

3. *Social Development*—John and I strongly support and request that the District employ a social skills curriculum that could serve children having the same need as Jack. Only with a carefully constructed curriculum, shared with all professionals delivering services and interacting with Jack, will the message get across and internalized.

4. Writing Whole Sentences—There remains a question as to whether there are processing or other issues in Jack's ability to write whole sentences easily. I will review the summer schedule with the speech therapist and our psychologist to determine if we should evaluate Jack during this period to try to identify the nature of this difficulty.

As we discussed, please provide me with a general response to the above areas as soon as possible. Finally, we understand that the resource room will consist of five boys and one girl in the home room. The three boys currently in the class will remain. Since emotionally difficult or behavior problem situations are the worst environment AS people can be in, we understand that the resource class will not have any children with emotionally-based disorders or strong negative behaviors which could impact or influence Jack's emotional development. To this point, would you please let us know what the nature of the other children's issues are, and what their academic capabilities are. This will give us peace of mind and assure us that the base classroom will continue to meet Jack's needs.

Thank you all for your hard work during this school year. We are quite pleased with Jack's progress and hope that he continues to show considerable gain next year as well.

Letter to School and Private Team
at Beginning of Academic Year

TO: School personnel including teachers at the therapeutic day school Jack is attending, therapists, my counterpart at the dept. of education, and Jack's private therapists

FROM: Anne Addison

RE: Review of Summer Experiences and Fall Plans

DATE: Going into fourth grade

The purpose of this memo is to review Jack's progress since June and to discuss our plans outside of school for the fall. John and I believe that this school year will be very critical for Jack. Jack has come so far along. We are keeping our fingers crossed, hoping for many more behavioral and emotional strides this year. We know that all of you will be working very hard on Jack's behalf this year; please know that we are so very, very thankful.

A fair number of issues cropped up this summer that we would like to review with you. We would also like to begin thinking about the transition plan from Jack's current out-of-district placement back to our home school. The meeting should probably be an IEP meeting.

A REVIEW OF SUMMER ACTIVITIES

Summer Day Camp
The majority of Jack's summer experience centered around a day camp for children with learning disabilities, ADD, ADHD, Asperger's Syndrome and other disorders on the autism spectrum. The camp was forty-five minutes away at a college campus. Jack was driven to the camp by one of the counselors; he left home at 8:20 a.m. and returned home at 4:20 p.m. It was a long day.

In the beginning of camp, the counselors reported that Jack kept very much to himself, catching butterflies and playing Gameboy (they didn't really allow children to play Gameboy, but for the first few weeks let Jack do this as he adjusted to the program). There were seven boys in Jack's group and three counselors. Apparently, many of the boys were physically aggressive; Jack gave me examples of this and the counselors relayed this in the daily communication log. The first few weeks the counselors often praised Jack for using words and following directions.

Jack is never very verbal about what goes on at school or camp. However, this summer he began telling me stories about some of the aggressiveness of the other boys. After four weeks Jack said one day, "I'm sick of these bullies. If they hit me, I'm going to start hitting back." In a nutshell, the negative part of the camp experience was that Jack did start using his hands rather than his words and he was exposed to foul and sexual language and heard a good deal of rude talk. Luckily, he didn't try using the swear words, but he still has words and phrases like, "idiot," "stupid," "whatever," and "in your dreams" in his repertoire. I think that we all need to come down hard on Jack's use of bad language/phrases to extinguish them as soon as possible.

On the positive side, Jack became very social and began building some confidence around sports. He frequently invited friends from camp over to our house. Unfortunately, many of these boys used bad language or told inappropriate stories in my presence so I didn't see them as being good influences on Jack and didn't promote the friendships. To his credit, Jack told me after several play dates, "I guess we'll have to cross him off our list," so at some level he seems to understand what is and isn't acceptable behavior.

We hope there is a way that you can continue to have Jack build his sports skills—particularly in baseball and basketball, where he has shown an interest.

All in all, the counselors reported that Jack became a good participant in his group, was good humored and, eventually, learned how to avoid negative relationships. One day, the communication log said that Jack had gotten into a scrap with another camper. Jack had been telling me how mean this boy was all summer. I said to him, "Jack, these children have special needs. If someone really can't control his anger, just keep your distance." To which Jack replied, "Well, why am I at this camp?" He was really surprised to hear that he was at a special needs camp. I explained that while he did really well working alone, that in life, we also need to do well working in groups. Specifically, he needs to learn how to work well in a group, cooperate with others and follow directions. This was why he was at the camp and at the therapeutic day school.

Jack seems to understand that he has to accomplish these important things to move on. My overall sense was that the camp allowed Jack to spread his social wings but it came at a price of exposure to many things that we wished he hadn't seen first hand.

Fishing and Boogie Boarding in Georgia
We spent a family week in Georgia where Jack spent much of the time fishing and boogie boarding in the ocean. He learned quite a lot about various fish that might be useful for writing topics.

PRIORITIES FOR THE FALL

I believe that we have a good IEP in place for fourth grade, with goals that tie in to needs that we continued to see during the summer. To prioritize these needs, based on my summer observations, I would say the following are most pressing:

• *Learn how to manage frustration better.* As the summer went on, it seemed that Jack's fuse got shorter and shorter. He was a bit more impatient each time a question didn't get answered right away or he had to wait for something. While he didn't totally fall apart, we need to get him developing coping techniques so that he doesn't even get close to falling apart (he's gotten close in the last week or so).

• *Improve eye contact.* Eye contact seems like it's slipping again.

• *Greet people appropriately.* We continue to remind and prompt Jack to do so; this skill is still not in a natural pattern.

• *Strengthen social and communication skills.* OBVIOUSLY. I just didn't want you to think that I thought we had licked this one.

• *Strengthen writing abilities.* Jack was totally anti-writing all summer—even short thank you notes.

• *Type to Learn.* I couldn't get Jack to even try it this summer but it is in his book bag—the disc and the study guide.

• *Improve organizational abilities.*

STRATEGIES WE WILL BE USING AT HOME

Developing Friendships and Working on Social Skills
• *Friendships*-- Jack will continue to have Julien, the twelve year old who was with us last year, as his study buddy and "big brother" one day a week after school. We have seen Jack look towards Julien as a role model for cool, boy behavior. Julien and I talk about what behavior issues we are working on with Jack and he makes sure to address them when an opportunity presents itself.

We have recently moved into a house that has an eleven year old boy, Jason, living next door. I have told Jason a little bit about Jack's special needs and he is also very interested in big brothering Jack. The two have been spending a lot of time together at the stream that runs through our properties. I suspect this will be another good place for Jack to acquire, and practice, good social skills.
• *Chess*—Jack will continue to take private chess lessons with Rich, his chess coach, one day a week. Rich has received permission for Jack to join a chess club at a private school where he will be teaching on Tuesday afternoons at 3:00 p.m. I know this would mean that Jack would need to leave school fifteen minutes early to get to the chess club. However, we might want to consider the experience as a good opportunity for social skill development. Let's discuss this when we meet.

A BIG ISSUE

Jack recently gave up one month of Gameboy for something that he wanted to buy. By doing this, he has really reduced his interest in Pokemon, which has made him much more available to socialize with other children. The bus ride is long and boring. Could you allow him to do his reading homework on the bus? I know you do not like him doing his homework on the bus but it would teach him about using time well and give him something to do. PLEASE consider it.

Thank you so much.   Let us know how we can help you.

LETTER OF ENCOURAGEMENT TO THE TEACHER

Full address goes here

Date

Teachers name and address here

Dear Shannon,

I just wanted you, the assistant teachers, the specials (art, music and gym) teachers and the school administration to know how pleased John and I are with the progress that Jack is making. In reviewing Jack's second marking period report card we are particularly excited about the gains that he appears to be making in the areas of *Personal and Social Development* and *Work Habits and Attitudes.*

Last weekend, John and I attended the annual Orton-Gillingham conference where we participated in a seminar called "Social Values", run by the executive director of a special needs school in Dallas. The seminar reviewed a segment of the curriculum in this school that teaches children, in a very structured and carefully constructed way, social skills, healthy attitudes, and good work habits. Both the curriculum and the way it was woven throughout a child's experience during the day, in every setting, were impressive. I see the same constant focus and attention on these elements as critical for a child with Asperger's Syndrome. Obviously, it is working extremely well—as well as everything else you are doing.

This year has been one of steady gains, academically, but, more importantly, socially and emotionally for Jack. As our team of doctors and therapists has discussed with us many times, it is critical for Jack that: 1) the environment be safe, simple and comforting so that Jack is available for learning and, 2) that the teacher be intuitive, creative and insightful—which you certainly are.

What a difference this year is compared to last year! We are very encouraged that a formula for learning has been found that is effective for Jack. I think we have learned this marking period that although we still need to take baby steps in moving Jack into larger environments and more challenging social situations, that if we are patient and careful and remain on this strategic course for him, he will continue to show gains.

Many, many thanks to you and your extensive team for your continued work with Jack. Would you please be sure to convey our thanks to everyone who is part of Jack's world at school?

Letter for Transitioning from One School Program to Another

TO: School personnel including teachers, coordinator for special education at the school, school-based therapists, my counterpart at the dept. of education, and Jack's private therapists and psychiatrist

FROM: Anne Addison

RE: Transition to New School

DATE: Fourth Grade

This memo is to provide you with a recap of current services and perspectives from therapists who see Jack at school and privately. The objective of this report is to synthesize and share information among the various disciplines and to give all of you at-home observations of Jack at this point in time. This document was prepared to assist you in the education, behavior, developmental and medical programs and planning that you are managing for Jack.

One of my first questions is on the communication front. How can we, as Jack's parents, best support the behavioral strategies and priorities that the school is using? The more that we can focus on the same issues, in the same way, the stronger Jack will get the message.

I am also wondering if it makes sense to develop shorter-term goals which support the annual IEP goals. In first grade, the teacher had monthly goals. We met briefly each Friday morning to discuss how we were doing against these goals and to brainstorm ideas or discuss what professionals needed to be brought into the loop to help us resolve an issue.

From the work that Jack was doing at the hospital's school program and tying into our home goals, I have prepared a draft of some possible short-term priorities:

Proposed April Goals
• Follow directions with three prompts.

- Focus on his work with three prompts.
- Limit silly behaviors with just three prompts.
- Be a good friend; i.e. share and cooperate with others without being too competitive.
- Continue to build pragmatic language skills.
- Be safe.

Current Treatment Program

- Psychiatric Medication—Thorazine and Lithium were discontinued last week, due to a suspected drug rash. Although the rash turned out to be scarletina, Jack has remained off psychiatric medications. He is currently taking Amoxicillin (for scarletina), fish oil (for focus and depression), and Benadryl (for itch of scarletina).

    1. Language/Speech—According to the IEP, Jack will receive language therapy twice a week, focusing on pragmatic skills.

    2. Sensory Integration O.T.—IEP indicates once a week.

    3. Academic Program—CES school.

General Observations

- *Progress continues to be made across the board.* We believe that the highly structured academic program at the hospital and the strong behavior management system that Jack participated in at the hospital for twenty four weeks is a strong contributor to his willingness to follow directions, his improved ability to make transitions, and his lessened self-agenda. At home, we are closely following the goal sheet mechanism that was used at the hospital's academic program, and following their behavior management system.

- *Interactions with peers is improving—best chance for success is in highly structured/supervised format.* As shown in the goal sheets at the hospital and in our own observations, Jack can play fairly and cooperatively with children when it is a game with clear directions and rules such as board games. Jack has his greatest difficulty in semi-structured situations such as a pickup game of basketball or something that would just be invented by children. In such situations, he is easily frustrated if things don't go his way or he misreads social cues.

• *Jack is much more verbal about himself, his feelings, etc.* I take this as a positive development. In particular, Jack is able to tell me when he is anxious, using phrases like, "I'm scared," "I'm frightened," or "I'm worried." It is helpful for people to suggest to Jack that he might be feeling a certain way and then ask him for confirmation or denial. For example, the first day of school today I asked Jack if he was feeling scared. He affirmed that he was and then asked if he could bring a stuffed animal with him to school.

• *Mealtime, bedtime, and other routines are no longer battle zones.* This has only occurred since Jack's stay at the hospital. When Jack first returned from the hospital our nightly goals included coming to the dinner table when called and going to bed on time. He has now internalized these schedule pieces and is punctual and appropriately behaved.

• *The most difficult area at home is Jack's disorganized state of being when he is not engaged in a specific activity and the periods when he decides not to cooperate.* The disorganization referred to encompasses his quick rate of moving, silliness, fooling around, and messing about behavior. Jack's silliness is much more pronounced than it has ever been since his stay at the hospital.

• *Day one of the school experience was extremely successful*—Jack responds well to high structure, a calm, nurturing, warm teacher style and simple setting—all of which seem to be in place at CES. The more Jack feels unthreatened, supported, respected and valued, the more he will lose his anxiety and fear and relax. This is when you will see the best Jack. You will see his great sense of humor, good-naturedness and kindness—not to mention his intellectual spirit.

Letter During Transition Out of District to In-District

TO: School personnel including teachers, therapists, my counterpart at the Dept. of Education, and Jack's private therapists and psychiatrist

FROM: Anne Addison

DATE: Fourth Grade

Thank you all so much for meeting with me recently to discuss Jack's possible transition to North Street. As much as John (my husband) and I would be thrilled to have this occur, we need to be very sure that this would be the next best step for Jack. As I briefly explained, Jack can easily sink or swim. Going from a four person classroom to a twenty person classroom seems like a very big leap. While the resource room can add some relief, we found in second grade that the relief was not enough to offset the anxiety that built up at lunch, at recess and in the large mainstream experiences. we may need to make a bridge with another program before we can leap to a regular mainstream setting. This is just something for you to consider as you visit Jack's class.

In terms of the after school program, we are thrilled that Jack has been accepted into the Mad Science and Chess programs. While it will be difficult for me to get Jack on Tuesdays and Wednesdays so that he can make it to the class on time, and to act as the aide, I don't see any other choice. If we are considering this as one of the links to moving him to North Street, shouldn't the after school program be part of his IEP? Chuck, would you follow up with me so that we can discuss this. In the meantime, I am prepared to be with Jack as after school starts this week.

Jack's teacher would like to speak to someone to better understand the Reading and Writing curriculum that I passed along to her. Could the right person please call her at [give telephone number]? If you could follow up with her this week it would be greatly appreciated.

Again, many, many thanks for your interest and help with Jack. We will do our very best to assist you in the hopes that Jack can be part of your school and we trust that you will do the same.

IEP Meeting—Follow-Up Letter

TO: School personnel including teachers, therapists, and Jack's private therapists

FROM: Anne Addison

RE: Placement and Planning Meeting Recap

DATE: First Grade

This reviews the highlights of this morning's discussion and outlines the next steps that we agreed to. Please let me know if there are any misunderstandings with this memo, or if there are other ideas or suggestions that should be incorporated into the preliminary work of the IEP. John and I have been exceedingly pleased with Jack's progress during the past five months and are hopeful that your carefully constructed program will provide the appropriate support and structure to progress towards achieving his full potential.

We see this coming academic year as being critical for Jack and expect it to be as, or more, challenging than the one just completed. Given that many of Jack's weaknesses emerge when engaged in social and peer interaction, we can only stress our concern and hope that the plan for Jack will improve these areas of weakness.

NEXT STEPS

The next steps as I understand them are:

1. The district and school support team for Jack will consult with and coordinate goals and plans with the school's independent therapists in the following areas: (Here we put the names and phone numbers of our team).

2. Our occupational therapist will forward a copy of the most recent evaluation to the board of education.

3. A meeting to review the proposed IEP will take place in July. Please let me know who from the school and board of education will be attending the meeting.

PRELIMINARY PLANS

1. Jack will participate in the inclusion classroom, beginning this fall. I understand that the class will consist of eight typical children and five special needs children. The classroom will have a head teacher and two assistants.

2. Supplemental therapy and pull-out opportunities will be determined after the school's education team has had greater conversation with our current therapists.

3. Jack will visit the teacher's summer classroom on July 17th, 9:00 a.m., to assist him with the transition to the fall.

I can be reached at the following telephone number (put your phone number here). I will expect to hear from your office in the next few weeks for a July meeting date. Thank you for your assistance and care in helping us with Jack.

LETTER TO SCHOOL PERSONNEL AND PRIVATE TEAM FOLLOWING A REPORT CARD

TO: School personnel including teachers, therapists, and Jack's private therapists and psychiatrist

FROM: Anne Addison

DATE: Fourth Grade

RE: First Quarter Progress Report

Note: Jack was transitioning from the out-of-district therapeutic day school to our home school, attending both of these for part of each day, when this letter was written.

We have reviewed Jack's first quarter progress report. While it appears that he is achieving most academic goals, we are concerned about the lack of sufficient progress in social skills and writing. We are wondering what can be done to address these areas. Below, is a summary of the IEP goals for which Jack has attained only a "1" (Unsatisfactory Progress) or a "0" (No Progress), as well as some brainstormed strategies.

Please review this memo and let me know if you feel that we should meet. Thank you for your help.

• <u>Positive interactions with adults</u>
1. *Jack will verbalize needs and concerns when anxious or upset 80% of the time (Grade: 0)—How about role playing this?* Can you learn to verbalize feelings by practice? If we try to get Jack to demonstrate this skill when he is in the midst of being upset, it may be difficult for him to disengage from the emotion of the moment. Why not set up role plays for him to practice at times when he is actually in control of himself?
2. *Jack will accept an answer from staff thus reducing repetitive questioning 80% of the time (Grade: 1)—*What if you tried to do a stepped reduction with a goal that relates to the point system. For example, if he currently repeats a request

5 times, the first step would be to repeat a request only 3 times. Once Jack can ask only 3 times, then step it down to 2, etc. What if there is an immediate reward tied to controlling himself to not keep repeating a request?

• Jack will improve behaviors related to academic functioning as measured by the following objectives:

1. *Jack will decrease frequency of utilizing material objects as a distracter to no more than 3x/day and will decrease use of nonfood items in his mouth (Grade for both: 1)*—Does OT have any acceptable substitutes, such as squeezing a ball, to help Jack with this sensory need?

2. *Jack will make comment or ask questions directly related to the current topic of discussion 80% of the time (Grade: 1)*—When this happens at home we tell him why it is not on topic and ask him to ask a different question or make a different comment. I don't have any good suggestions here but maybe the ST has a thought.

• Jack will develop positive interpersonal relationships in school situations as measured by the following objective:

In group, Jack will identify his feelings at least once per group, and also attempt to identify peer feelings once per group. (Grade: 0). Perhaps starting with concrete vignettes—social stories with facial pictures—would be at a pace that would allow Jack to start reading feelings. Storybooks that are at a very low grade level which would have exaggerated pictures and simple text might allow Jack to see feelings more easily; we could then move him along to more subtle examples, using movies and role play. The inability to read feelings is one of the hallmarks of Asperger's Syndrome individuals. Tony Attwood, the noted psychologist who wrote *Asperger's Syndrome*, suggests the use of "feelings notebooks." Children who use these notebooks are asked to write down how they feel. Perhaps you could tell a short story and ask how a character might feel, or if there is a situation at school. Ask Jack to write one sentence on how he feels and how the other person involved in the incident might feel.

• Jack will increase positive social interactions as measured by the following objectives:

1. *Jack will accept and cooperate with suggestions presented by a peer 90% of the*

time (Grade: 1)—Carol Gray's *Social Stories* might help or role play might help, making this his personal goal for the week might help. Perhaps doing pair projects where they have to take specific turns accepting each other's ideas would be effective.

2. Jack will stop playing, listen when a peer is upset and try to resolve conflict 75% of the time. (Grade: 1) Perhaps the psychologist at our home school, the therapeutic day school, and the Board of education can put heads together to come up with some strategies for teaching empathy and reading feelings. At home, we stop and point out to Jack the situation and ask him to try to see when someone is upset and then have him try to generate an appropriate response. Of course, we are struggling with the same problem.

• *Establish eye contact when greeting an adult (Grade: 1+)*—I know we are all continuing to remind him of this.

• <u>Jack will develop and/or refine handwriting and written expression skills as measured by the following objectives:</u>
There are four deficits in this area:
1. *Indenting paragraphs, (Grade: 1)*
2. *Constructing a paragraph with a topic sentence and 3 supporting sentences, (Grade: 1)*
3. *Constructing a paragraph using four sequential sentences supporting one main idea, (Grade: 1)*
4. *Using graphic organizers to construct 2 or 3 paragraph compositions (Grade: 1)*

These deficits are of great concern as the fourth grade requirements in the public school are now at an essay level. I would suggest getting together with the reading specialist at our home school to discuss new strategies or ideas and perhaps increase the time spent on writing skills. Via this memo, I request that the appropriate contact person at our home school contact Eileen, Jack's teacher at the therapeutic day school.

An overall comment was made that although Jack is working well with peers during free periods, he is having a harder time during cooperative activities in academics. In first grade at the public school, we had Jack work with just one other student in academic activities; it seemed when we moved to more than one other student, Jack had great difficulty holding himself together. Perhaps, we should go back to pair activities, as this seems to be all that Jack can negotiate at the present time. Consistently, we see the same situation at home. Jack works well with one other child, but if we add a second child to a board game or science project he cannot sustain his focus.

As you know, this is a critical year for Jack's development. We are so grateful to you for putting your efforts behind Jack and brainstorming some new ideas that might help him overcome these areas of non-progress.

Please feel free to contact me if you need to.

Letter Thanking School Personnel When Jack Changed Schools

Date

Dear Eileen, Suzanne, Aides, Specials Teachers and Dan,

Wow! I hardly know where to begin. It is just incredible to look back and see the journey that Jack has taken in the past two years. I will never forget my first meeting in Dan's office, where I saw him review the thick file and oodles of reports, then look at me with his kind eyes and say, "Let's just give this kid a chance. He has had diagnosis after diagnosis. Let's get him here and just start working with him." We believe the beginning of Jack's turnaround began with that first meeting.

I wanted to give you all something to thank you for all that you have done for Jack but everything just seemed inadequate. So, on the next page, we leave you *Caring for One Lost Sheep,* and hope that it conveys how grateful we are.

Thank you for taking a child and looking at him as he is, without judgment and without reserve,

Thank you for taking the time to understand someone who looks at the world in a way that is different for us, but natural to him,

Thank you for taking the time to teach a child about what it means to be a friend and a student,

Thank you for your creativity; in finding new strategies to tap into one child's barriers,

Thank you for your sense of humor—for taking the time to be an audience to a boy's jokes and to bring some laughter to his day,

Thank you for not giving slack, when that might have been the easier immediate solution but not the answer to the bigger problem,

Thank you for the patience that was needed to break down the basics of life—like learning how to follow a direction—again, and again, and again, and again,

Thank you for living the belief that it is a process not a today's product, that matters in life,

Thank you for never letting molehills become mountains and reminding us that mountains can be climbed, if you just walk a little bit each day,

Thank you for living out the story of the one lost sheep. Each day, you demonstrated your genuine caring about what happened to one little boy. All the prestige and dollars in the world couldn't bring about the miracle that we witness today. We only hope that we can walk in the shoes that you did, to carry Jack this far.

With every blessing and thanks,

Anne and John Addison

Letter to the Insurance Company to Provide Background on Your Child

Date

Dear Insurance Company:

The purpose of this letter is to give you the medical background of our child, Jack Addison, so that you may better understand the reason for the bills that will be coming your way on a regular basis. Jack has recently been diagnosed with Attention Deficit Hyperactivity Disorder (ADHD). ADHD is a neurologically based illness, which has the following key symptoms: inattention and distractibility, impulsivity, hyperactivity, and difficulty with delaying gratification. This illness was diagnosed through an evaluation by a pediatric neurologist and a pediatric psychologist.

In addition to ADHD, Jack has deficits in the areas of speech and language and sensory integration. In order to help you understand Jack's case and medical requirements better, I have included in this packet the summary from the evaluations of the psychologist, speech therapist, and occupational therapist.

 Based upon the various therapists' evaluations, Jack's illness will require the following treatment program:
• Medication management using Ritalin, for the control of impulsivity and inattention.
• Speech and language therapy twice a week, to work on pragmatic language skills and oral motor stimulation.
• Occupational therapy twice a week to improve sensory integration and tactile defensiveness.

Please let me know if I can provide you with any further information to understand Jack's medical and emotional requirements. Thank you for working with us on managing Jack's case and reimbursing us for medical expenses on a judicious basis.

Sincerely,
Anne Addison

LETTER TO THE INSURANCE COMPANY TO ACCOMPANY LARGE STACK OF BILLS

Date

Dear Name of insurance company:

This letter is to provide you with an update as to Jack's progress over the last six months and to outline our treatment plan for the remainder of the year.

Progress Made
Jack reached some important milestones this last quarter:
• Jack has been able to string several sentences together and has begun to tell stories that have a logical beginning.
• Jack has shown significant improvement in his tactile defensiveness, allowing us to reduce the use of the "brushing program."
• Jack has continued to perform well in the integrated kindergarten.

Key Issues
The above gains have allowed us to make the following changes to Jack's treatment plan and set the next goals:
• Speech and language therapy will continue twice weekly, with the hope of increasing Jack's conversational ability to holding a conversation with an adult for three unprompted exchanges for 4 days in a row.
• Jack's occupational therapy sessions will be reduced to once a week, given his improvement in the tactile area, and will focus on sensory integration.

Thank you for your timely response to the therapy bills that we have submitted on a regular basis. We are implementing complementary home exercises given to us by the various therapists, in an effort to move Jack's progress as quickly as possible. Please be assured that we are doing everything that we can to assist his development, keeping costs down for you and maximizing his quality of life for us. Again, many thanks for partnering so effectively with us.

Sincerely,
Anne and John Addison

Preparation for Consultation with Doctor Specializing in Bipolar Disorder

Date

Dear Teacher's Name:

As you know, we are taking Jack for a consultation with a doctor who specializes in bipolar in pre-pubescent children on April 27th. In order to give her helpful information to reach her own conclusion, I think it would be good to have data from the school setting. Would it possible for you to keep mood charts or something similar to give her an idea of Jack's key issues, behaviors and moods? Let me know if you need chart forms.

Thank you.

Anne Addison

MEDICAL AUTHORIZATION TO THE SCHOOL

Date

On September 16-17th and October 2-6th, John and I will be out of town. Margaret Ross, a family friend and our babysitter for seven years, will be responsible for making all emergency decisions (should they occur) for Jack and Sarah during this time. She may be reached on my pager, (give pager number). You should first contact me on my cellular phone (your number) or John at his cellular phone (give phone number), before contacting Margaret.

Thank you for your assistance.

Sincerely,
Anne Addison

Elements of an Introductory Letter to a Doctor that you will be Visiting for a Second Opinion

Before you visit the doctor from whom you are requesting a second opinion, consolidate your child's background and the key questions that you have in the form of an introductory letter. The major sections of the letter might be:

• *The Purpose of the Visit.* Why you are going to this doctor for a second opinion. What you hope to learn.

• *Brief History.* Give the doctor a brief history of the relevant milestones, stages, school experiences, and other occurrences that you believe are important for a doctor to know about. Be sure to include your own hypotheses and feelings about what is going on with your child.

• *Examples of Your Child's Behavior.* Give some real examples of things that have happened that exhibit the behaviors or emotions that you are most concerned about.

• *Gathered Data.* Consider tracking your child's moods, behaviors or whatever things you want the doctor to take a look at. The doctor will only have a clinical impression. You can give her a feel for what your child is like in the real world.

Letter to a Babysitter When you are Going to be Away Overnight

MEDICATION:
Ritalin: 7:30 a.m. 10 mg. (1 blue pill)
            11:00 a.m. 5 mg. (1 yellow pill)

Every morning Jack takes 1 Vitamin E, 1 Vitamin C, and 2 fish oil (in the fridge, also called Omega 3)

At night, please give Jack two Benadryls at 7:30 p.m., to help him get to sleep.

IMPORTANT NUMBERS
• Your and your spouse's cell phone number(s) and where you will be staying.
• A friend's phone number. Be sure that you tell your friend that you will be away and that she is on your emergency list. Review doctors' phone numbers and emergency procedures.
• Important doctor's numbers—pediatrician, psychiatrist, dentist.

Dear Erika,

Jack has had a tiring camp experience around all special education kids, which, in retrospect, may have not been the best thing. I think our goal for these next four days is to get him relaxed and around typical children. The psychologist suggested that I allow more than my usual television and Gameboy limits due to his social exhaustion from camp. Now, we have to get him reconnected with live things and re-oriented—this won't be easy, as we don't want him to go into agitation mode. I would suggest that each morning or day you say, "Okay, you have two hours for Gameboy/television for the day (combined) so think about when you want to use it." I would add maybe thirty minutes of early morning cartoons when he just wakes up if he needs to unwind.

I have left money and beach cards in the green ceramic soup tureen on the shelf in the hutch in the kitchen. There is a newspaper of things to do in our area on my desk in my office. You decide what you want to do. Here are some thoughts:

- Renaissance Fair in Tuxedo Park.
- Take the ferry to the island that the Parks Department runs.
- St. Catherine's Church Fair.
- Zoo to see the new apes exhibit.
- Hiking at the Audubon Center (call them for directions).
- Children's Museum—look on–line you'll get directions.

Erika, I have been doing a little more negotiating with Jack lately. I am trying to listen to why he doesn't want to do something and have him come up with a compromise that will work for both of us. He's doing a nice job of this. Of course, if you need him to cooperate or behave a certain way, that's that. You can use no television or no Gameboy as a consequence.

He has been watching this cartoon, "DW" from 9:30-10 at night and then going to bed. I know it's late but he just hasn't been tired. We've been reading *Goblet of Fire* together, which I hope that you continue.

Jack might give you a hard time about taking a bath every day. He will say he can do a cloth wash. You can tell him proper hygiene is a daily bath, but if he's gone in the pool you may say okay to a cloth wash.

Please make sure he brushes his teeth in the morning and at night.

Thank you so much for helping me out. Have fun!!!!

BACKGROUND LETTER TO A COACH
WORKING WITH JACK

Date

Coach's Name and Address

Dear Robert,

This letter gives you a quick overview of Jack's needs and a few tips on how best to work with him. Thank you for being so patient and kind with him. Jack doesn't have a mean bone in his body but it can be frustrating at times if you don't know why he is distracted or not responding. I hope that this letter will make working with him a little easier; feel free to share it with the assistant coaches if you think it will help them as well.

Jack has Attention Deficit Hyperactivity Disorder (ADHD), which means that he gets very easily distracted, is impulsive, and runs in a high gear. It is a chemical imbalance in the brain and he takes a medication that helps with many of these behaviors. Jack has a second disorder which is less well known. It is called Asperger's Syndrome (AS). It is also a neurological disorder. Luckily, Jack has this on a mild level. People who have Asperger's are like Dustin Hoffman's character in the movie *Rain Man*. They process information very, very slowly (it takes Jack about three times as long to process directions as it takes a regular kid), and they pick up very few social cues. They learn social skills by being taught them and by learning from peers.

People with AS can get fixated on something to the point of obsession; Jack happens to be interested in nature and you may see him leave the baseball field to go investigate something on the sidelines that looks particularly interesting to him.

All this said, here are the five tips to get the most out of Jack:

1. Try to get near his eye level, ask him to look you in the eye and then tell him what you need him to do.

2. Add a pat on the back or other affirmation onto your requests, so he feels comfortable and not anxious.

3. If needed, give him a warning before he will need to make a change (like, "Jack, you are up to bat in two more turns.")

4. When pairing him, pair him with someone who has a mellow personality.

5. If you see Jack start obsessing over something (a bug, finding his ball, etc.) just tell him, "Jack, you are getting a little stuck on that. Do x,y,z and we will worry about it later." Unfortunately, once in a while he will just get stuck and have to complete whatever the thing is before he can move on.

Added to all of this, Jack was recently found to have a tick-borne infectious disease. It's a cousin of Lyme disease. Its symptoms are extreme fatigue, migraines, and sleeplessness. He is also suffering from bad allergies. As you've seen, he hunches down on the field once in a while, probably because he is tired; just keep reminding him that he needs to be ready at all times. Hopefully, the medications that he is now on will kick in soon.

As I told Marty, we wish we could have brought you a stronger player. My husband and I are sports nuts, as is our daughter. It is actually miraculous that he is finally able and willing to play on a baseball team. Now that he has shown an interest, we are working with him during the week to try to shape up his technical skills. He rarely, if ever, held a bat before last week or threw a baseball, so we have some work ahead of us.

You have no idea what a mark your working with him will make. To some kids it's just another season. For Jack, this is a major milestone. We can't thank you enough for your work with him. Let us know if you have any questions or if you need any help with the team.

With much thanks,
Anne Addison

Thank You To A Coach

Date

Dear Skip and Swim Program Gang,

I often find that it is easy to go through the paces of life without reflecting upon the impact that my actions and personality have on others. I think that this is true of many people. You all have profoundly affected both of our children this summer in ways that you cannot imagine. For this, John and I want to give you our deepest thanks.

As most of you know, Jack is a special needs child with a neurological wiring that has eluded definition by doctors across the country. Though he may look like a typical child, even the simplest direction or social interaction takes enormous energy and self-discipline for Jack. Needless to say, in addition to the trauma of endless therapies, examinations and a three month stay at the hospital this past year, he has had poor experiences and negative feedback so frequently that his self-image and esteem are very low.

Enter GCC pool.

Although Jack couldn't accomplish attending the day camp, we nervously decided to let him go to the pool each day when he came home from summer school—where he works on social skills and making up the academic work that he missed while at the hospital. I watched first with fear and then joy as each of you went from frustration to making a real effort to guide this child. I now love watching him as he enjoys simple interactions with other children, playing water games such as "Sharks and Minnows."

Where an afternoon of fun in the pool might be just another thing to do for most kids, it is HUGE for Jack to enjoy the company of other children and to be accepted, as many children have so graciously done this summer. John and I are only too aware of the extra effort that it takes to lifeguard when Jack is in the pool; you have no idea how much we appreciate your extra effort and patience with him. We have seen this little boy grow by leaps and bounds in terms of his confidence and enjoyment with life. He eagerly looks forward each day to seeing Sean, Scott, Andrew, Mike and all the other children who have patiently talked Pokemon to him to his heart's content.

You will never know the impact that you have had on him. We are hopeful that it will not be too many more years before he has made sufficient gains to be on the team. This achievement will be nothing short of a miracle for a child that could not even follow the simplest of directions or hold a conversation one year ago.

Equally important is the impact that you all have had on Sarah. With a brother like Jack—and the trauma that accompanies the hospitalization of a sibling—Sarah often gets less than her fair share of attention and bears more burden than the average nine year old. She came to the team a bit exhausted, worn down and without the spirited self-esteem and assurance that we always knew her to have. We don't have to tell you the effect that the team has had on Sarah's sense of self. To say that she has embraced the team is putting it mildly… they have helped her redefine herself.

The team has given Sarah a sense of belonging, a sense of value and worth. I will never forget watching Sarah swim her first meet this summer, and Skip— with the enthusiasm that only he can exude—rush up to her, cup her face between his hands, and tell her how terrific her swim was. What a sense of value to a little girl! This same enthusiasm and care is reflected by each of the swimming coaches in practice and at meets.

You all have made profound and lasting impacts on two children—and many more. I can't imagine a more valuable summer. You have redirected and influenced the path of those following you.

Thank You,

Anne and John Addison

Date

Camp Address

Dear Camp Director,

I am writing this letter to give you some background and insight into Jack. Since this is his first sleep-away camp experience, we want to be sure that it goes as well as possible. Please feel free to call me with any questions or concerns, after you read the letter.

As always many thanks for your interest in and care of Jack.

GENERAL DESCRIPTION OF JACK

Jack's personality varies quite a bit depending upon how comfortable he is in a situation and who else is in the situation. These past few months he has been transitioning from a special needs school to a regular elementary school. The move has been highly successful. Jack has been focused, relatively serious and very aware of what is acceptable behavior for children his age. He feels really good about himself at the school and is doing extremely well. Several things took place that set Jack up for success. The teachers laid a clear, visual structure out for Jack and were explicit in what their expectations were. But most important, the teachers gave Jack frequent praise, encouragement and understanding.

During this same period, I have seen Jack fixated on a topic, immature, and difficult to focus. This situation occurred when Jack was around other children with Asperger's and was in an academic setting that was not challenging.

SOCIAL DEVELOPMENT/PEERS

Though Jack's maturity level and tendency to fixate will vary greatly depending on those around him, you will find Jack always sunshiney. He doesn't have a mean bone in his body and has a great day-to-day sense of humor. However, he easily sinks to the lowest denominator. I can't stress enough the importance of keeping Jack around children who are easy going, don't fixate on topics (particularly Gameboy and Pokemon), and are kind.

Jack has several friends who are older (12) and are mentors to him. These boys are the ones who really guide Jack. Jack is still stuck in the Gameboy and Pokemon phenomenon; these boys are the ones who tell him to put it away and come shoot hoops, roller blade, and do other boy things. Jack does tend to seek out boys who like to do what he likes to do. These things are fishing and Pokemon. Our greatest concern about the summer experience is that Jack will spend the whole time with some other boys who are fixated on Pokemon and fishing and not branch out. We have seen that when he gets with other Asperger's type boys, they all reinforce each other's narrow mindset. When we are able to get him away from Pokemon or whatever box he is in, he can participate nicely with other children. In the past, Jack has been known to be a bit rigid in his play with children, needing things to be done a certain way. However, in the past year, we have seen Jack become much more flexible with his interactions with others.

SOCIAL DEVELOPMENT/ADULTS

Adults who are most successful in their interactions with Jack are first able to try to see the world through his eyes; second, they are very obvious in their support and encouragement of him (letting him know that they are on his side); third, they are firm but rational. Jack does not respond well to adults who are nervous, raise their voice, get agitated easily or are unwilling to talk things out. Sometimes, getting Jack to do something requires you to provide an explanation for him, so that he can understand why he can or can't do something. While it would be so much easier if Jack would just take a "yes" or "no" answer, sometimes, you need to just spell a situation out for him. As his latest report card notes, Jack sometimes does not take "no" for an answer and may ask a question repeatedly, hoping to get a different response. I find that if I am calm, consistent, and explain why the answer has to be a certain way, that he will accept my response.

Initially, Jack might not give adults eye contact or much interaction. Once he trusts the adult, he will interact much more. Jack may perseverate on a topic that he loves, like fishing or Pokemon. I would encourage the adult, at some point, say, "You know Jack, I enjoyed talking about Pokemon but I'm not a big fan. Let's move on to another topic." He needs to continue to work on meeting people wherever they are and not be so intent on his own agenda.

PHYSICAL SKILLS

Jack has great agility and some natural physical abilities. Unfortunately, the special education school that he has been at doesn't offer gym; thus, Jack has lost about three years of development in sports skills. He is very aware that he is behind in this area. While he is happy to play basketball, baseball, soccer and in-line hockey with another boy, I think he is reluctant to work in a group because he knows he won't be as good. Given the way this society operates, one of our goals for this summer is that Jack begins to really enjoy team sports. He has had a little tennis and squash in his background and says those are not top on his list. Perhaps you can make sure he tries all of the sports and then encourage him in what he most enjoys. I think that if the counselors kept giving him positive feedback and working with him, Jack would gain confidence and be more willing to try team sports.

JACK'S AREAS OF INTEREST

The things that Jack likes which we would like to encourage are:
• In-line hockey.
• Baseball.
• Water sports (he loves fishing, and as you'll see he's interested in learning all sorts of water sports).
• Science and nature.
• Fishing.
• Chess.

The things that Jack likes which we would like you to limit are:
• Gameboy and Pokemon.
• Computer games.

I realize that many of these children need the Gameboy and zoning out games to settle down, and that they also might be a way for the children to interact. However, for Jack, I would like you to set a limit of 1½ hours/day for Pokemon/Gameboy and computer games. I think you will make out best if the Gameboy is required to be put away for the day and can only brought out at certain times.

SPECIFIC SUMMER GOALS

• For Jack to become more independent and responsible in his personal care. I still prompt him to get dressed, comb hair, and brush his teeth. Hopefully, the summer experience will get him in a routine with these. He is good about making his bed and such; hopefully, you have requirements like this for the kids.

• For Jack to broaden his interests and find another passion or two. Jack has been in a very small special education school for the past three years. When he has the opportunity to do sports, etc. with other children he loves it. We are hoping that you can encourage and support him to find a team sport and other passions.

• Have fun with new friends. Jack has a great spirit and has become very social in the last year. We are hoping that he meets and makes some new friends.

• Have a really positive away-from-home experience. Our daughter looks forward to her camp experience all year long. We are hoping that Jack, too, will fall in love with a summer camp experience.

ACTIVITY AREAS TO SPECIFICALLY ENCOURAGE

• Team sports—whatever he gravitates to, but try to get him to try it all.

• Any activity that is not electronic and that is interactive with others. We would like to see Jack discover a few new passions.

• Developing good friendships.

PRIOR CAMP EXPERIENCE

This is Jack's first away from home camp experience. He did spend eighteen weeks as an inpatient at the hospital getting re-diagnosed, and handled being away just fine. His summer experiences are usually short sessions at the local aquarium, etc.

SPECIAL ALERTS

Medical: ADHD

Mild Asperger's

Easily gets poison ivy, and badly

Nutritional: Jack enjoys fish, pizza, meat, vegetables and pasta. He is least interested in fruit, though I make sure he eats some everyday (he likes pears and cantaloupe). Jack loves ice cream. He is also a sweet eater though I limit this greatly. I won't tell you no chocolate because I think that would be difficult if other children are having it; but I will say that chocolate revs him up. The fewer sweets, the better.

THANK YOU TO A SUMMER COUNSELOR

Date

Dear Counselor,

First, a big thank you for all of your hard work with Jack. We have seen Jack go from a child who came home and played by himself to walking in the door from a full day of camp with, "Can I have (camper's name) come over?" He is changing into Mr. Social.

We have one last favor to ask of you. In order to focus on the behaviors needing the most attention, we need to get a feel for where Jack is at. Since the end of school he has probably made some progress, held steady, or perhaps slipped a bit in various areas. YOU are in the best position to tell us where he is at since you get to see him in environments with others.

Thank you very, very much.

Sincerely,

Anne Addison

LETTER TO CHURCH TEACHERS AT BEGINNING OF SCHOOL YEAR

Date

Dear Deborah, Terry and Kate,

Thank you so much for continuing to teach the fourth grade class. Being comfortable and secure that people understand him is really helpful for Jack. You asked what is new with Jack since last year so I thought I'd just give you a brief review of where we are.

PROGRESS THAT JACK HAS RECENTLY MADE

• *Social Skills*—Jack has been fortunate enough to have a very kind eleven-year-old boy (Jason) living next door, now that we have finally moved into our home. The two boys share similar interests; Jason is very patient with Jack but doesn't hesitate to tell him when he is doing something that is inappropriate, too wild or too goofy. I think this has been our best source of social skill training yet. Jack has become aware that he is made a little differently; we've been talking about this a lot lately. He knows that his social brain isn't working correctly and that he needs to follow the guide of what he calls regular kids. Unfortunately, he sometimes looks at the incorrect behaviors of regular kids and then tells me it must be okay if those kids are doing something. It would be best if you could put him near some of the really calm boys—so that he can grasp some of the social nuances and correct manners that he should have.

• *Broadened Interests*—I have finally managed to make a deal and get the Gameboy/Pokemon away from Jack. He is supposed to get it back at the end of September but I'm hopeful we can make another deal. As you saw last week, Jack can always manage to find something to occupy him. Sometimes, he will obey me easily and leave the thing in the car to go to church, but other times, we can spend a good chunk of time discussing a deal that will allow him to bring a toy into church but won't play with it in Sunday School—it is just to keep his hands busy in church. I will try my best to keep toys out of the class and have told Jack that that's the rule.

If we do get in a power struggle and I lose, please just ask him to put the toy on a shelf when he walks into the Sunday School classroom. Just tell him that's the rule and that no other child in the class has a toy. Last week, he argued that he would have put it away but one of the regular kids had brought a snake in.

• *Focusing*—This is one of the biggest areas that we are still grappling with, particularly learning to raise his hand. A hand on his shoulder and reminder should be enough of a prompt if he gets out of line.

• *Silliness*—Probably the single most difficult behavior we now see is silliness combined with high energy. If you see any immature, silly behavior you can perhaps ask him to take space for five minutes to pull himself together if a couple of prompts and notes that others aren't acting this way don't do the trick.

I find that frequent, specific praise on social actions that are appropriate is now very helpful to Jack as feedback that he is doing the right thing. This is a critical year for us. We are trying to transition Jack out of the special education school that he is attending. To meet this goal, he'll need to make some very big social and behavioral leaps.

If everyone who interacts with him can continue to help him learn appropriate social cues and social interactions, we would be so grateful. Don't hesitate to remind him of some of the basics:

• Eye contact—remind him to look at you when he is speaking or you are speaking.

• Voice modulation—he can tend to talk too loud.

• Working with others—that he is sharing and interacting appropriately if he is working with another child (which would be great for him).

Finally, Jack enjoyed having Terry's son, Scott, in the class last week. If you think that this situation is helpful to Jack and/or the running of the class, we would be happy to hire someone (maybe Scott if he is interested?) to be a shadow for Jack. Just let us know.

A million thanks.

With much appreciation,

Anne (and John) Addison

Date

Ski School Address

Dear Name of Head of Adaptive Ski School Program,

I just wanted to tell you a little bit about Jack and the kind of instructor that would be best for him. He had a fabulous experience last year, all because of the ski instructor. Jack has ADHD and Asperger's Syndrome. Asperger's Syndrome is high functioning autism. People who have this disorder can get very fixated on something and have a hard time shifting gears. They also don't read social cues very well. Luckily, Jack has only a very mild case of this.

What you might notice first about Jack is that it will take him awhile to get ready. He has tactile sensitivities so he'll tell you that the boots are too tight or that something else doesn't feel right. The first day don't be surprised if I have to run out while you are on your way to the slopes to get something else for him that feels better.

Once skiing, you will see that he is a visual learner. It is best to use few words and try to use visual images. He learns by following. He will do a good job of following your directions, but he might get distracted spotting some wildlife, since animals are his passion. He will frequently ask you to take him on black runs if last year is any indication. Last year, he became stuck on getting better fast. I think it would be good to set a reasonable goal for the week and work towards it, like, "If we work hard we might get to do so-and-so run by Friday."

The best sort of instructor for Jack would be one who is very patient, lots of fun and flexible, but at the same time has requirements. Jack's lesson is as much about learning how to interact with others and practice good manners and social skills as it is getting better in the sport. We would love a guy (rather than a girl) for role modeling, if possible. Please tell the instructor to feel more than free to correct Jack's manners, if needed. If you need any further information, please let me know.

Thank you,
Anne Addison

Using Humor and Visuals to Make a Point To Jack

Dear Jack,

This is not a fast food restaurant. We are not McDonald's. Our family eats together.

For the last two nights you have ignored my requests to do homework and eat dinner with the family. I do not mind discussing doing homework a little later so that you can play after school. But you have not discussed this with me, as a responsible person should.

We eat dinner each night at 5:30. Each night that you miss dinner there will be no dessert or bedtime snacks for you. You can eat a cold dinner, which was hot at 5:30.

I am very disappointed.

If this behavior continues, we will go back to the point sheet.

I love you. I am excited that you want to play with neighborhood kids after school, but we need to talk about a schedule that fits the family.

Love, Mom

APPENDIX II
LOGS AND TRACKING TOOLS

Example of Daily Communication Log

(This was written in third grade when Jack was at the out-of-district, therapeutic day school)

From the Teacher:

Jack had a good day. Silly behaviors started near end of day (1:30ish). Not bad enough to be highly disruptive.

He started Type to Learn program this morning. He'll do it first thing in the a.m. on Monday, Wednesday and Friday.

We put the Legos away for awhile—there were a lot of sharing problems. Now, they're playing with cars and trucks.

For reading, Jack started reading *The Cay.* It's a 6th grade reading level. We'll see how he does. I'm going to try to give writing assignments every few chapters.

My Response (that Night):

Do you think Jack should take a second Ritalin dose at 1:30ish? Based on your notes to me of the last two weeks it sounds like 1:30 is about the time when he starts getting silly.

Jack made a child cry at after school chess by saying, "You're making stupid moves on purpose." He read the child's sadness only after the boy started crying—he did show empathy at that point.

Do you need Carol Gray's *Social Stories*? I can pick up a copy. I think they will be useful for social lessons such as the chess one. I am calling our public school today to get their reading/writing curriculum as we discussed. I hope that you'll be able to get Jack on roughly the same book list as his counterparts at the public school. Let me know what you think after you look at it.

Sample Medication Log

Date	Medication/Daily Dosage	School Behavior	Home Behavior Questions
Fall 1995-96	Ritalin 15 mg.	Learning cooperation and sharing; no anger or aggressive behaviors noted.	Transitions still difficult, can get frustrated easily, self-agenda stronger than following directions for daily routine.
Summer	Ritalin 20 mg.	Following own agenda vs. following the group, not aggressive or agitated.	Following own agenda, poor eye contact, not interested in social interactions.
Fall 1996-97	Ritalin 20 mg.	Generally cooperative, little aggression seen, doing nicely in mainstream.	Eye contact starting to improve, social interaction a little better, transitions still difficult.
February, '97	Adderall 20 mg.	Frustrated and physically aggressive/ not following directions. Transitions and eye contact going downhill.	Same at home as at school.
April, '97	Ritalin 27.5 mg.	Rocky at school, lots of acting out, aggression	Not as cooperative as previous year.
June '97	Amoxicillan 750 mg. (Lyme) Ritalin 27.5 mg. Buspar 15 mg. Clonidin 0.1 mg.	Generally following own agenda but not as agressive as late winter.	Same as at school.
Fall, '97	Ritalin 20 mg. Buspar 20 mg. Desyrl 50 mg. Amoxicillan 750 mg.	Improving eye contact, improving social contact. Working on transitions. Following directions are steadily improving.	Steady uphill progress although inconsistent with cooperation and following directions at speech therapy, occupational therapy and in extracurricular activities.
March, '98	Ritalin 30 mg. Buspar 20 mg. Deseryl 25 mg. Amoxicillan 750 mg.	Best developmental period ever. Very good growth period socially and emotionally Little trouble with transitions but handling mainstream and special ed class well.	Better cooperation at home. Still difficulty or unevenness with after school therapies and programs.
July, '98	Ritalin 30 mg. Amoxicillan 750 mg. (Lyme) Buspar 25 mg. Deseryl 25 mg.	Camp at country club, very social. Completes full day about 60% time, a little silly but can respond to prompts.	During course of summer becomes more and more silly and less cooperative. By August, is self-agendaed again.

Sample Medication Log

Date	Mediction/Daily Dosage	School Behavior	Home Behavior Questions
Sept. , '98	Ritalin 20 mg. Amoxicillan 750 mg. (Lyme) Buspar 25 mg. Deseryl 25 mg.	Handles mainstream with some difficulty (2 hours first thing in day) and goes downhill from there. Anxious, uncooperative, "leave me alone" which becomes physically fight and flight by 10/8.	Spends much time alone doing computer activities; a little more irritable but none of the aggression that is being seen in school. More self-agendaed than spring and early summer in outside activities (tennis, squash, church school and speech therapy).
Sept. 26, '98	Ritalin 20 mg. Buspar 25 mg. Deseryl 25 mg.	Becoming increasingly agitated, see teacher's chart tracking behaviors.	Same as above.
10/8/98	Ritalin 30 mg. Risperdal 0.5 mg. Deseryl 25 mg.	In incident where Jack ends up at emergency room, he is given Rispderal to calm down and physically restrained.	Extremely upset about incident. Read attached note to see what incident was about.
10/26/98	Ritalin 30mg. Zoloft 12.5 mg. Deseryl 25 mg. Buspar stopped	Much variability but generally fleeing or fighting after mainstream class. Six subsequent inci dents where mom had to be called to get William under control. Mom could get him under control immediately, once out of school.	Generally following directions, fuzzy, groggy, seems sad or lethargic. Clearly upset about school. No aggression but unsafe behaviors (climbing, etc.)
11/9/98	Zoloft 25 mg. Ritalin 30 mg. Deseryl 25 mg.	Same as 10/26/98	
11/18/98	Zoloft 25 mg. Ritalin 30 mg. Risperdal 1 mg. Desyrl 25 mg.	From 10/8/98-12/6/98 worst period William has ever had, both home and school. Much more angry, aggressive, volatile, with no tolerance level.	From 10/8/98-12/6/98 worst period Jack has ever had, both home and school. Much more angry, aggressive, volatile, with no tolerance level.
12/3/98	Zoloft removed Ritalin 30 mg. Deseryl 25 mg. Risperdal 1 mg.	Much variability but generally fleeing or fighting after mainstream class. Six subsequent inci dents where mom had to be called to get William under control. Mom could get him under control immediately, once out of school.	Generally following directions, fuzzy, groggy, seems sad or lethargic. Clearly upset about school. No aggression but unsafe behaviors (climbing, etc.)

Sympton Tracking System

This system gives you a way to gather and analyze behavioral and emotional information on your child. It can be used to better understand symptoms, test diagnosis hypothesis, and as a guide for educational and health care professionals working with your child. If you know how to use Microsoft Excel, you will be able to use data to create a line chart that will allow your doctor and other team members to see how your child is functioning over a period of time. I like to use at least two week time period, so that we can see any weekly patterns that might be there.

Instructions for Creating Your Own Sympton Tracking System

Step 1: Determine what goals you are trying to achieve. In this example, I wanted to better understand the major behavioral issues in Jack's ADHD. I identified the major behaviors to be studied, than assigned a rating using a five point scale for that behavior every half hour that I observed Jack. The data was then averaged for the day and plotted on a chart.

Step 2: Using the format of the *Hourly Behavior Tracking Sheet* create a similar form that will help you monitor the symptons that you are interested in studying.

If the rating scale that the *Hourly Behavior Tracking Sheet* uses does not accurately reflect the character of your child's reactions, feel free to change the ratings.

It is very important that the data is taken every half hour, as indicated. If someone else is working with your child, try to observe the interaction so that you can rate that time period. If it is not possible (such as during school hours), make sure that the teacher, teacher's aide, or whoever will be doing the rating, is using the same scale, with the same definitions for each rating that you are.

Step 3: Find the daily average for each symptom by adding up all the numbers in a column and dividing that number by the total number of enteries in the column. For example on the *Hourly Behavior Tracking Sheet* for May 3rd that follows, the total score for the day for Hyperactivity is 88. Divide 88 by the number of times that you took the data, 26 periods. 88 divided by 26=3.52.

Step 4: Write the average for the day in Step 2 for Hyperactivity on the *Daily Behavior Tracking Sheet.* Follow the process for each of the symptoms that you are tracking. Set up hourly and daily data sheets similar in format to mine, with all of the symptoms that you want to track.

Step 5: Once all of the Daily Tracking Sheet data is input onto an Excel spreadsheet, follow the Excel instructions for creating a line chart. You will be able to clearly see which symptoms are present in your child and to what degree.

Hourly Behavior Tracking Sheet

Time	Hyperactive	Impulsive	Inattentive	Setting	Medication	Comments
7:30-8:00	4	3	3.5	home	nothing	Running outside, wouldn't get dressed
8:00-8:30	3	3	3.5	home	Ritalin, 10 mg.	
8:30-9:00	3	2	3.5	home		Waited for Ritalin in system 20
9:00-9:30	3.5	2	3	school		min., asked to dress then.
9:30-10:00	3	1	3	school		
10:00-10:30	2	1	2	school		
10:30-11:00	2	2	2	school		
11:00-11:30	2	2	2	school		
11:30-12:00	4	2	2	school		
12:00-12:30	3.5	2	3	school		Teacher reported no incidents,
12:30-1:00	3.5	2	3	school		but unusually high energy level
1:00-1:30	3.5	2.5	3	school		
1:30-2:00	3	2.5	2	speech therapy	Ritalin, 10 mg.	
2:00-2:30	3	2.5	2	errands		Not cooperative in store
2:30-3:00	3	2.5	2	home		
3:00-3:30	3	2.5	2	home		
3:30-4:00	3	2.5	2	home		
4:00-4:30	3.5	2.5	2	home		
4:30-5:00	3.5	2.5	2	home		
5:00-5:30	4.5	2.5	2	home		
5:30-6:00	4.5	2.5	3	home		
6:00-6:30	4	3	3	home		Started teasing Sarah, became physical
6:30-7:00	4	3	3	home		
7:00-7:30	4	3	3.5	home		
7:30-8:00	4	2.5	3.5	home		
8:00-8:30	4	2.5	3.5	home	Benadryl, 25 mg.	
Daily Average	3.52	2.42	2.76			

Rating Scale
1= Appropriate behavior for 7-8 year old.
2= Mild amount of behavior or mood. Needed more than 2 prompts to stop behavior and was responsive or mood lasting less than 10 minutes.
3= Clearly see this behavior or mood. Needed frequent prompts to stop behavior but could be redirected. Mood lasting 10-20 minutes.
4= Frequently see this behavior or mood. Needed constant redirection and at least 1 time out to stop behavior. Mood lasted 20-30 minutes.
5= See this behavior and mood constantly. Needed time out or quiet space more than once. At least one tantrum, lasting more than 30 minutes.

338

Daily Behavior Tracking Sheet

Date	Hyperactive	Impulsive	Inattentive	Medication	Comments
May 3	1.5	2	2	Ritalin 10 mg, 2x/day	
May 4	4	3	5	"	
May 5	2	2.5	3	"	
May 6	3.5	2.4	2.8	"	
May 7	3.8	2.8	2.5	"	
May 8	4	2.9	2.7	"	3 hours sleep, unusually difficult
May 9	3.8	2.7	2.6	"	
May 10	3.5	3	2.8	"	
May 11	3.6	2.8	2.6	"	
May 12	3.5	2.5	2.8	"	
May 13	3.25	2.75	2.8	"	
May 14	3.5	2.4	3	"	Started limiting sugar in diet
May 15	3.25	2.7	3.5	"	
May 16	3.5	2.4	3	"	
May 17	3.8	2.2	2.6	"	
May 18	4	2.6	2.5	"	
May 19	3.6	3	3	"	

339

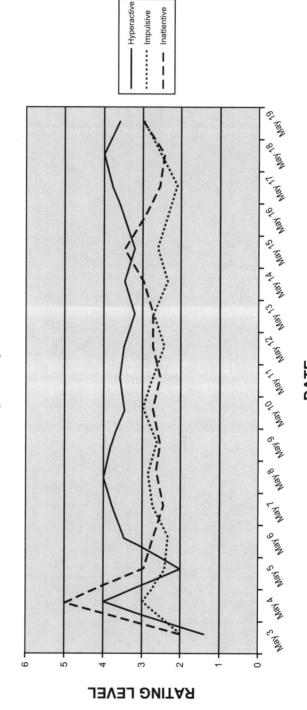

ADHD Symptons Tracking for Jack Addison
May 3 - May 19

DATE

RATING LEVEL

Hyperactive
Impulsive
Inattentive

340

Appendix III
Medical Information

Descriptions of Medical Professionals

Developmental Pediatrician—A developmental pediatrician is also board certified in developmental disabilities. Some pediatricians call themselves developmental pediatricians but really aren't. Many families are beginning to use developmental pediatricians as the primary coordinator of their professional team. In addition to having a good grasp of therapies, developmental pediatricians can assist with vitamins, diet, and other things.

Neuropsychologist—A neuropsychologist compliments a regular psychologist by evaluating how your child's disorder impacts his ability to learn. The neuropsychologist will work with you and your child's teachers to develop strategies and tools to help your child learn effectively.

Occupational Therapist—An occupational therapist assesses and treats sensory processing, visual perception and visual motor integration skills. The occupational therapist works on integrating the sensory processing and visual motor skills needed for daily living activities and school-based activities. In the Attention Deficit Disorder (ADD), Attention Deficit Hyperactivity Disorder (ADHD), Pervasive Developmental Disorder (PDD), and autism arena, the occupational therapist focuses on two major areas. One is sensory integration. Motor planning, balance, coordination and tactile defenses (sensitivity to the feel of certain fabrics, materials, etc.) are typical areas of weakness for a child with poor sensory integration. The second is visual motor and fine motor skills. An occupational therapist who is certified in sensory integration can conduct an in-depth evaluation and recommend a treatment plan.

Pediatric Neurologist—A neurologist looks at the physical brain functioning of a child from a hard-wiring perspective. She will complete an office examination that includes reflex testing, physical overview, history of pregnancy with the child, delivery and developmental milestones. Based upon her review and clinical observations she may or may not recommend further brain study such as an MRI or CAT Scan. Researchers have just begun to distinguish differences in the structure of the brain for some of these disorders. They have even begun to identify the genes which may trigger the disorders.

PHYSICAL THERAPIST— A physical therapist concentrates on improving the use of major muscle groups, such as those in the arms and legs. Many children with special needs may be clumsy and have coordination problems. A physical therapist can help a child learn how to adapt and/or strengthen his body to increase his physical abilities.

PSYCHIATRIST—Psychiatrists are often the gatekeepers in your array of professionals. The psychiatrist will review all of the evaluations that your child has had, and is the one who will ultimately make the diagnosis (in consultation with the other professionals) and determine a treatment plan, including the option of medication. The psychiatrist is an M.D. and therefore can manage any medication used to treat your child's disorder.

Knowledge of the brain is growing exponentially. By the time this book reaches you, the discovery of the specific genes that trigger Asperger's Syndrome (just to pick one recent finding) will be old news. The field of psychiatry is reorganizing itself, often around specific disorders. Finding the psychiatrist with a patient population that is largely diagnosed with what your child has can be enormously helpful.

PSYCHOPHARMACOLOGIST—A psychiatrist who specializes in the study of medications in behavioral and neurological disorders.

PSYCHOLOGIST—The psychologist looks at the cognitive functioning of your child. He is the one who will decipher your child's thinking and learning styles. In an initial evaluation, a psychologist will conduct a series of tests that look at a range of functioning, such as emotions, anxiety, anger, attention, impulsivity, memory, etc. The psychologist will determine what battery of tests are appropriate for your child based upon interviews with you and your spouse, the pediatrician, other doctors who have seen the child, and clinical observation.

The evaluation period depends upon the number of tests, cooperation and stamina of the child, and the length of each session. At the completion of testing, the psychologist should provide you with a detailed written report.

She should also sit down with you to review her findings, give recommendations and to answer your questions. The report should be easy to understand, detailed, and action-oriented. In other words, you should be able to determine your next steps and begin to develop an action plan. The sorts of questions that the report should answer are:

- What is my child's diagnosis?
- What are his areas of strength and weakness?
- Does my child need additional testing in a specified area?
- Should we bring in a psychiatrist to explore medication alternatives?
- What kind of therapies would my child benefit from?
- How should the school environment and classroom be structured?

If your psychologist recommends that a psychiatrist and/or appropriate therapists be brought in, gather two or three names in each discipline, interview them, and then continue on your data-gathering mission. Note: a psychologist is not an M.D. and cannot prescribe medication.

SPEECH AND LANGUAGE THERAPIST—Many children with special needs have communication disorders as well. A child might have trouble with the physical exercise of speaking, might be unable to process what he hears, might not be able to respond to another person and may be unable to hold a conversation. A speech and language specialist can conduct an evaluation to break down what is interfering with your child's communication process, and recommend a treatment plan.

APPENDIX IV
RESOURCES

ORGANIZATIONS
AND THE NEWSLETTERS THAT THEY PUBLISH

AHEAD WITH AUTISM
Promotes better understanding and awareness of autism around the world, funds projects that will enable parents and professionals to obtain information about autism, and related disorders worldwide.
PO Box 599
Riva, MD 21140
Phone: 410-956-5882
www.aheadwithautism.com

ASPERGER SYNDROME COALITION OF THE U. S. (ASC-US)
Publishes The Source, a quarterly newsletter. National non-profit organization formed to increase the awareness of, and provide support for, individuals affected with the following neurological disorders: Asperger's Syndrome; High Functioning Autism; Hyperlexia; Nonverbal Learning Disorder; Pervasive Developmental Disorder and Semantic-Pragmatic Disorder.
P. O. Box 351268
Jacksonville, Florida 32235-1268
Phone: 866-427-7747
E-mail: info@asc-us.org Website: http://www.asperger.org

ASSOCIATION FOR BEHAVIORAL ANALYSIS
Dedicated to promoting the experimental, theoretical and applied analysis of behavior. Disseminate public and private information. Publishes a newsletter and two journals.
213 West Hall
Western Michigan University
1201 Oliver Street
Kalamazoo, MI 49008
Phone: 616-387-3841

AUTISM ASPERGER RESOURCE CENTER
Quarterly newsletter, The Autism and Asperger's Disorder Connection
4001 HC Miller Building
3901 Rainbow Boulevard
Kansas City, Kansas 66160
Phone: 913-588-5988/Fax: 913-588-5942/E-mail: aarc@kumc.edu

AUTISM FOUNDATION OF NEW YORK
Non-Profit organization representing families affected by autism & autism spectrum disorders
Sandy Levine – Executive Director
1050 Forest Hill Road
Staten Island, NY 10314
Phone: 718-370-8200

AUTISM RESEARCH INSTITUTE (ARI)
 Publishes Autism Research Review International (quarterly newsletter).
Primarily devoted to conducting research, and to disseminating the results of research, on methods of preventing, diagnosing and treating autism and other severe behavioral disorders of childhood
Dr. Bernard Rimland – consulted on Rain Man
4182 Adams Avenue
San Diego, California, USA 92116
Phone: 619- 281-7165
www.autism.com/ari

AUTISM SOCIETY OF AMERICA
Dedicated to providing support to persons with autism. Founded by a small group of parents in 1965, it now has 20,000 members and is a leading information source on autism.
7910 Woodmont Avenue Suite 300
Bethesda, MD 20814-3067
Phone: 301-657-0869
www.autismsociety.org

CHADD (Children and Adults with Attention-Deficit/Hyperactivity Disorder) National organization supporting ADHD families.
8181 Professional Place Suite 201
Landover, MD 20785
Phone: 301-306-7070

Child and Adolescent Bipolar Foundation
Provides education, support and advocacy for children and adolescents and their families.
e-mail: wwwbpkids.org

Child Development Institute
Robert Myers, Ph.D. (Clinical Child Psychologist)
17853 Santiago Blvd, Suite 107-328
Villa Park, California 92861
Phone: 714- 998-8617
e-mail: webmaster@childdevelopmentinfo.com

Community Services for Autistic Adults & Children (CSAAC)
Newsletter and online book store
Dr. Christine Caselles, Director Intensive Early Intervention
Paul Livelli, Director Community School of Maryland
CSAAC Foundation
751 Twinbrook Parkway
Rockville, MD 20851
Phone: 301- 762-1650
e-mail: csaac@csaac.org

Council for Exceptional Children (CEC)
Publishes member newsletter, CEC TODAY
Professional association of special education teachers and administrators; related service providers such as school psychologists, occupational therapists, and social workers; university professors, undergraduate and graduate students; and parents. The association works to advance the educational success of students with disabilities and/or gifts and talents and support those

who serve this special population.

The Council for Exceptional Children
1110 North Glebe Road, Suite 300
Arlington, VA 22201-5704
Toll-free:1-888-CEC-SPED
Phone:703-264-9478
e-mail lyndav@cec.sped.org

CURE AUTISM NOW
Publishes quarterly newsletter.
Organization of parents, physicians and researchers dedicated to promoting and funding research with direct implications for the treatment and cure of autism
5455 Wilshire Blvd
Suite 715
Los Angles, CA 90036
1.888.8.autism
www.cureautism.org

DIVISION FOR EARLY CHILDHOOD (DEC) OF THE COUNCIL
FOR EXCEPTIONAL CHILDREN
Publishes the journal *Exceptional Children*
Barbara Smith, DEC Executive Director
DEC Executive Office
1380 Lawrence Street, Suite 650
Denver, CO 80204
Phone: 303-556-3328
E-mail: dec@ceo.cudenver.edu

DIVISION FOR LEARNING DISABILITIES (DLD) OF THE COUNCIL
FOR EXCEPTIONAL CHILDREN (DLD/CEC)
Barbara Wozney, DLD Membership Chair
1625 Park Overlook Drive
Reston, VA 20190-4920
E-mail: joewozney@aol.com

LEARNING DISABILITIES ASSOCIATION OF AMERICA (LDA)
Publishes quarterly newsletter
4156 Library Road
Pittsburgh, PA 15234
Phone: 412-341-1515/Fax 412-344-0224
www.Ldaamerica.org

MAAP (MORE ADVANCED AUTISTIC PEOPLE) SERVICES INC.
Publishes the MAAP newsletter quarterly
Dedicated to assisting family members of more advanced individuals with autism by offering information and advice on autism, and by providing the opportunity to network with others in similar circumstances.
Susan Moreno
MAAP Services
P.O. Box 524
Crown Point, Indiana 46307
Phone/Fax: (219) 662-1311 E-mail: chart@netnitco.net
www.maapservices.org

FAMILIES FOR EARLY AUTISM TREATMENT (FEAT)
Publishes daily e-mail newsletter.
Non-profit organization of parents and professionals, designed to help families with children who have received the diagnosis of Autism or Pervasive Developmental Disorder (PDD NOS)
P.O. Box 255722
Sacramento, California, 95865-5722
(916) 843-1536   www.feat.org

FEDERATION FOR CHILDREN WITH SPECIAL NEEDS
A nationwide Parent Training and Information (PTI) Project that provides services to parents of children with special needs and professionals. The Federation offers services including: information, referral & technical assistance, specialized workshops, a quarterly newsletter, resource library and speakers bureau.
www.fcsninfo@fcsn.org

The Morning News
Edited by Carol Gray, Director of The Gray Center, a nonprofit foundation dedicated to individuals with Autistic Spectrum Disorders and those who work alongside them to improve mutual understanding. She is the author of several books.

Carol Gray, Editor
The Morning News
Jenison High School
2140 Bauer Road
Jenison, Michigan 49428
Phone: 616-457-8955

NATIONAL AUTISTIC SOCIETY
Publishes the magazine *Communication* and quarterly newsletter, *Asperger United*
393 City Road
London EC1V 1NG
United Kingdom
Phone: 44 0 20 7903 3595
Nas@nas.org.uk
Asperger United: Asp.utd@nas.org.uk

NATIONAL COALITION FOR PARENT INVOLVEMENT IN EDUCATION (NCPIE)
Sue Ferguson, Chair
3929 Old Lee Highway, Suite 91-A
Fairfax, VA 22030-2401
Phone: 703-359-8973
Fax: 703-359-0972
Email: ferguson@ncea.com

NATIONAL DEPRESSIVE AND MANIC-DEPRESSIVE ASSOCIATION (NDMDA)
A toll-free national information line providing information and resources for depression, manic depression, and related disorders.
730 N. Franklin St. Suite 501
Chicago, IL 60610-3526
Phone: 800-826-3623

NATIONAL MENTAL HEALTH ASSOCIATION (NMHA)
Provides brochures on clinical depression and other mental health topics.
1021 Prince St.
Alexandria, VA 22314-2971
Phone: 800-969-6642
www.nmha.org

National Institute of Mental Health (NIMH)
NIMH is part of the National Institute of Health. Information, resources, and educational materials are available on a wide range of mental health disorders.
NIMH Public Inquiries
5600 Fishers Lane, Room 7C-02, MSC 8030
Bethesda, MD 20892-8030
Phone: 301-443-4513
www.nimh.gov/publicat/index.htm

PARENT TRAINING AND INFORMATION CENTERS
Parent centers in each state provide training and information to parents of infants, toddlers, school-aged children, with disabilities and the professionals who work with their families. This assistance helps parents participate more effectively with professionals in meeting the educational needs of children and youth with disabilities.
Alliance Coordinating Offices:

NORTHEAST REGIONAL CENTER
Parent Information Center
P.O. Box 2405
Concord, NH 03302-2405
Phone: 603-224-7005 E-mail: picnh@aol.com
Judith Raskin, Regional Director
Mary Trinkley, Technical Assistance Coordinator
CT, DE, DC, ME, MD, MA, NH, NJ, NY, PA, Puerto Rico, RI, US VI, VT

MIDWEST REGIONAL CENTER

Ohio Coalition for the Education of Children with Disabilities (OCECD)

Bank One Building

165 West Center Street, Suite 302

Marion, OH 43302-3741

Phone: 740-382-5452 E-mail: ocecd@gte.net

Margaret Burley, Regional Co-Director/Dena Hook, Technical Assistance Coordinator

CO, IL, IA, IN, KS, KY, MI, MN, MO, NE, ND, OH, SD, WI

South Regional Center

Exceptional Children's Assistance Center (ECAC)

907Barra Row, Suite 102/103

Davidson, NC 28036

Phone: 704-892-1321 e-mail: sregionata@aol.com

Connie Hawkins, Regional Director

Judy Higginbotham, Technical Assistance Coordinator

Johnny Allen, Multicultural TA Coordinator

AL, AR, FL, GA, LA, MS, NC, OK, SC, TN, TX, VA, WV

WEST REGIONAL CENTER

Matrix Parent Network and Resource Center

94 Galli Drive, Suite C

Novato, CA 94949

Phone:415-884-3535 e-mail: alliance@matrixparents.org

Nora Thompson, Technical Assistance Coordinator

Patricia Valdez, Multicultural TA Coordinator

AK, AZ, Department of Defense Dependent Schools (DODDS), CA, HI, ID, MT, NV, NM, OR, Pacific Jurisdiction, UT, WA, WY

THE RESOURCE FOUNDATION FOR CHILDREN WITH CHALLENGES

P.O. Box 1405

Santa Clarita, CA 91386

Phone: 661-298-2610

THE SIBLING INFORMATION NETWORK
Publishes newsletter
The Sibling Information Network
1776 Ellington Road
South Windsor, CT, 06074

THE SIBLING SUPPORT PROJECT
Publishes *The Sibling Support Project* Newsletter.
Donald Meyer, Director; The Sibling Support Project located at Children's
Hospital and Regional Medical Center in Seattle, Washington;
Children's Hospital and Medical Center
PO Box 5371
CL-09 4800 Sand Point Way,
NE Seattle, WA 98105.
Phone: 206-527-5712

TEACHER EDUCATION DIVISION (TED) OF THE COUNCIL FOR
EXCEPTIONAL CHILDREN
Publishes classroom-oriented magazine *TEACHING Exceptional Children*
Mary Little - TED Membership Chair (2001-2004)
Department of Human Services and Wellness
Daytona Beach Campus
1200 International Speedway Drive
Daytona Beach, FL 32114-0800
Phone: 904-255-7423 x4067/E-mail: Mlittle@mail.ucf.edu

ZERO TO THREE: NATIONAL CENTER FOR INFANTS, TODDLERS, AND FAMILIES
Publish bulletin Zero to Three
National Center for Infants, Toddlers and Families
2000 M Street, NW, Suite 200
Washington, DC 20036
Phone: 202-638-1144 /e-mail: fenichel@zerotothree.org.

Book Catalogues Specifically Targeted to Special Needs

A.D.D. Warehouse
300 Northwest 70th Ave. Suite 102
Plantation, FL 33317
954-792-8944
1-800-233-9273
www.addwarehouse.com

Brookes Publishing
P.O. Box 10624
Baltimore, MD 21285-0624
1-800-638-3775 North America
1-410-337-9580 International

EP Library (Published by Exceptional Parent)
1-800-535-1910
www.eplibrary.com

Future Horizons
Future Horizons, Inc
721 W. Abram St.
Arlington, TX 76013
1-800-489-0727
817-277-0727
www.FutureHorizons-autism.com

Magazines

Attention!
A magazine for families and adults with ADHD.
CHADD
8181 Professional Place, Suite 201
Landover, MD 20785
301-306-7070

Autism/Asperger's Digest Magazine
Published six times a year by Future Horizons
721 W. Abram St.
Arlington, TX 76013
1-800-489-0727
 817-277-0727
www.FutureHorizons-autism.com
www.autismdigest.com

Exceptional Parent
Published eleven times a year for parents of children with a wide range of disabilities.
65 Route 4
River Edge, N.J. 07661
1-877-372-7368
www.eparent.com

Websites

Applied Behavior Analysis Resources (ABA) reviews and sells books
E-mail: RichardSaffran@hotmail.com
phone: 508-490-0957

AspergersSupport
A support list for parents of children with Asperger's Syndrome.
To join, send an e-mail message to the following address:
AspergersSupport-subscribe@yahoogroups.com
For more information contact list owner:
AspergersSupport-owner@yahoogroups.com

AS/PDD/HF Autism
A moderated Listserv e-mail support group for families of/persons with AS/PDD/HF Autism
To join send a message to Lisa McMahan at:
LTobaben@aol.com
Include a note explaining that you would like to join the AS/PDD/HF Autism list.

AS-and-Proud-of-it

List for those with Asperger's Syndrome or their families designed to exchange information and provide support.

AS-and-Proud-of-it-subscribe@yahoogroups.com

For more information contact list owner: AS-and-Proud-of-it-owner@yahoogroups.com

ASLearningAtHome

List for mom's who home school their children who have been diagnosed with Asperger's Syndrome (AS) (mild autism). This list is only for those who currently home school or are SERIOUSLY considering home schooling.

To join, send an e-mail message to the following address:

ASLearningAtHome-subscribe@yahoogroups.com

For more information contact list owner: ASLearningAtHome-owner@yahoogroups.com

Asperger

Mailing list for discussions of all aspects of Asperger Syndrome and other forms of high-functioning autism, including Pervasive Developmental Disorder. Subscription requires owner approval. A high volume list. Instructions: Send the message, SUBSCRIBE ASPERGER to List owners: Head List owner - Ellen Dietrick Dietricks@home.com; Co-list owners - Karen Reznek Karen.reznek@idealink.washington.dc.us; Sandy Sebree Sanseb@aol.com; Phil Schwarz pschwarz@ix.netcom.com; Dave Spicer dspicer@charter.net; Tee Forshaw dtlfor@foryou.net; Barry Conner consultmac@connerconsulting.net

Autisminfo.com – reviews and sells books

Provides parents, particularly those with newly diagnosed kids, a good source of information.

Brad Middlebrook

bradmidd@aol.com

Autism Today – newsletter and online bookstore

Attention: Angela

Phone: 877-482-1555/e-mail: info@autismtoday.com

AUTINET

Discussion list on autism, especially high functioning autism. An active list. Need List owner's approval to join. Instructions: Write to autinet-request@iol.ie In the SUBJECT heading, send these words: SUBSCRIBE AUTINET and in the body of the email explain your interest. List owner: Peter Wise pw@shannon.tellabs.com

NATIONAL ALLIANCE FOR AUTISM (NAAR) ON-LINE BOOKSTORE

Families and Scientist providing biomedical research on autism

99 Wall Street

Research Park

Princeton, NJ 08540

609.430.9160

www.naar.org

THE O.A.S.I.S. (ONLINE ASPERGER SYNDROME INFORMATION AND SUPPORT)

Provide essential information for families of children diagnosed with Asperger Syndrome and related disorders, as well as to educators who teach children with AS and professionals working with individuals diagnosed with AS.

Barbara L. Kirby

E-mail:bkirby@udel.edu

www.udel.edu/bkirby/asperger

SHADOWSYNDROMEKIDS

This list is intended for parents of MILDLY affected children of varying syndromes/disorders To join, send an e-mail message to the following address: ShadowSyndromeKids-subscribe@yahoogroups.com

For more information contact list owner: pamrose@mindspring.com

SPECIAL CHILD – ONLINE MAGAZINE

Publication dedicated to parents of children with special needs

Lisa Baker, Editor –in-Chief

baker@specialchild.com

www.FIRSTSIGNS.ORG

A non-profit organization dedicated to educating parents and physicians about the early warning signs of autism and other developmental disorders in early childhood.

First Signs, Inc.

P.O. Box 358

Merrimac, MA 01860

Telephone: (978) 346-4380/ Fax: (978) 346-4638/Email: info@firstsigns.org

www.ONSPECIALED.COM

An informational site for parents, teachers, students, and professionals that has developed into the largest web site for special education and learning disabilities in the world. Included is detailed information on 100's of learning disabilities, physical disability's that effect learning. Additionally it supplies information for parents on parenting, private schools, summer camps, books and educational materials.

Dr. Glazer

P. O. Box 346

Edwards, Colorado 81632-0346

Telephone: 970-926-5600

E-mail: webmaster@OnSpecialEd.com

WWW.WRIGHTSLAW.COM

newsletter and online bookstore

Parents, advocates, educators, and attorneys come to Wrightslaw for accurate, up-to-date information about effective advocacy for children with disabilities.

APPENDIX V
THE POINT SHEET SYSTEM

Daily Point Sheet for School Days

A.M. Expectations	Point Bonuses/Losses
Get dressed Make bed Brush teeth Eat breakfast Take pills... ...then TV until bus	100 To Start Bonus/Loss Points:

Money in bank for a.m.:

P.M. Expectations	Point Losses
Homework done Homework checked Dinner Bath Pajamas... ....then TV/Gameboy In bed when told	100 To Start Bonus/Loss Points:

Money in bank for p.m.:

Daily Total

Total for Day _____

Percentage for Day (divide points earned by 200)_____

Total Points for Week To Date _____

Bonus points

+5 points
Responding to someone when involved
Playing appropriately
Helpful Hints
Making a good choice

+10 points
Following directions the first time
Making a really good choice

+15 points
Showing initiative
Helping
Talking through feelings
Making a very, very good choice on own

POINT LOSSES

-1 point
Not following a directive

-5 points
Yelling

-10 points
Banging, kicking, etc.

-15 points
Arguing
Lying
Not telling where going
Mean language

-20 points
Not doing the things on the list with 2 prompts

-30 points
Being unsafe
Destruction of property
Not participating in required activity

APPENDIX VI
INDEX

Index

FROM THE AUTHOR

If you have stories that you would like to share or strategies that you have found helpful, we would love to hear them. You may send them to Anne Addison at AnneAddison@aol.com or to the author in care of Stacey McLaughlin Communications, 21 West St., #23L, New York, New York, 10006.

Please direct all comments, suggestions and stories to onesmallstarfish@aol.com **instead** of the AnneAddison@aol.com address given in the above note from the author.